Regulating Spanish Banking, 1939–1975

Regulating Spanish Banking, 1939–1975

M.A. PONS BRIAS

Routledge
Taylor & Francis Group
LONDON AND NEW YORK

First published 2002 by Ashgate Publishing

2 Park Square, Milton Park, Abingdon, Oxon OX14 4RN
711 Third Avenue, New York, NY 10017, USA

Routledge is an imprint of the Taylor & Francis Group, an informa business

First issued in paperback 2016

British Library Cataloguing in Publication Data

Pons Brias, Maria Angeles
Regulating Spanish Banking, 1939–1975.
(Studies in Banking History)
1. Banks and banking–Spain–History.
2. Banking law–Spain. I. Title.
346.4'6'082

Library of Congress Cataloging-in-Publication Data

Pons Brias, Maria Angeles
Regulating Spanish Banking, 1939–1975 /
Maria Angeles Pons Brias.
p. cm. (Studies in Banking History).
Includes bibliographical references (alk. paper).
ISBN 0-7546-0194-3
1. Banks and banking–Spain–State supervision–History–
20th century. I. Title. II. Series.
HG1778.S7P66 2001
332.1'0946'09045–dc21 2001022166

ISBN 13: 978-0-7546-0194-4 (hbk)
ISBN 13: 978-1-138-27287-3 (pbk)

Contents

List of Figures

List of Tables

Acknowledgements

A book is never written without the help of others. I am heavily indebted to my supervisor D. James Foreman-Peck for long discussion, his guidance and critical assessment of this study. My research would not have been possible without his analytical skills and patience. I would like to thank Professor Feinstein, who assumed supervision of my thesis in the last part of my research. Furthermore, I am grateful to Pablo Martín Aceña who kindly assumed external supervision of my thesis; his comments benefited my work significantly. I also thank Professors Valpy Fitzgerald and Michael Collins for comments and discussion.

I would like to extend my gratitude to Leandro Prados and the rest of the members of the Economic History Department at the Carlos III University who encouraged me to study at the University of Oxford. I also want to thank Jordi Palafox and the rest of the members of the Department of Economic History at the University of Valencia, who helped me at the beginning of my research; they read portions of my dissertation and not only provided valuable comments, but also pushed me to develop ideas for further research. I would like to mention Charles Powell for his help. I benefited from discussions with Gabriel Tortella, Jose Luis García Ruiz, Daniel Díaz, and many others. Jose Emilio Boscá has provided invaluable assistance with the computing of this work. I specially thank my husband, and my family and all the extraordinary friends I met in Oxford for their support (especially Dolores Cullen, Carolina Labarta and Orlando Ochoa).

The staff of the Bank of England Archives, the Bank of Spain Archives and the *Biblioteca del Banco de España* provided expert help. Lastly, I am grateful for the financial support which I received from the Ministry of Education in Spain. The responsibility for any error is mine alone.

List of Abbreviations

BSL	Banking Supervision Law ('*Ley de Ordenación Bancaria*')
CECA	*Confederación Española de Cajas de Ahorro*
CEN	*Consejo de Economia Nacional*
CPI	Consumer Price Index
GDP	Gross Domestic Product
GDPpc	per capita GDP
GNP	Gross national product
GNPpc	per capita GNP
INE	*Instituto Nacional de Estadística*
INI	*Instituto Nacional de Industria*
IMF	International Monetary Fund
IPI	Industrial Product Index
IRI	*Instituto di Reconstructione Italiano*
M0	notes + coins
M1	notes + coins + non-interest bearing deposit
NI	National Income
OEEC	Organisation for European Economic Cooperation
PTAs	pesetas
SBC	Supreme Banking Council ('*Consejo Superior Bancario*')
SMI	Stock Market Index
RAI	Register of Unpaid Sellers
WPI	Wholesale Price Index

Introduction

The main purpose of this study is to examine the impact of financial regulation on the Spanish banking system performance from the end of the Civil War (April 1939) to the mid-1970s. At the end of the Civil War, and because of the economic damage that it had caused, the Franco government introduced many measures to reorganise the economy. Franco's economic programme was intended to achieve the accelerated industrialisation of Spain. In the post-war years the government considered different strategies of development. One of them was based on the encouragement of agriculture and light industry. However, the Franco authorities chose a very different growth option. The most important objective of their preferred economic programme was the maximisation of industrial production, especially in the basic industries (electricity generation, iron and steel industry and chemicals, among others).

The economic programme was promoted by state intervention and was intended to encourage self-sufficiency. To maximise industrial production and to achieve autarky, the government established a substantial legislative framework. A huge interventionist apparatus was erected. Controls were used extensively in the early nationalist period and they pervaded the whole system until the late 1960s; naturally, the banking sector was no exception.

In the financial field, the legal expression of this reorientation of the economy was the passing of several laws to address the main financial consequences of the war as well as to provide a framework for the pursuit of the economic objectives of the regime. Regulation controlled entry to the banking sector, interest rates, banking expansion through branches and mergers, cash dividends, the characteristics of assets and liabitities and other banking activities.

In 1962 an attempt was made to liberalise the banking system; new banks and branches were permitted and interest ceilings were modified. But the transformation of the regulatory framework was not as great as had been generally assumed and public intervention remained the main characteristic of the banking sector.

The changes in the banking regulatory framework – the pre-war situation, the period of strongest financial restriction in Spain between 1939–1962, and the reform efforts between 1962 and 1975 – offer an instructive case study. This research has three main objectives. The first part of this book discusses the reasons for regulation: why the Franco government maintained a very restrictive banking regulatory framework. To understand the government's decisions on the financial legislative framework, Chapter 1 provides a general view of the situation of the Spanish economy from the end of the Civil War to the 1970s. This chapter analyses the main political and economic choices made by the Franco regime and the consequences of these decisions. Chapter 2 describes the main characteristics of the Spanish financial system in this period in terms of size, diversification or concentration. Chapter 3 examines the regulatory framework and the institutions which implemented this legislation. Moreover, this chapter summarises the main traditional views on the role of the Spanish banking system in this period. Chapter 4 explains the reasons for regulating the Spanish banking system under the Franco regime. The public interest and capture theories attempt to summarise the literature about the causes of regulation. According to the public interest theory, regulation emerges as a solution to avoid market failures (lack of information, allocation problems and so on). In capture theory, regulation is the result of interest group pressures. Lobbies consider regulation as a means of using state power in their own interest. Given these different theoretical reasons for regulation of the banking system, Chapter 4 discusses the possible explanations of the emergence of the Spanish regulatory framework from 1939 to the mid-1970s. The conclusions reached argue that the financial regulation was the result of two different pressures: the interests of the banking sector looking for a regulatory system which closed the market, reduced competition and eliminated uncertainty, and the interest of the authorities who tried to involve the banking system in their general strategy of development.

The second purpose of my research has been to assess the results of intervention. Chapter 5 is more specifically concerned with how factors external to the bank influence its behaviour. A financial institution is viewed in the literature as a firm that attempts to maximise profits by trading in financial assets and liabilities. It chooses quantities (deposits and loans) and prices (interest rates) as control variables. But banking behaviour depends also on how regulatory constraints restrict the choice of assets and liabilities and the 'strategic' or control variables banks can choose to maximise profits. This chapter develops a model of banking behaviour both with and without regulation – I present the basic model, show my results and discuss further implications.

After defining the implications of changes in regulation on banking behaviour from a theoretical point of view, the objective of this work is to empirically estimate the response of profits, concentration and other significant variables to changes in the regulatory framework. Chapter 6 examines a number of hypotheses that have been commonly proposed to account for the evolution of the Spanish banking industry in this period. One of these hypotheses relates to the 'structure-conduct-performance' theory and links concentration with profitability. A more concentrated banking system diminishes the cost of collusion. These collusive agreements reduce competition and increase profitability. The second hypothesis concerns the existence of scale economies in the banking sector. It focuses on the relationship between size and profitability. This chapter considers a general explanation for the evolution of the Spanish banking profitability in those years where I incorporate the possible effects of changes in regulation on the profit function.

Chapter 6 also deals with the impact of regulation. It is divided into three parts. Part 1 focuses on the effects of interest rate controls on Spanish banking behaviour. Part 2 aims to explain the main determinants of Spanish banking profitability and the influence of regulation. Part 2 is further divided into three sections. Section 1 examines the relationship between profitability and concentration, a general conclusion of the 'structure-conduct-performance' literature. Section 2 analyses the Spanish banking profitability in nominal and real terms and the existence of 'super-normal' profits in the banking industry. It also examines profits derived from the issues of shares or *plusvalias*. Section 3 is concerned with a general profit equation for the Spanish banking sector in this period. The important question in this final section of Part 2 is whether there is empirical evidence that profit-maximising behaviour was altered by regulation. Part 3 examines the possibility that regulation affects firms, not by changes in profitability but through risk. The firm may be a profit-maximising or a risk-averse investor. In this sense, regulation may allow banks to obtain not higher but less risky profitability rates.

Regulation does not only have an impact on financial behaviour but also on growth, inflation and the balance of payments. These questions, however, were not examined in this research. The absence of data on key variables and the relatively small sample do not allow consideration of these questions. My main interest has been in developing an explanation of how regulation affected financial markets. Hence, the particular questions which this research seeks to answer are: why did the Franco government regulate the banking sector? How was regulation undertaken? How did regulation affect banking behaviour? How did regulation affect banking investment decisions?

These questions have only been examined in Spanish studies in a fragmentary way. The most widespread claims in the 1960s and 1970s about Spanish banking during the Franco regime were:[1] 1) the financial system failed to provide the capital required in some sectors. Conservative lending practices of banks – their predilection for short-term loans and credit discrimination – supposedly delayed the recovery of the Spanish economy during the 1940s and 1950s, 2) banks discriminated in favour of those sectors in which they were involved: oil, electricity or the iron and steel industry, 3) banks behaved monopolistically in setting deposit and lending rates, and 4) the dominance of banks was ensured by regulation and reinforced by interlocking directorates of the largest banks.

According to these studies, the Spanish banking sector was a closed financial system, protected from external competition, controlled by a small number of banks (the 'Big Five') which owned substantial parts of industry. Banks protected from external competition were inefficient: lack of innovation, unsophisticated techniques and very high costs were the main characteristics of these financial institutions in this period. In exchange for this lack of competition (which gave banks high profits and low risks) banks were required to provide loans to specific priority sectors (a policy of 'privileged circuits'). They were also obliged to hold public debt both at and below market rates (in particular they were compelled to invest in long-term government securities which could be automatically discounted with the Bank of Spain without additional costs).

The main shortcoming of past research on the Spanish banking system under the Franco regime has been: a) the absence of a theoretical model to identify the main effects of regulation on banking behaviour, and b) the lack of empirical analysis about the possible effects of regulation on profits, risk, and banking modernisation. For these reasons, this study seeks to introduce two new elements in the analysis of the Spanish banking system during the Franco regime: a theoretical model of banking behaviour and empirical estimate.

A formidable difficulty, which bedevils any study of the Spanish economy in this period, is the lack of information in many areas. This problem is especially serious in the case of the banking industry. The private archives of the main banks are not open to researchers, although some banks are organising their archives at this moment.[2] My attention has thus concentrated on the information from the Bank of Spain Archives (until 1955),[3] the data published by the Superior Banking Council (SBC) and the Bank Annual Reports. Other sources of information of which I made use were the Bank of England Archives, SBC circulars, and other secondary sources.

One very important point should be mentioned here with regard to reconstructing data. Banks did not have homogenous accounts and they presented their economic results in very different ways. Thus, the first objective of this study has been to develop a general model of profit and loss account to obtain consistent profit figures. With this model we were able to obtain accurate information about the evolution of banking profitability, an essential variable for understanding banking sector behaviour in this period.

CHAPTER ONE

The Development of the Spanish Economy, 1939–1975

In this chapter I will discuss the main characteristics of the Spanish economy during the Franco regime. The purpose is, first, to explain the economic environment of the banking system at that time and then second, to analyse the main basis of the economic programme of the regime. To understand the role of the Spanish banks it is necessary to consider two factors: the first is the evolution of the Spanish economy in this period and the second factor is the economic policy of the regime.

With regard to the evolution of the Spanish economy we assume there to be a strong relationship between the economic conditions of a country and the evolution of the banking system (Goldsmith 1969). The main function of financial intermediaries is to take deposits and to transform them into loans and other financial assets. In this sense, the main 'input' of banks is deposits, which in turn depend upon savings. Thus, it is necessary to understand the evolution not only of income, but also savings and other macroeconomic variables, to explain the behaviour of the banking system.

With regard to the second factor, the economic policy of the regime, we assume that financial regulation is only a small part of the legal framework, and that it is therefore necessary to study the links between the policy choices of the government in foreign affairs, agriculture, industry, etc., as well as in financial regulation.

An understanding of the economic programme of Franco's government is essential to any explanation of banking regulation in this period. The purpose of the present chapter is therefore to give a general overview of the political objectives of the regime. The relationship between the legal financial framework and other government policies will be examined later in Chapter 4.

I. Introduction: Spain at the end of the Civil War

The Spanish economy after the Civil War was in a very difficult position. Although the Franco authorities explained their lack of economic success in the 1940s by emphasising the catastrophic effects of the Civil War, the physical destruction was less than that suffered by other European countries which were involved in the Second World War (Catalán 1992: 366). The railway network, the road system and housing were badly damaged, but these costs may have been overestimated. The most important loss was that in human lives, and this destruction of human capital had serious effects on economic activity. According to Díez Nicolás (1985: 41–55), the number of deaths during the three years of the war was around 344,000. A further 214,000 deaths occurred in the period 1940–1942 as a consequence of hunger, poor living conditions and political repression. Moreover, this demographic catastrophe had serious consequences for the birth rate. To these human losses we must add the number of people who went into exile during the first months of 1939 and the post-war years.

The economic consequences of the Spanish Civil War may be classified into the following categories:

a) The destruction of human capital.
b) Shortages (of raw materials, foods, capital goods, electricity, animals, oil, fertilisers and so on).
c) The destruction of physical capital. The First Development Plan of 1964 evaluated these costs as being: the destruction of 250,000 houses, and serious damage caused to another 250,000 houses; heavy losses suffered in the railways (around 40 per cent of all locomotives and wagons were destroyed and 61.2 per cent of all passenger carriages). Unfortunately, there are no accurate estimates of the losses incurred to industrial plant and equipment (Comisaría del Plan de Desarrollo Económico 1965: 9).
d) A decrease in savings and investment.
e) Inflation.

There are not many quantitative indicators of the economic situation in the post-war years, but we can compare the Gross National Product (GNP) and the working population structure before and after the Civil War:

As we can see in Table 1.1, after the Civil War the Spanish economy experienced an increase in the percentage of population working in the agrarian sector. Some authors consider that this was the result of the 'agrarian rhetoric' of the Franco government. During the formative years of the regime certain of its ideological supporters argued that agriculture was the essential element to achieve reconstruction (Carande 1941: 43–82). However, the Franco government chose a very different way to stimulate economic growth. The increase in the percentage of population working in the agrarian sector was more a consequence of the greater destruction and difficulties in the industrial areas, than an effect of government intervention. If we consider the productivity differential between agrarian and non-agrarian activities, the Civil War was an important cost for

Table 1.1 The sectoral structure of the Spanish economy before and after the Civil War (%)

	Working population		GNP structure	
	1930	1940	1935	1940
Primary sector	47.3	51.9	34.5	30.4
Secondary sector	30.9	24.1	31.7	30.2
Tertiary sector	21.7	24.0	33.8	39.4

Source: Alvarez Llano (1984: 43).

economic modernisation because of this misallocation of resources. Table 1.1 shows that in spite of an increase in the population working in the agrarian sector, the share in production of the Spanish primary sector decreased.

To analyse the consequences of the war, Catalán (1992: 359–95) made use of indicators of the degree of economic recovery. He examines the number of years that Spain, Portugal and Italy needed after the war – the Civil War in the case of Spain and the Second World War in the cases of Italy and Portugal – to recover the maximum level of real National Income (NI) that they had achieved in pre-war times. Catalán (1992: 266) affirms that the destruction of physical capital during the Spanish Civil War was lower than in Italy during the Second World War. The situation in Portugal was different because it was a non-combatant country, but nonetheless, it had serious economic problems after the Second World War in terms of shortages, inflation, etc. Catalan's study seeks to examine whether the differences in the economic situation in each of these countries were the result of the post-war destruction or a consequence of the different economic policies adopted by their respective governments. He shows that Portugal needed six years, Italy ten and Spain twenty-two years to regain the pre-war levels of real NI. The result is similar when we compare, for example, levels of food consumption in calories in these three countries. In the period 1934–1938 the country with the highest levels of calories consumed per person per day was Spain at around 2760 calories, but by the period 1953–1955 Spain was the country with the lowest levels of calories consumed. From the period 1934–1938 to 1953–1955 Italy had a rate of growth in the level of calories consumed of 2.4 per cent, Portugal had an increase of 9.6 per cent and Spain had a negative growth rate in the level of calories consumed of −10.4 per cent. The main conclusion to be drawn from the estimates of this author is that the economic policy of the Franco government retarded the process of reconstruction of the Spanish economy compared to the policies adopted in Italy and Portugal. Carreras (1984: 144–5) and García Delgado (1987: 167) came to a similar conclusion. To further understand these findings it is necessary to analyse the basis of the economic policy of the Franco government.

After the Civil War the Franco authorities faced several choices (Comín and Martín Aceña 1991: 68):

a) To choose an economic programme based on either the agricultural sector or the industrial sector.
b) To adopt a strategy of economic growth promoted by private enterprise and market forces or by the state.
c) To stimulate 'balanced' or 'unbalanced' economic growth.
d) To follow a strategy of 'inward-oriented' or 'outward-oriented' growth.

In the following pages I will examine the options that were finally chosen.

II. The main options of the Franco economic programme

The agriculture – industry option

One of the regime's options for economic development showed a preference for agriculture and light industry. The influence of the 'Falange'[1] can explain the defence of the social and moral values of the rural sector and so of this growth alternative. However, the winning option implied a very different strategy of development. The main objective of the Franco government was to maximise industrial production, regardless of the cost, and major legislation was passed to achieve this end.

There are some indicators of this government interest in stimulating accelerated industrialisation. After the Civil War the authorities introduced some privileges for firms declared to be of 'national interest' and the agrarian sector was not considered as a 'priority sector'. The main characteristic of the agrarian sector in the 1940s was scarcity: there was an important decrease in cultivated land, in production and yields. The Franco government explained this situation as being a result of wartime destruction, adverse climatic conditions (a prolonged drought) and a lack of foreign exchange resources to import machinery and fertilisers. However, recent research offers an additional factor to explain this disaster: agrarian policy (Barciela 1981: 383–484). Some contemporary reports also agreed with this claim. As Laurence (1950: 1) indicates:

> After the war, although many commodities were in short supply, one would have supposed that the main effort of the Spanish Government would have been directed to restoring Spanish agriculture to the state of

> efficiency obtained before the Civil War. Unfortunately this has not been the case. The main effort of the Spanish Government has been directed to industrialising the country, for which end the National Institute of Industry was set up, and only secondary consideration at best has been given to the needs of agriculture. Promises have indeed recently been made that something will be done for the farmers, but results have not yet been very impressive.[2]

Although Pelham (1950: 3–4) includes other complementary factors to explain the difficult situation of the agricultural sector he comes to a similar conclusion:

> Apart from admitting that the country has been afflicted by drought over the last three years, it is tempting to say that the regime has neglected agriculture in favour of grandiose schemes of industrialisation, but this would probably be only partially true. Many of the problems are deep-rooted and complex and even in the most favourable circumstances could only be solved over a number of years. The remedying of material shortages, such as the lack of fertilisers and agriculture machinery, would tend to some quick results, but the Government has been handicapped by the shortage of world supplies, and more recently by Spain's slender resources of foreign exchange. Nevertheless, it has shown itself less energetic in dealing with the problems of agriculture than with those of industry ... the Authorities have done little more than to impose largely negative controls over many of the phases of agriculture production, and that part of their industrial programme designed to supply the needs of agriculture has made little progress towards fruition.

State interference – discrimination against the agrarian in favour of the industrial sector and the rigid controls to regulate output, prices and wages – discouraged investment in the agrarian sector. The government designed various interventionist measures to stimulate the production of wheat and olive oil, especially in terms of protection and guaranteed prices. Results were bad in wheat and modest in olives. Growers reoriented their investments toward non-controlled or less controlled crops[3] and regulation stimulated the black market – known as the *estraperlo*. In spite of the *estraperlo*, low yields and food shortages were not avoided (see Tables 1.2 and 1.3). With many crops, the black market was even larger than the official market and *estraperlo* prices were three times as high as the official ones. The main effect of this situation was that in the black market the revenue per hectare rose. However, this 'positive' effect did not affect all farmers. Small farmers had few possibilities of avoiding interventionism. It was the *latifundista* (owners of extremely large areas of land) who were in a better position to participate in the black market as they had places to hide the crops, means of transport and financial resources to bribe civil servants (Barciela 1981: 396).

The government interest in accelerated industrialisation was evident in legislation. Several Acts were passed in 1939 to help the expansion of existing firms and to encourage new enterprises.[4] In addition the government introduced an economic programme to help specific sectors: nitrogen, man-made fibres and vehicle production. It included some privileges for these industries by way of tax reductions and lower tariffs to import machinery. The government also fixed a minimum guaranteed yield of 4 per cent on investments in these privileged sectors.

Table 1.2 Cultivated land, 1931–1949 and an index number of the evolution of this variable (1931–35 = 100)

	Thousand hectares				
	Wheat	Barley	Vineyard	Olive	Oranges
1931–35	4557	1895	1439	1903	75
1940–44	3716	1654	1392	1964	76
1945–49	3912	1553	1399	1993	71
	Index number of the cultivated land				
1931–35	100	100	100	100	100
1940–44	81	87	97	103	101
1945–49	87	82	97	105	95

Source: Barciela (1981: 386).

Table 1.3 Yields of the main crops, 1931–1949

	Wheat	Barley	Vineyard	Olive	Oranges
1931–35	9.5	12.6	13.7	1.83	139
1940–44	8.7	11.7	13.6	1.62	110
1945–49	8.0	11.7	11.5	1.66	102

Source: Barciela (1981: 386).

Until the end of 1941 the government believed that indirect measures of encouraging private investment were enough to stimulate growth. However, the poor results of these measures – shortages in consumer goods, low investment, lack of foreign exchange and inflation, among others (see Tables 1.4 and 1.5) –

forced the authorities to change and they decided to reinforce interventionism in a similar fashion to that used by the Italian government. Imitating the IRI, the Franco government set up the National Institute of Industry (INI), a state holding company intended to promote industrial development by direct action, particularly in those sectors concerned with the 'basic' industries (electricity, steel, shipbuilding, railway material, chemicals, cars, lorries and aircraft).

The INI was to promote 'economic autarky' by establishing industry where private enterprise had failed to and improving in efficiency what to date had proven inefficient – either through a lack of resources or incentives – and in the areas where the government considered it was essential to act.

Market forces or state control

The kinds of instruments the government used to promote industrialisation are linked with the second option I have mentioned: to adopt a strategy of economic growth promoted by the state or by private enterprise. The Franco authorities bet on a strategy of industrialisation under state control. The main problem of this public interventionism was that there was no coherent plan of industrialisation. Most of the projects were undertaken for reasons of national prestige or for military objectives, with little regard for their opportunity-cost.

The first official statement about the main 'future' characteristics of Franco's economic policy was made by the Ministry of Industry in a report on 22 March 1939 (Viñas et al. 1979: 294–7). In this report, the declared intention was: a) to nationalise the basic industries and b) to balance the balance of trade. The report remarked on the crucial role of state intervention to reallocate resources. State interventionism had been a constant characteristic of successive Spanish governments from the 1890s. The main difference between Franco and previous governments is that after the Civil War the degree of intervention was even greater. Moreover, the military component of government spending was also higher.

In the 1940s and 1950s the involvement of the state in the functioning of the economy was high in many European countries in the industries of coal, electricity, railway, civil aviation and telecommunications, among others. In fact the participation of the public sector in the Spanish economy was lower than in France, the United Kingdom and Italy (Comín and Martín Aceña 1991: 603). However, the main differences between Spain and other European countries were:

a) An autarkic strategy of development. In most European countries controls were understood to be emergency measures in the post-war years or for use in a very difficult economic situation (Cairncross 1992: 66). However in Spain these controls were conceived to be an essential part of Franco's strategy of development.

b) The degree of control. The government wanted a planned economy and planning was impossible without control. The use of direct controls was impressive: Spanish producers were subjected to regulations at almost every point in the production process. These controls pervaded the whole system: barriers to entry in the industrial sector, imports, investment, and labour conditions were all regulated by the Franco authorities.

c) The political regime. In other European countries the objective of increasing the role of the state in the economy was made within a democratic framework but in Spain the political system was a dictatorship and this difference has important consequences. The strong links between the Franco government and other interest groups (industry, banking groups and other members of the élite) facilitated rent-seeking behaviour, as it is easier for the elite to control the state in a dictatorship than in a democracy. Democratic regimes are responsible to an electorate at regular intervals and thus tend to act to the benefit of the electorate. A dictatorship, on the other hand, needs the support of influential interest groups to maintain in possession of power. I will discuss this problem in more detail in Chapter 4 where the causes of financial regulation in Spain in terms of the 'capture theory' are examined.

So far I have discussed the choices made in the first two options – to develop an economic programme based on the agricultural or the industrial sectors and to stimulate a strategy of economic growth promoted by the state or market forces. We have seen that Franco's economic programme was based on stimulating the industrial sector and that economic growth was promoted by the state. To examine the rest of the options I have mentioned ('balanced' versus 'unbalanced' growth and the role of foreign markets) it is necessary to explain in more detail how the government planned this strategy of industrialisation.

'Unbalanced' versus 'balanced' growth

The Franco authorities promoted 'unbalanced' growth. State interventionism was crucial in the industrial sector; however, there was no plan to help the consumer goods industries. As Table 1.4 indicates, from 1945 some industrial sectors achieved a rapid increase in output (chemicals, metallurgy and mining), but consumer goods suffered a slower growth.

In the 1940s NI and industrial output grew at very low rates – in fact, there were negative rates of growth in some years – as Table 1.5 indicates. Some

Table 1.4 Index of Spanish industrial production in different sectors, 1940–1958 (rates of growth in %)

	Energy	Mining	Chemical	Metallurgy	Consumer goods
1940–45	3.8	–2.7	3.2	–3.6	2.1
1945–50	5.0	7.4	18.0	7.7	–0.5
1950–55	7.4	8.2	12.7	9.0	7.3
1955–58	10.5	8.0	8.7	11.9	6.1

Source: Morella (1992: 129).

authors consider this period (1935–1950) to be the origin of Spanish economic backwardness and that during these years the 'gap' in terms of development between Spain and other more developed European countries increased (Carreras 1984: 144). However, this decade of low growth rates also coincided with an important structural change. As Table 1.4 shows, it was in the second half of the 1940s that the energy, mining, chemical and metallurgy sectors had very high growth rates in contrast to the consumer goods sector. We cannot establish a causal relationship between this evolution of industrial output and state interventionism; however, what we can affirm is that there was an important structural change in the 1940s where the process of accelerated industrialisation in this period was made at the expense of a strong reduction in consumption and a regressive income distribution (Morella 1992: 131). As Laurence (1950: 1–2) indicates:

> Industry needs capital, and when this has to be found from Spain's own resources it can only be at the expense of the consumers. Hence the general standard of living has steadily fallen and inflation has correspondingly increased, and there is no sign that either of these trends is being arrested.

All available information indicates that the Franco authorities bet on an 'unbalanced' economic growth and that the regulatory measures – preferential interest rates, tax reductions and other policies – helped basic industries. It is important to note, however, that the expansion of basic industries was not kept in step with the government's plans. Although expansion of electricity production was very important – in 1953 Spain had a productive capacity of electricity almost two-and-a-half times as great as it was in 1939[5] – this production was unable to keep up with the demands of industrial and other consumers. The same problem applied to other basic industries such as iron, steel or cement.[6] As I will explain

Table 1.5 Main economic indicators, 1941–1950 (rates of growth in %)

	Real NI[1]	Real IPI[2]	Real GNP[3]	NI[4]
1941	1.4	1.2	0.4	
1942	7.1	2.1	0.4	7.7
1943	–0.3	3.8	3.1	14.3
1944	2.5	3.6	2.5	10.7
1945	–2.3	–8.6	–3.7	17.7
1946	11	8.9	1.8	15.1
1947	1.8	–0.4	1.9	12.3
1948	–0.6	0.9	–1.2	15.5
1949	1.1	0.7	0.8	15.5
1950	5.1	3	1.5	13.8

Notes: (1) constant prices 1958, (2) constant prices 1958, (3) constant prices 1980), (4) Fixed capital formation/NI.

Sources: (1) and (2) Carreras, ed. (1989: 553–570), (3) Prados de la Escosura (1995), (4) Farré-Escofet (1980: 5).

in the next section, these serious problems of the basic industries were linked to Franco's foreign policy.

'Inward-oriented' versus 'outward-oriented' growth

A self-sufficient economy protected from external competition was the pattern of development chosen by the Franco government after the Civil War. There is controversy about the reasons for the isolation of the Spanish economy. Some authors consider that it was a consequence of: a) the diplomatic and economic boycott imposed by the 'democratic' countries on a 'fascist' state – for example, the United Nations decision to impose an economic boycott on Spain was taken in 1946 and not lifted until 1953. This boycott implied the exclusion of Spain from the Marshall Aid Plan of 1949 and b) the Second World War (Anderson 1970: 34–5 or Velarde 1962: 7). This argument coincided with the 'official' excuse of the Franco government.

Other authors claim that this isolation was a result of the ideology of the Franco regime itself (Tamames 1970: 230). The nationalist policy makers sought to promote self-sufficiency and they introduced important tools to achieve 'economic autarky'. As González (1979: 46) indicates, the Franco government rejected an American credit of 100 million dollars in the 1940s and Beaulac (1986: 102) explains how on 22 June 1940 Franco told the American ambassador in Madrid that Spain did not need American aid.[7] Abroad, the international community used economic aid to Spain to keep Franco from becoming a war ally of Hitler: in 1941 the United States authorised the shipment of wheat to Spain. The most generally held opinion is that, in the years immediately after the war, necessity and ideology determined the policy strategy developed by the regime.[8] From the beginning of the 1950s autarky was a matter of choice.[9]

Autarky was not justified by the regime in economic terms. The Franco government faced some ideological constraints. Nationalism was an essential element of the regime and so self-sufficiency was presented as a political ideal and economic reasons were relegated to second place.

To sum up, autarky, state interventionism and the promotion of accelerated industrialisation were the basis of Franco's economic programme until the beginning of the 1950s. However, inflation, public deficit and external disequilibrium were the result of the limitations of autarky and interventionism.

In the post-war years, the need for reconstruction and the presence of acute shortages in foodstuffs and raw materials explain rising prices. Inflation was also generated by the permissive monetary policy of the government which allowed the financing of the public deficit. In this period government expenditure increased continuously but revenues failed to meet this expenditure. The public deficit increased rapidly and imposed a heavy financial burden on the budget in terms of interest and redemption.[10] These deficits had an extraordinary influence on government decisions. Part of the gap between revenues and expenditure was financed by the issue of government bonds, for which the government looked for the collaboration of the financial system, as we shall see later in Chapter 4. Moreover, the government had access to the mint, allowing an extraordinary increase in the circulation of notes. The result was inflation.

With respect to the foreign sector, the Spanish economy had a serious disequilibrium in the balance of payments. Inflation restricted the country's export capacity and thus hindered its ability to import; foreign exchange control limited the growth of exports. Moreover, in the 1940s the peseta remained overvalued at the official exchange rates and this overvaluation hindered the growth of exports while it stimulated imports.[11] These problems explain the economic difficulties of the Spanish economy in the 1940s.

The government restricted imports and exports grew at a slower rate than in other European countries. For example, from 1948 to 1958 the rate of growth of real exports was 4.5 per cent in contrast to the 13.4 per cent in Italy (Tena 1992: 349). What were the reasons of these poor international trading results?

1. Quantitative restrictions were the main instrument in controlling imports. These government controls restricted the imports of raw materials, energy and other basic products. They had very negative consequences for the evolution of the agricultural and industrial sectors. In other European countries such as Portugal or Italy, after the war, the government reduced or even removed quantitative restrictions to obtain the necessary flow of imports. Spain faced two different problems. First, the government's interest in achieving autarky, and second, the lack of resources to finance an increase in imports. In Portugal, the government financed imports with its foreign exchange reserves, Italy, with external aid and an increase in exports, but Spain lacked the necessary financial resources. The final effect of these import restrictions was the impossibility for the Spanish economy to increase productivity in some basic industries.
2. Spain had many difficulties in achieving the recovery of exports. The reasons for this poor performance by the foreign sector were: a) the exchange rate policy. The Franco government established a policy of 'hard' currency. The peseta was overvalued and this foreign exchange policy was a disincentive for exporting, b) import controls limited the expansion of some essential inputs such as fertilisers, raw materials or machinery and c) the composition of exports. The percentage of agricultural products in total Spanish exports was higher than in other European countries. After the Second World War the demand for industrial goods recovered faster than the demand for agriculture products. Hence, Spain, with a low rate of productivity in the industrial sector, did not manage to benefit from the expansion of the international demand that took place during this period.
3. As I indicated above, the idiosyncrasy of the Regime and the boycott of the international community limited foreign financial aid. In the post-war years, other European countries such as Italy received an important amount of external resources to modernise the industrial sector. In Spain this foreign aid did not come until the 1950s. For this reason, the Franco authorities looked for an alternative source to finance their industrialisation programme and they chose the banks.

III. The transformations of the 1950s: the Stabilisation Plan

The decade of the 1950s started with relative economic and political openness. In 1950 the rate of growth of NI was low but inflationary pressures were very strong (Fontana and Nadal 1980: 146). In March 1951 there were important strikes in Barcelona. All these circumstances forced Franco to change the cabinet in July 1951. There are some signs of policy reconsideration in this change, showing a certain liberalising character, especially in the economic area. Furthermore, with the 'cold war', the United States initiated a process of 'rapprochement' to Spain. In 1950–1951 an American bank, the Export-Import Bank, provided a long-term credit of 62.5 million dollars to the Spanish Government and this credit was later extended by an additional 24 million dollar loan.[12] In 1953 Spain and the United States signed a military bases agreement under which the United States gained permission to build bases in Spain in return for considerable economic aid.

Moreover, in the early 1950s a group of young economists, linked to the Faculty of Political Science and Economics of the University of Madrid, entered political life. They considered that liberalisation was a precondition for development and they even proposed educational and political reforms. The identification of their programme with the 'Falange' notions allowed them to have considerable influence on the Franco government. In the same vein, a group of liberal managers, bankers and economists linked to the *Opus Dei* began to develop.[13] They supported the price mechanism as a central instrument of the economy and rejected interventionism. Both 'pressure' groups had a great influence on the political changes at the end of the 1950s.

Thus, it is evident that the Spanish economy experienced a considerable transformation in the 1950s. Different quantitative estimates show that the change in the economic structure was significant and that the rates of growth were high in comparison to the 1940s (see Tables 1.6 and 1.7). García Delgado (1987: 170–77) offers various estimates of GNP which indicate a rapid economic growth in this decade. Prados' estimates (1995: 65) are less optimistic and he considers that 'the 1950s, a decade of generalised growth in Western Europe, could be associated in Spain with incomplete catching-up, as the ups-and-downs in real output per head and the comparison with Germany and Italy tend to suggest.'

If we compare Spanish economic structures in 1940 and 1960 we see a substantial change. In this period there was an important transfer of the working population from the primary to the secondary and tertiary sectors (Table 1.6). The main result of this change was a substantial increase in productivity. In the agricultural sector there was a vast reserve of unemployed labour with a marginal productivity close to zero. The reallocation of resources and the occupation of this work force in the industrial and service sectors had positive effects on the rates of growth of the Spanish economy (Martínez Serrano and others 1982: 39–40).

On the one hand, these economic results were the consequence of the structural changes that took place in the second part of the 1940s as Table 1.4

Table 1.6 Spanish economic structure, 1940–1960 (two different estimations)

	a. Working population (%)			*b. GDP structure (%)*		
	1940	1950	1960	1940	1950	1960
Primary sector	50.5	47.6	36.6	29.8	29.7	23.7
Secondary sector	22.2	26.5	30.2	21.7	25.8	25.8
Tertiary sector	27.3	25.9	33.2	48.5	44.3	42.1

Source: Rodríguez (1977).

	a. Working population (%)		*b. GDP structure (%)*	
	1940	1960	1940	1960
Primary sector	51.9	41.6	30.4	22.6
Secondary sector	24.1	30.2	30.3	36.7
Tertiary sector	39.4	40.8	24	28.1

Source: Alvarez Llano (1984: 43 and 49).

highlights and, on the other hand, American aid also had positive effects on economic growth. Finally, the relative political change – in comparison to the previous decade – marked by a slight liberalisation which stimulated an increase in competition and efficiency could be another factor in explaining these improved economic results (Fanjul 1981: 135–42).

However, in spite of the relative economic improvements of the 1950s, in 1956 the limitations of autarky became increasingly apparent and Spain's economic difficulties reached crisis proportions. Relative price stability prevailed from 1952 to 1956 but the rate of inflation climbed to 9.14 per cent in 1956 and 16.62 per cent in 1957. The problem of this new price explosion was that it was unexpected and it shattered the expectations of stability which had been created after four years of relative price stability. This burst of inflation was generated by several causes. The magnitude of public deficit – and the way of financing this deficit with public debt which could be automatically discounted with/by the Bank of Spain without additional costs, a decreed wage and salary increase and the lack of elasticity of the supply explain accelerated inflation (González 1979: 49–82). The external value of the peseta fell and the balance of payments recorded a series of deficits. In these circumstances public discontent with

Table 1.7 Main economic indicators, 1951–1963 (rates of growth in %)

	Real NI[1]	Real GNP[2]	Real GDP[3]
1951	10.9	9.5	8.5
1952	6.8	9.6	7.4
1953	1.4	0.7	2.4
1954	7.2	8.1	8.5
1955	4.8	5	5.7
1956	7.2	6	6.9
1957	3.8	4.1	3.8
1958	5.2	3.9	3.2
1959	–2.7	6.3	–1.9
1960	1.3	3.2	3.1
1961	12.4	N.D.	13.1
1962	10.1	N.D.	10.7
1963	9.2	N.D.	9.2

Notes: (1) Constant prices 1958, (2) constant prices 1958 and (3) (Gross Domestic Product), constant prices 1980.

Sources: (1) and (2) Carreras, ed. (1989: 553–70), (3) Prados de la Escosura (1995).

economic and political conditions was very important (with student protests, and strikes in the North of Spain) in contributing to the political change that took place in 1957.

The Franco government had two options: to maintain the general political lines of nationalism – interventionism and autarky – or to change the main economic foundations of the regime and to initiate a process of gentle liberalisation of the Spanish economy. The change in the cabinet in February 1957 shows that Franco chose the second option. Franco never explained or justified his cabinet choices, and therefore it is very difficult to know whether he was conscious of the importance of this change. It would probably be inappropriate to see this cabinet change as a deliberate choice of a new political model but the limitations of the nationalist economic programme were by then evident and Franco did not have many alternatives.

The period from 1957 to 1959 was characterised by a series of initiatives by the government. In spite of this, at the end of the 1950s Spain faced a number of serious problems: inflation continued, the balance of payments was in a very difficult situation and social instability (strikes, student protests) was growing.

Foreign pressures and internal problems were the basis of the Stabilisation Plan of 1959 (Fuentes Quintana 1986: 131–57). The reforms affected also the banking sector through the *Ley de Bases* (Banking Reform Law) of 1962 and the subsequent laws.

This Plan was the first measure adopted to change the 'foundations' of the Franco regime in twenty years: autarky and interventionism. The first signs of this political change appeared when Spain became a member of several international institutions. Spain joined the Organisation for European Economic Cooperation (OEEC) in January 1958 and it also became a member of the International Monetary Fund (IMF) and the World Bank in the same year. The Franco government compromised by agreeing to economic reforms with these international institutions. By the end of June 1958 the Franco government sent a copy of the economic reforms it was prepared to adopt to the IMF and the OEEC. The government hoped to use these institutions as instruments for consultation and as a source financial aid.

Although the government had an interest in obtaining technical information, this consultation was also used as a sign to show to Spanish society and to the rest of the world that the government had clear intentions of starting a new 'era'. Moreover, people might be better disposed towards the negative effects of this reform if reputable institutions supported the Plan. Finally, the government received important financial support for the Stabilisation Programme.[14]

The Plan had a central objective: to achieve economic growth but avoid inflation, and a disequilibrium of the balance of payments. At the same time, the Plan set out to liberalise external trade and introduce market mechanisms. This economic and political change had an effect on the legislative framework of the banking system, as I will show in the following chapters.

The stabilisation programme worked successfully. The balance of payments improved spectacularly and inflation was controlled. This positive effect on prices was accompanied by a moderation in the growth of the money supply and a decrease in public deficit, although initially there was a recession which caused a fall in income, an increase in unemployment and a worsening in the purchasing power of the working class. However, recession was transitory.

The change in the direction of Spanish policy was perhaps not so great as has generally been assumed (Anderson 1970: 232–50). The government had no intention of abandoning control and the power it gave to those in charge of managing the economy. However, the economic and social situation forced them to reform their economic and political programme in order to strengthen the regime. For this reason the liberalisation process was timid.

After the severe recession associated with the Stabilisation Plan the Spanish economy had very high rates of growth. As Table 1.8 indicates, the rates of

Table 1.8 Main economic indicators, 1964–1974 (rates of growth in %)

	NI[1]	GDP[2]	NI[3]
1964	5.8	8.3	29.7
1965	7.1	6.8	30.9
1966	7.4	7.0	31.6
1967	3.7	5.6	30.7
1968	5.9	6.5	30.9
1969	6.3	9.3	34.9
1970	5.7	4.9	32.9
1971	5.0	5.6	30.4
1972	7.8	8.1	32.2
1973	8.8	8.6	33.7
1974	5.2	7.4	39.0

Notes: (1) (constant prices 1958), (2) (constant prices 1980), (3) Fixed Capital Formation.

Sources: (1) and (3) Carreras, ed. (1989: 553–70), (2) Prados de la Escosura (1995).

growth of the GNP (at constant prices 1980) were around 5–8 per cent. The literature speaks about the 'economic miracle' of the 1960s (Harrison 1993: 23). The quantitative evidence shows that the process of development of the Spanish economy was more gradual than the traditional literature has considered it to be. The low rates of growth of the 1940s were accompanied by a considerable structural change and during the 1950s there were high rates of growth which must be taken into account in interpreting the economic changes of the 1960s. That is why it is necessary to be more precise when we analyse the reasons for the economic evolution of the 1960s.

The reappearance of market forces linked to the Stabilisation Plan acted as a stimulus to economic growth. First, the liberalisation of foreign trade permitted the incorporation of new technologies and exposed Spanish firms to international competition. These two factors induced many firms to increase efficiency by the modernisation of their methods of production. Second, liberalisation allowed Spanish firms to benefit from a favourable international context. The 1960s were a period of high economic growth in many European countries and fortunately the changes introduced by the Franco government allowed the Spanish economy to benefit from this international situation. Western Europe was a huge market for Spanish goods and provided rising earnings from tourism.

Finally, other 'exogenous' variables such as emigrant remittances and foreign investment played a decisive role in this 'economic miracle'.

Spain suffered a severe economic recession in the mid-1970s. After 1974, the downturn in economic growth was substantial. Although many European countries suffered the oil crisis, the difficulties of the Spanish economy were aggravated by other internal problems: the limits of a planned economy and the unbalanced growth. Liberalisation efforts were insufficient and regulation avoided exposing the Spanish economy to market forces with the corresponding increase in efficiency that this measure would have encouraged.

If we consider the evolution of the Spanish economy from 1939 to 1975 we must mention two important aspects:

a) Although the literature speaks about the 'economic miracle' of the 1960s, the process of development of the Spanish economy was gradual. After the economic recession of the 1940s the Spanish economy achieved a considerable recovery as the rates of growth of the 1950s and 1960s indicate.
b) There is no accurate information about the growth of savings and investment in the first years of the Franco regime. The estimates of Rafart Febrer (1959: 35–50), Plaza Prieto (1971: 243–51) or Farré-Escofet (1980: 7), indicate that in the 1940s savings grew at a very low rate. The evolution of deposits in these years shows that they increased at a lower rate than NI. For example, the ratio 'deposits (banks and saving institutions)/NI' had a positive trend from 1940 to 1945 although from 1945 to 1950 there was a smooth negative trend. The ratio 'deposits/GDP' using Prados' data was lower than the ratio 'deposits/NI' although there was a positive trend from 1940 to 1949 – it was around 0.3 in 1940, 0.4 in 1945 and 0.44 at the end of the 1940s. With respect to the evolution of the proportion of savings in the hands of financial intermediaries, the ratio 'deposits/NI' in 1960 was 0.69 and the ratio 'deposits/GDP' was 0.58 and both indicators had a positive trend until 1975. Thus, these results show that with the exception of the 1940s, we cannot consider the Spanish economy as having a low rate of growth of savings during this period. One of the objectives of this research is to analyse the relationship of the evolution of deposits and the regulatory framework and whether regulation had a negative effect on the incentive to save. In Chapter 7 I will deal with these problems in detail.

IV. Conclusions

After the Spanish Civil War the Franco regime introduced many measures to reorganise economic activity. These political and economic measures reveal the basis of the economic policy of the regime. Although we must not exaggerate the consequences of the Civil War in terms of physical destruction, in the post-war years Spain was in a very difficult economic situation. Human losses and inflation were some of the main characteristics of Spain in this period. NI grew at very low rates and national savings were not sufficient to stimulate investment. The 1940s were a decade of stagnation and for this reason some authors (Carreras 1989: 127–57) speak about the 'failure' of the Franco economic programme to achieve the recovery of Spain.

The resources to finance the Spanish economic reconstruction were scarce. On the one hand, the external boycott and the political option of the Franco regime limited the amount of foreign resources available[15] – in terms of loans and other financial aid. On the other hand, the economic measures established by the regime had very unsatisfactory results and they impeded the flow of internal resources to finance the process of industrialisation.

The problems of the Spanish economy in the 1940s were linked to the economic programme of the Franco government. The Franco authorities bet on a strategy of development based on the industrial sector. In some areas there was no break with pre-war economic policy. In the 1920s, the Primo de Rivera dictatorship established a wide range of interventionist measures. This government outlined a very important plan of structural reforms and restricted competition in many areas. These measures were not only maintained but also reinforced in the 1940s. The main difference between the Franco regime and the preceding governments was the degree of control and intervention. Although some industries received a very important stimulus, the main result of this state interference was the very low productivity of the Spanish economy and the low rates of growth of the 1940s.

To summarise the situation of the Spanish economy in the post-war years, the government tried to achieve industrialisation through an increase in intervention and an 'inward-oriented' or 'autarkic' policy. However, this political economy of the regime caused serious bottlenecks. The low rates of growth of the 1940s were not only the consequence of this high degree of intervention but they were also linked to the strategy of national 'self-sufficiency'.

In these circumstances the government assigned a very important role to the financial system. The report of the Bank of Spain (1933–1945, D-6421) remarked on the importance of credit in the task of reconstructing Spain. The collaboration of the banking system – in terms of political and economic aid –

was essential for the Franco regime. In Chapter 4 I will explain how the government made use of regulation to achieve this collaboration. I will try to demonstrate how the legal framework was the result of different pressures: the interest of the banking system in eliminating competition and increasing profits – not only in banking activity but in other industrial sectors where banks made their investments – and the interest of the government in obtaining political support and developing a strategy of growth based on achieving autarky and the accelerated industrialisation of the country.

In the 1950s a process of liberalisation of the Spanish economy began and these measures had a considerable effect on the evolution of income and productivity. The important rates of growth in savings from the mid-1950s were a consequence of these positive economic results. Nonetheless, the Spanish economic situation had many contradictions as the 1956 crisis shows. Then, political and economic instability forced the Franco authorities to adopt the Stabilisation Plan. The reflection of this new economic environment created by the Stabilisation Plan of 1959 in banking regulation was the *Ley de Bases* of 1962.

In general terms we can affirm that the Stabilisation Plan was successful. The timid liberalisation linked to this Plan had a positive effect on economic growth in the 1960s. However, as explained in this chapter, the transformation of Franco's policy after 1959 was not very important. In some areas the authorities reinforced government intervention and they maintained an economic programme which contained many contradictions. These results show that the liberalisation efforts were insufficient. However, we cannot minimise the important structural changes in the Spanish economy in the 1950s and the high rates of growth in the 1960s.

In the financial area, with the Stabilisation Plan the Franco authorities made the first serious attempts to control monetary policy. They took the first steps towards liberalising interest rates and implemented policies to stimulate competition (Lukauskas 1992: 228). In this research I will analyse whether these political and economic changes affected banking behaviour too. I will examine whether the *Ley de Bases* of 1962 had a positive effect on banking competitiveness and efficiency.

Notes

1 The 'Falange' was an extreme nationalist political group founded in Spain in 1933 by Jose Antonio Primo de Rivera.

2 In 1950 M. Pelham, Commercial Counselor at the British Embassy, wrote a Memorandum about the economic situation in Spain. P.H. Laurence sent several comments on this Memorandum. See Laurence (1950: 1–2).

3 The most controlled crop was wheat to solve the problem of hunger in the 1940s. All other crops were controlled but less so than wheat.

4 See 'Decreto 8–12–1939 sobre Instalaciones de Nuevas Industrias y Ampliación de las Existentes' – an act to stimulate new firms and to help existing firms – 'Ley 24–10–1939 sobre Protección y Fomento de la Industria' and 'Ley 24–11–1939 de Ordenación y Defensa de la Industria'.

5 Carreras (1992: 177), indicates that the electricity sector grew faster than the rest of the sectors of the Spanish economy in those years. The electricity production in 1935 was 3272 kW, in 1940 3617 kW and in 1956 13740 kW. In spite of this growth, the weight of this sector on the whole economy was low. Catalán (1992: 219) affirms that the electricity sector was not a priority sector of the Franco government until the mid-1940s. The volume of public investment in the electricity sector was lower than in other sectors such as iron or steel. Furthermore, the incentives of the private sector to invest in electricity were very low because prices were regulated and the profits of private firms decreased in this period. Only from the mid-1940s when the government reoriented the economic policy by increasing public investment and reducing controls, the growth of the electricity sector was significant.

6 Many economic reports in this period made references to the modest results that the industrial program had in these basic industries. For example, the Annual Reports of the Banco Vizcaya in 1944, 1947, 1948 and 1949 made continuous references to the shortages in electricity production, iron, steel and cement. The Annual Reports of the Banco Bilbao made similar references in 1944 and 1949.

7 Beaulac was working in the USA embassy in Madrid in this period.

8 See, for example, Estapé (1966: 42).

9 There is an excellent survey about this controversy in Gamir (1975: 13–20).

10 The public sector under the Franco regime was very small. In fact, the ratio 'Public Expenditure/ GNP' was small until the mid-1980s. It was around 18 per cent in the postwar years and around (8–11) per cent in the 1950s, 1960s and 1970s (Comín 1994: 297). However, the main problems of this public expenditure were: a) the inflationary methods of financing the deficits, and b) the composition of the public expenditure. An important proportion of public expenditure was to pay interest and redemption and defense costs, but the amount of public investment was very low.

11 The official rate of exchange from 1939 to 1948 was:
1 dollar = 44.13 pesetas. However, in the free market the rate of exchange was:
1941 ... 1 dollar = 101.1 pesetas (PTAs)
1943 ... 1 dollar = 47.4 PTAs
1945 ... 1 dollar = 71.7 PTAs
1948 ... 1 dollar = 113.3 PTAs
As the Bank of England Report indicates (Bank of England Archives, OV61/4, 3 November 1947: 1): 'The Tangier value of the peseta of 129 pesetas = £1 as compared with the official rate of 44 pesetas = £1 is obviously no guide to the peseta's real value but that a very heavy appreciation is necessary to restore normality to Spanish trade is undisputed.'

12 From 1962 to 1972 the Spanish government received American aid of 2,900 million dollars. 35 per cent of this aid was in the form of loans, 45 per cent in the form of donations and the rest through other kinds of aid. To provide an idea of the quantitative importance of this aid, in 1953 the total aid was 12 per cent of the total of

foreign exchange obtained from exports. This percentage was 55 in 1956. See, for example, Fanjul (1981: 161).

13 The *Opus Dei* is an important order of Catholic laymen.

14 The Franco government received 75 million dollars in IMF drawing rights – a unit of account of the IMF, a basket of currencies weighted according to the international trading importance of each contributing country – 100 million dollars in OEEC credit and 70 million dollars in commercial credit from the Chase Manhattan and First National Banks. There were other additional financial aids. Moreover, the IMF gave financial assistance for a programme of currency devaluation. See Tamames (1976: 282).

15 Initially Spain received some help (especially in form of exports) from Germany. However, after the defeat of Hitler, only Argentina gave aid to Spain. The Peronist government sent 264.3 million dollars, which was used to buy wheat, maize and frozen beef (Viñas 1982: 89).

CHAPTER TWO

The Spanish Financial System, 1939–1975

Countries differ with respect to their financial structure (for example, level of diversification, types of financial instruments), modes of operation and relative size of the financial market. We can expect the differences in development to be reflected in this financial structure (Goldsmith 1969). It is the main task of this chapter, first, to describe the main characteristics of the Spanish financial system from the end of the Civil War to the mid-1970s and, second, to explore the main differences that exist between the Spanish financial sector and other countries.

In Section I I examine the relative size and diversification of the Spanish financial sector from a comparative perspective. Section II looks at the banking sector and in particular the nature of 'universal' or 'mixed' banks in this sector. Finally, in Section III I explain the main characteristics of the savings institutions.

I. The Spanish financial structure: size and diversification

To analyse the Spanish financial system, it is important to know its relative size, the relationships between the various types of existing financial institutions and how this financial structure changed over time. In this section, therefore, I will describe the Spanish financial system itself, and also provide a comparative perspective in order to obtain some indication of its level of development.

How a financial system is composed is as important as its relative size. The nature of a country's financial structure is influenced by the relative importance of different types of financial institutions. Commercial banks are normally the first financial institutions to emerge in a process of economic development. However, the development of non-banking institutions has an important influence on the intensity of competition. The role of foreign banks is another important differentiating characteristic of developing countries. Although some developing financial systems were dominated by foreign banks, in other countries foreign banks were prohibited or were restricted in their operating which inevitably affected competition and profitability.

Size

With respect to size, we can use two indicators: a) 'total assets financial intermediaries/GDP' and b)' total deposits/GDP'.[1]

The total financial assets / GDP ratio

The relationship between a country's financial structure and its real structure is reflected in the financial interrelations ratio.[2] This ratio is obtained by dividing the total value of all financial assets by the total value of tangible assets (for example, national wealth or gross national product). We can assume, as Goldsmith (1969: 373) indicates, that developed countries had a higher ratio 'total financial assets/GDP' than less developed countries. If we compare the relationship between total financial assets and GDP in Spain and the UK (see Table 2.1), we observe that after the Civil War the Spanish financial sector was less developed than the British financial sector. These differences were reduced in the 1950s; in this period the financial assets in Spain grew faster than the GDP, in contrast to those in the UK. When inter-

Table 2.1 The financial assets/GDP ratio in Spain, 1948–1975

	Spain (million PTAs)			UK (million £)		
	Financial Assets	GDP	Financial Assets/ GDP (%)	Financial Assets	GDP	Financial Assets/ GDP (%)
1948	133,636	140,817	94.90	18,263	11,820	154.5
1952	284,483	276,682	102.82	21,006	15,810	132.9
1957	621,068	506,109	122.71	26,299	22,110	118.9
1962	1,211,401	850,934	142.36	34,708	28,800	120.5
1967	2,392,515	1,754,434	136.37	58,362	40,520	144.0
1970	3,138,013	2,462,986	127.41	99,362	51,590	192.7
1975	7,824,966	5,902,156	132.58	209,722	106,350	197.2

Sources: Spain: Martín Aceña (1988), Boletín Estadístico del Banco de España, Balances de la Banca Privada (SBC), Memoria Crédito Oficial, Anuario Estadístico de España, Dirección General de Seguros (1962–1975) and Prados (1995) and the UK: Sheppard (1971), Financial Statistics, Capie and Weber (1985) and Liesner (1985).

preting this fact it is necessary to compare the relationship between the 'banking assets/GDP' ratio (Table 2.4) and 'total financial assets/GDP' ratio. In the British case, the decline of private banks coincides with the increase in importance of other financial intermediaries (building societies, trustee savings banks, finance houses, etc). In the UK, the 1950s and 1960s were periods of financial diversification, in contrast with the situation in Spain where private banks consolidated their position.

There are three main conclusions we reach about the size of the Spanish financial system. The first is concerned with the relatively small size of the Spanish financial system in the post-war years in comparison to other more developed countries (measured by the value of the ratio 'financial assets/GDP'). Although it is true that the financial sector in Spain was less developed than the British,[3] or the German financial systems (Table 2.2), following Goldsmith's estimates the ratio 'financial assets/GDP' in Spain in 1948 was higher than in both France and Italy (Goldsmith 1969: 209). The second concerns the strong growth of the Spanish financial system in the 1950s and 1960s. This rapid growth is a direct consequence of the low level of departure in the 1940s. In the 1970s this trend changed and the UK financial system grew faster than the Spanish one. Much of the expansion of the British financial institutions was due to the very rapid growth in foreign currency business (Committee to Review the Functioning of Financial Institutions 1980: 404). Third, Spanish banks controlled an unusually high percentage of the assets of all the financial institutions

Table 2.2 The financial assets/GNP ratio in different countries (Goldsmith's estimates) (%)

	1938	1948	1963
France	130	63	104
Germany	99	107	124
Great Britain	158	184	162
Greece	66	37	83
Italy	137	67	174
Spain	81	83	105
All countries	109.8	95.4	114.5
Developed countries	159.5	132.5	155.9
Less dev. countries	49.5	51.3	65.4
Less dev. European countries	75.2	62.7	108.5

Source: Goldsmith (1969: 208–9).

Table 2.3 The banking assets/GDP ratio in Spain and the UK, 1948–1975 (%)

	Spain	UK
1948	54.25	64.81
1952	53.57	50.01
1957	68.04	38.32
1962	76.24	35.01
1967	78.32	52.57
1970	61.66	105.86
1975	69.90	131.84

Source: See Table 2.1.

combined, in contrast with other more developed countries where the level of diversification of the financial system was broader.[4]

Deposits/GDP

Following Figure 2.4, the 'total deposits/GDP' ratio shows two different patterns of evolution: between the end of the Civil War and 1955, and from 1955 to 1970. In the first period, Spain had a smaller volume of deposits in relation to GDP than the UK. Although there was a considerable growth in the 'total deposits/GDP' ratio (with an annual rate of growth of this ratio at around 4 per cent from 1942 to 1950) the differences in size between Spain and the UK were very significant.

In the UK, in the second half of the 1940s, in spite of inflationary pressures, there was an important increase in the volume of deposits in the hands of financial intermediaries. Gibson (1967: 20–23) considers that in the post-war years people tried to compensate for physical and financial asset losses associated with the Second World War by increasing the saving rate. There existed an exceptional period when people increased savings to maintain the value of their assets. The Spanish case is very different. In Spain the two circumstances mentioned (war destruction and inflation) coincided, however, the evolution of deposits is different. In the post-war period the slow growth of the GDP and the high rates of inflation impeded a substantial increase in the level of deposits (Overseas Economic Surveys 1948: 4). In spite of this, the annual rate of growth of the ratio 'total deposits/GDP' from 1945 to 1950 in Spain (around 1.4 per cent) was higher than that of the UK (around 0.5 per cent).

From 1950 the UK financial system was transformed: there was a decline in the percentage of deposits in the hands of banks and a substantial increase on the volume of deposits in the hands of other non-banking institutions (especially building societies and insurance companies). Banking deposits and Post Office

Table 2.4 The total deposits/GDP ratio in Spain, the UK and Italy, 1942–1975 (%)

	Spain	UK	Italy
1942	31.15	86.11	58.85
1945	40.54	107.81	38.32
1950	43.51	110.47	35.30
1955	48.53	85.63	45.19
1960	58.94	81.82	58.10
1965	69.71	82.86	56.46
1970	74.18	71.51	64.17
1975	83.66	72.14	n.d

Note: Figures in Italy include banking and savings deposits, but not insurance companies and other non-banking institutions.

Sources: Spain: see Table 2.1, the UK: Sheppard (1971), Financial Statistics, Capie and Weber (1985) and Liesner (1985) and Italy: Ercolani (1978), International Financial Statistics and Liesner (1985).

Table 2.5 The banking deposits/GDP ratio in Spain, the UK and Italy, 1942–1975 (%)

	Spain	UK	Italy
1942	21.92	45.31	28.85
1945	27.24	56.68	24.34
1950	28.79	57.24	20.36
1955	32.99	40.22	26.88
1960	37.22	35.13	35.38
1965	42.39	31.55	33.71
1970	49.77	28.27	55.21
1975	55.63	39.61	70.00

Sources: See Tables 2.1 and 2.2.

deposits suffered the highest decreases (see Table 2.6) whereas other financial institutions such as insurance companies and savings banks maintained the proportion 'deposits/GDP' and other financial intermediaries such as building societies increased it.[5]

In Spain, from the beginning of the 1950s the total volume of deposits in the hands of private banks increased substantially (Table 2.5). The deposit rate of growth between 1945 and 1965 was around 15–18 per cent in comparison to 4 per cent in the UK. This late development of the Spanish financial system is an indicator of the level of underdevelopment of the financial market in the post-war years. In a period when we observe a process of banking disintermediation

Table 2.6 Financial diversification in Spain and the UK, 1942–1975 (Percentage of deposits in hands of different financial intermediaries)

Spain	Banking institutions	Insurance companies	Post Office	Savings institutions
1942	70.39	3.85	2.02	23.75
1945	67.21	3.01	1.63	28.15
1950	66.18	3.08	1.22	29.52
1955	67.97	2.33	1.19	28.51
1960	63.15	2.54	1.35	32.95
1965	60.81	2.04	1.74	35.41
1970	67.10	1.37	2.04	29.49
1975	66.50	0.61	1.77	31.12

UK	Banking institutions	Insurance companies	Post Office	Trustee savings banks	Building societies	Others
1942	52.62	21.98	12.17	4.54	8.37	0.322
1945	52.57	18.84	16.04	5.45	6.87	0.236
1950	51.82	20.19	13.41	6.30	8.10	0.187
1955	46.97	24.52	10.26	6.32	11.76	0.169
1960	42.94	28.51	8.12	6.24	13.97	0.211
1965	38.07	31.44	6.13	6.80	17.29	0.273
1970	29.83	34.77	4.06	5.11	24.54	1.685
1975	41.01	27.26	2.97	2.77	25.31	0.677

Sources: See Tables 2.1 and 2.4.

in modern financial systems, in Spain during the same period, the consolidation of banking power took place.

Diversification

Table 2.6 shows the main differences in the composition of the financial systems in Spain and the UK.

Comparisons with Italy are more difficult to make as a consequence of the very different financial structure of this country.[6] The Italian financial sector was more diversified than the Spanish financial sector. For example, in Italy, in 1945, 40 per cent of deposits were in the hands of the public law banks and the national interest banks, 27 per cent were in ordinary credit institutions and co-

Table 2.7 Financial diversification in different countries, 1948 and 1963 (% of assets)

		1948	1963
France	banks	42.07	39.82
	savings banks	9.00	10.49
	other credit institutions	48.94	49.69
UK	banks	34.60	21.44
	savings banks	12.91	7.22
	other credit institutions	52.48	71.34
Italy	banks	35.92	36.25
	savings banks	14.82	18.17
	other credit institutions	49.26	45.58
Spain			
Goldsmith	banks	62.40	71.36
	savings banks	11.04	16.52
	other credit institutions	26.56	12.13
own estimates	banks	61.2	67.9
	savings banks	13.7	12.5
	other credit institutions	25.1	19.06

Sources: Goldsmith (1969: appendix IV) and Table 2.1.

operative people's banks, 17 per cent in savings banks and the remaining 15 per cent in special credit institutions (Ercolani 1978).

We can draw two main conclusions from Table 2.6. First, the central position of banks in Spain, and second, the lack of Spanish non-banking institutions in comparison with the UK with the exception of savings banks. Results are very similar if we look at the percentage of assets in different financial institutions (Table 2.7).

Table 2.7 shows the level of diversification of the financial system in terms of assets in different countries using Goldsmith's estimates. As Table 2.7 indicates, the diversification of the Spanish financial system is less than in France, Italy and the UK. Moreover, the diversification of the non-banking institutions is broader in these other countries too. In my research I will try to link this distribution with the Spanish regulatory framework and to show how this lack of diversification affected competition and banking profitability.

To understand the size and diversification of the Spanish banking system, it is necessary to take into account the importance of the capital market. Sardá (1967: 33–42) showed that the Spanish financial structure was nearer those of underdeveloped countries than industrialised ones for two reasons: a) in underdeveloped countries the percentage of assets in the hands of the banking sector is higher (see Table 2.8), and b) the small size of the capital market. Sardá

Table 2.8 The percentage of resources in different financial intermediaries in less developed countries

	Banks	Savings banks	Special institution	Capital market	Total
Greece (1965)	68	13	11	8	100
Portugal (1963)	56	15	6	23	100
Spain (1964)	52	18	9	21	100
Turkey (1965)	43		17	40	100
Yugoslavia (1965)	42.4	0.8	56.8	n.d	100
Average industrial countries (a)	35.3	18	8.2	38.5(b)	100

Notes: (a) it includes Germany, Belgium, Denmark, USA, France, Italy, Holland and the UK.
(b) it includes (capital market + insurance companies).

Source: Sardá (1967: 36–37).

emphasises the fact that in underdeveloped countries not only is the capital market smaller but the performance of this capital market is very different (in terms of lower levels of transactions, lower levels of participants, etc).

Moreno (1954: 220) explained how from the end of the Spanish Civil War the capital market was characterised by the scarcity of voluntary savings in relation to the demand for capital, especially between the years 1945 and 1950. As we can see in Table 2.9, in spite of the improvements in the 1960s, the percentage of resources in the capital market in Spain (21 per cent) was considerably lower than in more developed countries (38.5 per cent).

II. The Spanish banking system

Banks operating in Spain were classified according to their nationality, Spanish or foreign according to their category as official or private banks; the latter were divided into national, regional or local banks. With respect to official banks, we can distinguish between the *Banco de España* (the central bank) and a group of official credit institutions which were designed to play an important role in the execution of the government's economic programmes. These financial institutions were (Ridruejo 1954: 171–80):

- the *Banco Exterior de España*, a public bank which was designed to promote foreign trade.
- the *Banco de Crédito Industrial*, which was established to finance small and medium firms. The beneficiaries of loans had to be always enterprises which were declared officially as of national and public interest owing to the nature of the services or of the production in which they engaged.
- the *Banco Hipotecario*, which was designed to provide mortgages. This financial institution specialised in long-term credit.
- the *Instituto de Crédito para la Reconstrucción Nacional*, an institution designed to repair the damages of the Civil War. It was closely linked with Franco's building policy (especially houses) and naval construction.
- the *Banco de Crédito Local*, which was established to finance local authorities, municipalities, provincial boards, etc.
- the Agriculture Credit Service (*Servicio Nacional de Crédito Agrícola*), which was transformed in 1962 into the *Banco de Crédito Agrícola*.
- the Fisheries Credit Institution (*Caja Central de Crédito Marítimo y Pesquero*).

The contribution of these financial credit institutions to the total financing of the economy in the 1950s and 1960s was around 9–11 per cent and it decreased in the 1970s to 6–8 per cent (see Table 2.9). This percentage is lower if we

Table 2.9 Total credits granted by different financial institutions, 1941–1975

	Private banks	%	Savings banks	%	Public banks	%	Total
1941	4,737	77.6	624	10.2	747	12.2	6,108
1945	6,462	70.7	1,058	11.6	1,622	17.7	9,142
1950	18,043	75.4	3,722	15.6	2,158	9.0	23,923
1955	37,806	72.7	8,569	16.5	5,654	10.8	52,029
1960	71,527	68.5	21,422	20.5	11,506	11.0	104,455
1965	145,504	54.5	72,691	27.2	48,588	18.3	266,783
1970	301,065	50.8	243,519	41.1	48,331	8.1	592,915
1975	1,202,010	57.3	712,112	34.0	182,186	8.7	2,096,308

Source: *Balances de la Banca Privada* (SBC), *Boletín Estadístico del Banco de España* and *Memorias del Crédito Oficial.*

consider the commercial bills and bills of finance held by the private banks. Although the bill portfolio contained commercial bills of exchange covering genuine commercial transactions, it also included a very considerable number of bank loans which were guaranteed in the form of bills. Therefore, the bill portfolio consisted more of short-term loans than of commercial bills of exchange. If we include the bill portfolio in the total volume of loans supplied by the private banking sector, the percentage of loans supplied by public banks is lower. These official banks raised their funds through the issue of government guaranteed bonds (for example, *Cédulas de Crédito Local* in the case of the *Banco de Crédito Local, Bonos para el Fomento de la Industria Nacional* in the case of the *Banco de Crédito Industrial*, or *Cédulas para la Reconstrucción Nacional* in the case of the *Instituto de Crédito para la Reconstrucción Nacional*).

In some areas these public institutions had a privileged position with respect to private banks as the general manager of the *Banco Hispanoamericano* indicated in a visit to the Bank of England (Bank of England Archives 1945, 0V61/4, 16 May, p. 1):

> Asked about the monopolistic position in Spain of the Banco Exterior, Moreno said that this was still a source of irritation to the Spanish banks who were doing all they could to circumvent it. The Minister secured a privileged position for the Banco Exterior in foreign trade, because the bank is specifically authorised to carry out in Spain all banking operations connected with the interchange of goods, services and capital between Spain and foreign countries.

There is controversy about the level of autonomy of these public institutions. On the one hand, Tamames (1966: 350) and Muñoz (1969: 168–206) consider that these official banks were controlled by the main private banks to avoid the development of public financing and to restrict competition. The main evidence of this control is in the links between private and public banks, especially where members were common to the boards of directors of both these kinds of financial institutions. On the other hand, the Directors' Minutes of some official banks, such as the *Banco Hipotecario*, show the lack of independence of these institutions; they reflect how their activities were directed by the government to fulfil its political objectives (Lacomba and Ruiz 1990: 389). I will show later that both factors (the interest of the banking sector in controlling the market and the objective of accelerated industrialisation of the Franco government) had a strong influence on the development of the Spanish financial system in this period. The links between the industrial, financial and political sectors made it extraordinarily difficult to delimit the real influence of these two factors.

The volume of loans supplied by the official banks in Spain was lower than in France (where the four largest banks were nationalised in 1945) and in Italy (where the public law banks and the national interest banks supplied in the 1950s around 45 per cent of total loans). However, it was higher than in the UK and similar to Germany (Opie 1962: 69–71). Therefore, the discussion about the role of public banking institutions in Spain during the Franco regime is actually part of a more general discussion between the proponents and opponents of public banks in the financing of industrialisation, at least in the case of less developed countries.

As mentioned above, Spanish private banks were officially classified into three categories: national banks, regional banks and local banks. According to the 1946 BSL, national banks were those which had total funds of more than 500 million pesetas in paid-up capital, reserves and deposits and regional banks, those which had at least 200 million pesetas in paid-up capital, reserves and deposits. The remainder were considered local banks. Nine banking zones were defined by the authorities. National banks had to operate in at least three of the zones or in any ten Spanish provinces and regional banks in at least one of the nine zones. All the remaining banks which did not satisfy these criteria were considered local banks.

Foreign banks were represented in Spain by the branches of the Bank of London and South America, the *Credit Lyonnais* and the *Banca Nazionale del Lavoro*, all in Madrid; and *Societé Generale de Banque pour l'Etranger et les Colonies*, in Barcelona and Valencia; in addition, both the *Banco Nacional de Mejico* and the *Banco Español Mejicano* were authorised to maintain an agency in Madrid, under express prohibition of engaging in banking or business operations. After the Civil War the operation of foreign banks in Spain was restricted and it was not until 1978 that barriers to entry were removed, and even then not completely.

Spanish banks were 'mixed' or 'universal' banks. The nature of mixed banks had its origin in the nineteenth century but after the Civil War the links between banks and industry were consolidated. As Edwards and Fischer (1994: 1) indicate, the term 'universal bank' does not have a single agreed definition. A universal bank is one which provides a complete range of commercial and investment services. The term 'universal bank', however, is also used to define German banks, where all banking activity and corporation ownership can be carried out by one incorporated bank. For this reason, it has sometimes been suggested that the key feature of universal banking is a holding of shares large enough to monitor corporations as equity owners, such banks can influence non-bank industries through equity ownership, the exercise of proxy voting rights, and supervisory board membership (Steinherr 1996: 4 or Krummel 1980: 35).

The following pages examine the main characteristics of the Spanish banking system, with particular reference to concentration and the consideration of Spanish banks as 'universal' banks.

Number of banks and branches

The number of banks at the end of the Civil War was 114 with an important decrease in the post-war years, with a minimum number in 1944 of 102 banks. Nevertheless, later there was a considerable increase in this number and in 1950 there were 134 (Table 2.10). This relative banking 'expansion' was not on the whole significant as the small size of most of these banks meant that the Spanish

Table 2.10 Number of banks

1923	106
1935	115
1946	114
1950	139
1955	124
1960	109
1965	126
1970	111
1975	111

Source: *Anuario Estadistico de la Banca Privada*, SBC.

banking structure, where a small number of banks controlled all financial business, was not affected by their entry.

The Big Five banks were: the *Banco Español de Crédito*, *Banco Hispanoamericano*, *Banco Central*, *Banco Vizcaya* and *Banco Bilbao*.

The number of mergers between 1960 and 1970 was 109. As Table 2.11 indicates, mergers were more frequent before 1960 than after. Mergers were a typical strategy of the national banks to increase in size in a market where branching expansion was restricted. For this reason, after the 1962 Banking Law, the relative branching liberalisation was reflected in a reduction in the number of mergers. The most significant aspect of these mergers was that there were no mergers among the 'core banks'.[7] In 1965 the *Banco Central* and *Banco Hispanoamericano* tried to merge but the Finance Ministry opposed the merger. In fact, they fixed a tax to be paid on this merger that was confiscatory (García and Tortella 1993: 30).

Table 2.11 Number of mergers

1941–1970	109
1941–1950	52
1950–1960	38
1960–1970	19

Source: *Anuario Estadístico de la Banca Privada*, SBC.

Regulation not only introduced barriers to entry but controlled the expansion of banks through branches (see Chapter 3). Initially, the reaction of the main banks was negative (Annual Reports *Banco Vizcaya* 1943 and 1944, and Annual Reports *Banco Bilbao* 1942, 1943, 1944). The SBC in a report about the Bill of the BSL of 1946 (Bank of Spain Archives, Report of the SBC about the Bill of the 1946 BSL 1946: 14[8]) considered that this law seriously restricted branching expansion and they demanded the removal of these controls. After the BSL of 1946 it is not possible to find these kinds of complaints in the banking reports.

The effect of the 1962 Banking Law on branching was quite considerable. The total number of branches and agencies rose in a spectacular way, especially from 1963 (see Table 2.12). In this period the proportion of branches of the large banks decreased in comparison with the regional and local banks (Table 2.14). As I will explain later, as price competition was limited, the opening of branches was used as an instrument to increase the volume of deposits by location and advertising.

To obtain an indicator of the size of the branch network the 'number of branches/10,000 inhabitants' ratio was estimated. Table 2.13 shows that the

Table 2.12 Number of branches

1936	1903
1948	2157
1950	2226
1955	2449
1960	2647
1965	3421
1970	4291
1975	7218

Source: *Anuario Estadístico de la Banca Privada*, SBC.

Table 2.13 Number of branches per 10 000 inhabitants

Years	Spain	UK	Italy
1936	0.79	2.44	1.80
1948	0.78	2.24	n.d
1950	0.80	2.19	1.66
1955	0.84	n.d	1.68
1960	0.87	2.35*	1.88
1965	1.07	2.40	1.98
1970	1.27	n.d	2.04
1975	2.03	n.d	2.12

Note: (*) year 1962.

Sources: *Anuario Estadistico de la Banca Privada* (SBC), Alhadeff (1968), Mitchell (1988), Liesner (1985) and Barina and Carletti (1986).

number of branches in Spain until 1965 was clearly lower than in other countries such as Italy or the UK. However, the opening of branches from the middle of the 1960s was such that by the mid-1970s the differences were insignificant.

Branch expansion was more important in the national banks than in the local and regional banks. As Table 2.14 indicates, between 1950 and 1960, the Big Five banks opened 62 per cent of total new branches and between 1960 and 1970 this percentage was 51. In 1960 the Big Five had 67 per cent of total branches in Spain. In the United Kingdom the percentage of total branches in hands of the Big Five was also high: in 1938 the Big Five had 84 per cent of

Table 2.14 The percentage of branches in different banking institutions

A. – The Spanish banking system

Year	National banks	Regional banks	Local banks	Big Five banks
1950	85.5	9.2	5.2	70.9
1960	87.6	8.6	3.8	66.8
1965	81.6	11.1	7.3	60.8
1975	75.6	12.6	11.8	56.7

B. – The Italian banking system

Year	Big banks (*)	Cooperative	Other banks (**)
1950	46.5	14.7	38.7
1960	45.5	16.0	38.4
1965	45.3	16.6	38.0
1975	44.3	18.3	37.4

Notes: (*) Public banks, banks of national interest and ordinary credit banks are the big banks in Italy.
(**) includes savings institutions and other financial institutions.

Sources: *Anuario Estadístico de la Banca Privada* (SBC), Aldaheff (1968), and Barina and Carletti (1986).

total branches, 84 per cent, again, in 1951 and 85.7 per cent in 1962 (Alhadeff 1968: 246).

In Italy, from 1938 to 1945, the total number of branches decreased, although the big banks – the public banks, banks of national interest and savings banks – increased their branches. After the Second World War, the authorities authorised an increase in the number of branches; however, in this period the big banks increased their branches to a lesser extent than the small and medium-size banks. This change in the initial trend was the result of government intervention; the Italian government decided to stimulate the opening of new banks and branches in backward and rural areas, places where big banks had shown no great interest (Alhadeff 1968: 17–9). That is why in 1965 national interest banks plus public banks – the biggest banks – had only 22.5 per cent of total branches.

Structure of assets and liabilities: the nature of mixed banks

Spanish banks are mixed or universal banks. As mentioned above, their equity ownership, the exercise of proxy votes and their involvement in supervisory board membership of non-banks are the defining characteristics. As also indicated above, the term universal bank is used to define German banks. In this latter case the concept of mixed banks is linked to two additional features: a) a large part of the funds for investment are provided in the form of bank loans and most of these loans are long-term loans and b) banks closely monitor the performance of their firms (Edwards and Fischer 1994: 1). If we accept that these five aspects are the main characteristics of universal banks, then the main question is to decide whether Spanish banks were indeed universal banks according to this general definition.[9]

The significance of bank loans in the finance of aggregate investment in Spain

Spain had a very low level of self-financing in comparison with other European countries. The Report of the Chambers of Commerce (*Ministerio de Hacienda* 1961: 7) indicated that the level of self-finance of Spanish firms was around 25–28 per cent. As Collins (1991: 60–63) shows, in the UK retained profits as a proportion of capital employed were invariably in excess of 60 per cent and on occasions more than 70 per cent. Edwards and Fischer's estimates (1994: 54–5) of the sources of finance for investment in Germany over the period 1950–1989 show that internally-generated funds were the largest source of finance for investment (around 64 per cent between 1950 and 1959 and 62 per cent between 1960 and 1969). On the contrary, the principal source of finance for Spanish firms was borrowing and the evolution of capital investments was closely linked to credit conditions. Lluch (1974: 57) calculated self-finance as a percentage of total industry finance in selected firms (see Table 2.15).

Sardá (1968: 43) estimated the level of self-finance of some of the less developed European countries such as Greece, Portugal or Yugoslavia between 1963 and 1965 and he found that the level of self-finance in Spain (27 per cent) was closer to Greece (31.2 per cent) and Portugal than to the more developed countries (with an average of around 50 per cent). Therefore, empirical information shows that the proportion of investment financed by loans in Spain is higher than in other countries with a mixed banking system such as Germany or Italy. In this case we can categorise Spain as having a more 'bank-based' system of investment finance than Germany or Italy.

Table 2.15 The percentage of self-finance as a percentage of total industrial financing

Spain (1964–1970)	27
West Germany (1968–1970)	49
England (1969–1970)	42
Italy (1968–1970)	41
Sweden (1967–1968)	56
USA (1967–1968)	54

Source: Lluch (1974: 57).

The composition of loans

One of the defining aspects of mixed banks is the importance of long-term loans. The Spanish data are not easily comparable to the German or the Italian data because of different accounting criterions concerning the maturity of loans. There are two main problems when comparing these different banking structures. First, the maturity of long-term loans in Spain was very short in comparison to other countries. The 1946 BSL, the Bank of Spain statute and the Commerce Code restricted banks to providing only short-term credit (credit of less than 90 days). Only credit for some national interest or privileged sectors was excluded from this general rule. After the Decree Law 7/1960 this restriction was removed. Therefore, the series of long-term loans from the *Balances de la Banca Privada* (SBC) are not homogeneous for the period 1942–75 and it is not possible to know the total volume of long-term loans (loans granted for a period exceeding 90 days) supplied by Spanish banks.[10] Second, Spanish banks provided an important part of short-term credits in the form of 'bills of finance' (Prados Arrarte 1958: 46). According to the balance accounts of Spanish banks (*Balances Consolidados de la Banca Privada* (SBC), in Spain the percentage of long-term loans with respect to the total volume of credit in 1946 was around 68 per cent, and it increased to 69.54 in 1970. If we consider the ratio 'long-term loans/(total loans + bills)', the percentage of long-term credit is considerably lower: 36.96 per cent in 1946 and 22.51 per cent in 1970.

Sanchez Pedreño (1961) re-estimated the volume of long-term loans, to make the series comparable with the German and the Italian data, although he admits that he was probably underestimating the total volume of long-term loans. The results are in Table 2.16 (Martin Aceña and Pons 1994: 133–4).

According to Table 2.16, in Spain the proportion of long-term credit with respect to total assets was lower than in Italy and Germany. The differences are

Table 2.16 Banking structure in Germany, Italy and Spain, 1959

	Spain (a)	Germany (b)	Germany (c)	Italy (d)	Italy (e)
ASSETS					
1. Cash and balances with central bank	7.9	9.2	4.6	13.4	14.8
2. Short-term assets	59.7	52.6	28.8	42.4	35.9
2.1. Discount (bills)	33.9	20.5	6.8	21.4	17.8
2.2. Short-term credit (loans and advances)	25.8	32.1	22	20.9	18.1
3. Investment	31.2	27.4	46.6	27.5	32.9
3.1. Long-term credit	1.4	14	37.1	8.5	12.8
3.2. Industrial securities	7.2	11.6	7.7	8.7	9.6
3.3. Government bonds	22.6	1.8	1.8	10.3	10.4
4. Real assets	1.2	10.8	20	18.9	16.4
TOTAL ASSETS	100	100	100	100	100
LIABILITIES					
1. Current account and demand deposits	66.2	26.5	18.2	41.9	40
2. Time deposits and other long-term resources	8.4	44.9	61.7	41.7	43.8
3. Central bank credit	17.5	2.5	2.4	4.1	2.1
4. Capital and reserves	6	7.2	6	9.4	2.5
5. Other liabilities	1.9	18.9	11.7	2.9	11.6
TOTAL LIABILITIES	100	100	100	100	100

Notes: (a) private banks, (b) only commercial banks, (c) commercial banks, savings banks, credit cooperatives, postal banks and other institutions, (c) ordinary credit banks, (d) all institutions: ordinary credit banks, public law banks, banks of national interest, cooperative banks and savings institutions.

Sources: For Spain, Sanchez Pedreño (1961: 6–8). For Germany: The Handbook of Statistics, Federal Republic of Germany, 16 (1961): 123 and for Italy, Cerani (1962: 138) and *Annuario Statistico Italiano* (1961).

very important: only 1.4 per cent of the assets of Spanish banks were in the form of long-term loans in contrast to 14 per cent in Germany (more than 37 per cent if we include other financial institutions such as savings banks or credit cooperatives) or 8–12 per cent in Italy. In this sense, the Spanish banking system had a more similar asset structure to commercial banks (such as the UK banks) than to universal banks.

From the balance accounts of Spanish banks we obtain a very different result (see Table 2.17). According to this information, in Spain the percentage of long-term loans with respect to the total volume of credit in 1946 was around 68 per cent, and it increased to 69.54 in 1970. The main problem with this information is similar to that indicated above, that is, a very significant share of these long-

Table 2.17 The percentage of long-term loans with respect to total credit

	1942	1946	1955	1960	1965	1970	1975
Hispano	46.36	53.33	57.48	59.87	51.29	47.37	53.12
(a) LC/TC							
(b) LC/TC+B	27.25	21.76	18.95	20.35	14.07	11.89	17.95
Español	68.82	81.35	80.82	75.85	67.53	72.83	61.02
(a) LC/TC							
(b) LC/TC+B	52.44	47.82	71.50	34.75	25.30	29.05	20.17
Central	8.61	73.98	77.24	80.50	67.70	63.57	48.44
(a) LC/TC							
(b) LC/TC+B	6.02	41.20	25.44	27.57	16.00	36.87	13.31
Bilbao	37.10	73.89	59.82	65.67	73.86	77.04	65.40
(a) LC/TC							
(b) LC/TC+B	26.61	47.00	13.22	14.96	12.43	20.96	21.96
Vizcaya	71.18	63.64	73.53	83.18	84.10	77.84	68.91
(a) LC/TC							
(b) LC/TC+B	55.69	58.99	27.81	30.94	22.30	17.99	27.86
Urquijo	42.00	55.49	63.23	64.39	54.19	69.45	65.63
(a) LC/TC							
(b) LC/ TC+B	24.96	33.06	18.85	15.53	9.35	22.20	41.73
Average banking system							
(a) LC/TC	61.77	68.23	70.61	73.16	71.96	69.54	65.24
(b) LC/TC+B	38.03	36.96	30.71	30.31	22.45	22.51	25.27

Notes: (a) LC/TC: Long-term credit/Total credit, (b) LC/TC+B: Long-term credit/ (Total credit + commercial and financial bills)

Sources: *Balances de la Banca Privada* (SBC) and *Boletín Estadístico del Banco de España*.

term loans were actually short-term loans. From Table 2.17 we can draw two conclusions: 1) the most universal bank, the *Banco Urquijo* had a percentage of long-term loans below the average of the banking system, although it increased the percentage in this period and 2) there are significant differences among banks. Table 2.17 shows that the more 'industrial-oriented' banks (such as the *Banco Bilbao* or *Banco Vizcaya*) increased the percentage of long-term loans with respect to the total volume of loans, in contrast to the more 'commercial-oriented' banks (such as the *Banco Hispanoamericano*) which had a lower percentage of long-term loans.

Therefore, the importance of short-term loans in the Spanish banking industry is unquestionable. Although in practice banks renewed short-term credits continuously and they transformed short-term credits into long-term credits (Prados Arrarte 1958: 45, Bank of Spain 1961, D-20748: 19 or Bank of Spain Annual Report 1967, June, Chapter 10), this type of lending caused insecurity, especially in small firms which lacked other means of finance. As indicated before, in Spain the level of self-financing in comparison with other countries was quite low. In other countries where a small number of banks dominated the banking system, a monopolistic market did not mean a monopoly over the entire range of credit provision. In Spain where there were no alternative sources of finance – because of the lack of diversification of the financial system and the small size of the capital market – banks had extraordinary market power in this area – although this power was considerably reduced after the 1962 Banking Law and the development of savings institutions in the 1960s and 1970s.

The regulation of Spanish banks determined the structure, not only of assets like public bonds, but also liabilities such as loans. The government encouraged banks to invest in new issues of Treasury Bonds who in fact took up the bulk of them. As shown in Table 2.16, in the case of German banks, the volume of funds transferred to the public sector represented less than 2 per cent, while for Italy and Spain the proportions were relatively larger at around 10 and 23 per cent respectively. Thus, the contribution of Spanish banks to the financing of the public sector is clearly higher than that of the Italian or German banks.

Equity shares in bank portfolios

Another characteristic of mixed banks is the holding of non-banking shares. There are two different aspects we must observe. First, the importance of non-banking equities. Second, how Spanish banks were able to exercise proxy votes on behalf of the shareholders who had deposited their shares with the banks for safekeeping (*guarda de valores*). It is therefore necessary to distinguish between 'ownership' and 'control'. The combination of these two mechanisms will show us the total 'degree' to which Spanish banks controlled industrial firms.

The industrial portfolio of Spanish banks is smaller than the German or the Italian ones, although the differences are not very significant (Table 2.16). Spanish banks' holdings of industrial securities represent only a small percentage of total assets throughout the entire period and furthermore this percentage decreased continuously from 1943 to 1970 – this especially contrasts with the importance of public securities' holdings (see Table 2.18). The only bank with substantial differences is the *Banco Urquijo*: in 1943 the *Banco Urquijo* had 26.8 per cent of its total assets in industrial securities, in 1955, 21.56, and in 1969, 8.9.[11] With the Big Five banks, the most 'commercial-oriented' bank was the *Banco Hispanoamericano*, in terms of holdings of industrial securities. The most 'universal' banks were *Banco Vizcaya* and *Banco Bilbao* (Table 2.19).

Table 2.18 The evolution of the investment in industrial securities (% of total assets)

	Industrial securities/ Total assets		Industrial securities/ Total credits	
	Total banks	Big Five	Total banks	Big Five
1943	7.95	6.94	40.10	32.01
1949	6.87	5.66	37.32	30.45
1955	4.52	4.02	26.69	29.31
1958	4.47	3.95	28.66	28.96
1961	3.97	3.37	25.04	22.01
1965	2.56	2.13	19.35	14.61
1970	2.30	2.46	20.59	22.36
1975	2.55	2.55	18.23	19.62

Source: *Balances de la Banca Privada* (SBC), several years.

What about 'proxy' votes or *guarda de valores*? Many shareholders, especially private individuals, use the banks' securities deposit service for the safe custody and administration of their shares. Banks which hold shares for depositors can exercise the voting rights attached to these shares. Table 2.20 shows the total volume of shares in bank deposits for the total banking system and the Big Five banks. These estimates are based on the nominal values of the shares.

As we can see in Table 2.20, around 55–70 per cent of total securities were deposited in the Big Five banks. How important were these 'proxy' votes? For

Table 2.19 Industrial securities, Big Five banks

	1943	1955	1965	1970
Central				
(a) I/A	8.81	3.61	1.84	2.52
(b) I/L	3.99	31.13	17.35	31.79
Español				
(a) I/A	5.54	2.51	1.61	2.31
(b) I/L	23.39	14.56	11.05	14.68
Hispano				
(a) I/A	2.80	2.66	1.75	1.98
(b) I/L	13.09	18.74	12.78	17.85
Bilbao				
(a) I/A	9.70	6.54	3.27	2.33
(b) I/L	49.43	85.94	40.17	24.94
Vizcaya				
(a) I/A	16.14	8.78	3.26	2.27
(b) I/L	86.44	66.68	27.65	24.68

Notes: (a) I/A: ratio 'Industrial securities/Total assets' × 100.
(b) I/L: ratio 'Industrial securities/Total loans' × 100.

Source: *Balances de la Banca Privada* (CSB).

Table 2.20 Banks' securities deposit service

	Total banks	Big Five banks	% Big Five/Total banks
1941	29,195,407	15,859,209	54.32
1948	59,741,277	40,965,333	68.57
1955	136,721,898	100,496,811	73.50
1960	229,761,875	114,387,940	49.79
1965	389,305,740	258,151,720	66.31
1967	533,617,001	341,496,639	64.00
1970	814,482,688	528,923,839	64.94
1975	1,727,394,558	1,031,202,691	59.70

Sources: 1941–1948, *Anuarios Financieros y de SA* and 1948–1975, *Balances de la Banca Privada* (SBC).

example, in 1965 the banks' securities deposit service was of 389,305,740 PTAs and of this 258,151,720 in the Big Five banks. In this year the total value of the shares of the limited companies in Spain was 474,841,900 PTAs (securities and bonds). As we can see, the Big Five banks had the security deposit service of 53.96 per cent of total securities of the limited companies in Spain and the entire banking system 81.37 per cent of these total securities. Therefore, Spanish banks were the group with the largest holdings of shares in Spanish enterprises. The main problem is that we do not have any information about the degree of bank control of equity voting rights due to proxy votes, although some important bankers such as Ignacio Villalonga (1962: 108), from the *Banco Central* indicated that many shareholders (especially, small shareholders) delegated their votes to the banks where they had deposited their securities, in particular for the election of shareholder representatives to the supervisory boards. He recognised the 'power' that these proxy votes gave to Spanish banks in terms of the control of the management boards.

Bank supervisory board representation

The supervisory board of a firm has the function of controlling its management. Then, depending on the extent of their control of equity voting rights, banks can have a significant influence on the outcome of votes at shareholders' meetings, and in particular on shareholder representation on supervisory boards.

As an indicator of the connections between the main 'mixed banks' and industry I have included Table 2.21. This table gives a detailed analysis of the number of sectors, the number of participating firms, the numbers of seats (*consejeros*) and how many members of the supervisory board of a bank were presidents of another industrial firm. There is an important problem in interpreting this data. Many banks had a significant number of seats on the boards of directors of industrial firms. However, as in most cases the 'power' of these *consejeros* was very limited, the number of presidents on the firm's board of directors is more significant than the number of members.

In 1944 the bank with the highest number of seats was the *Banco Vizcaya*. In 1944 and 1967 the bank with the highest number of presidents was *Banco Español de Crédito*, followed by *Banco Vizcaya* and *Banco Central* respectively. Again the most 'commercial oriented' bank was the *Banco Hispanoamericano*, with the lowest number of *consejeros* and presidents in industrial firms.

In the 1920s the main interests of private banks were located in electricity, railways, mining, iron and steel and tobacco. According to De la Sierra (1953: 37–63), in the 1940s the sectors with the highest banking participation were: coal, steel, electricity, cement, fertilisers and chemicals. Although the large

Table 2.21 Spanish banks' representation on the supervisory boards

	1922		1944 (2)		1967		
Bank	Firms	Seats(1)	Firms	Seats(1)	Sectors	Firms	Seats(1)
Hispano	28	36	15	30 (1)	30	143	184 (53)
Español	47	63	25	41 (8)	46	271	358 (95)
Central	–	–	10	23 (3)	41	220	354 (69)
Bilbao	91	128	15	31 (5)	40	232	388 (78)
Vizcaya	64	150	19	60 (5)	44	254	429 (90)
Urquijo	67	107	13	24 (6)	36	178	219 (66)

Notes: (1) It includes the total number of interlocking members of the board of director + top members (president, vice-president and directors). The numbers between parentheses refer to the number of members of the board of directors who were presidents of a firm. (2) There is no information about the total number of firms and seats in 1944 because De la Sierra (1953) only studied a sample of firms.

Sources: 1922: Muñoz, Roldán and Delgado (1973), 1944: De la Sierra (1953) and 1967: Muñoz (1969).

banks participated in a wide variety of sectors, the main links between banks and industry were in the cases of the *Banco Central* in electricity, the *Banco Español de Crédito* in electricity and cement, the *Banco Bilbao* in steel, electricity and coal, the *Banco Vizcaya* in electricity and the *Banco Urquijo* in steel, coal and fertilisers.

If we consider the main sectors where banks had interlocking directorates in the 1960s, we see that the main investments of the *Banco Central* were in electricity, followed by machinery and metallurgy, and property companies. The interests of the *Banco Español* were concentrated in machinery and metallurgy, chemicals, and electricity. With respect to the rest of banks: the *Banco Bilbao* was involved in machinery and metallurgy, mining, and chemicals, the *Banco Vizcaya* in electricity, machinery and metallurgy, and chemicals and, finally, the *Banco Urquijo* participated in electricity, machinery and metallurgy, and electric material.

The two most significant differences between the post-war years and the late 1960s were: first, an increase in the number of sectors where banks participated. Other new sectors such as insurance companies, property companies, or the car industry were added to the traditional sectors (electricity, steel and mining). Second, an intensification of the links between banks and industry. Table 2.22

Table 2.22 The number of members of the boards of directors of banks in the electricity, steel and mining sectors

	Electricity 1944(1)	1967	Steel 1944(1)	1967	Mining 1944(1)	1967
Español	4F,6M	18F,26M	2F,2M	4F,4M	2E,2M	14F,10M
Central	5F,6M	17F,36M	1F,1M	–	2F,2M	14F,26M
Bilbao	2F,7M	17F,25M	4F,7M	10F,16M	2F,3M	21F,55M
Vizcaya	6F,18M	26F,67M	1F,2M	3F,8M	–	19F,35M
Urquijo	1F,1M	25F,30M	6F,10M	4F,6M	2F,5M	15F,17M
Hispano	–	11F,17M	1F,1M	4F,4M	–	3F,6M

Notes: (F): number of firms, (M): number of members in the boards of directors (including presidents and vice-presidents).
(1) In 1944 there is no information about the total number of firms and seats because De la Sierra (1953) only considered a sample of firms.

Sources: De la Sierra (1953: 37–62 and 92–104) and Muñoz (1969: Appendix 3 and 4 and pp. 491–643).

compares the information offered by De la Sierra with Muñoz's data. There was a significant increase in the number of firms where banks had members on their board of directors, and an increase in the number of seats too. In both years banks were more interested in big corporations. For example, in 1921 directors of the then seven largest banks could be found on the boards of 274 companies, whose combined capital amounted to 49 per cent of the paid-in capital of all Spanish corporations, although numerically this only represented 7.2 per cent of all corporations (Muñoz, Roldán and García Delgado 1973: 263). In 1967, directors of the then six largest banks (*Español de Crédito*, *Hispanoamericano*, *Central*, *Bilbao*, *Vizcaya*, *Urquijo*) could be found on the boards of 955 firms, which although numerically only represented 4.6 per cent of all Spanish corporations, their combined capital amounted to 70.6 per cent of the paid-in capital (Muñoz 1969: 235 and 292).

In terms of industrial participation there are important similarities to be found in the industrial participation of both the Spanish and German mixed banks. In both cases the 'leading' mixed banks concentrated on large industrial concerns and on few sectors of industry (steel, electricity, machinery, motor industry, etc). The main difference is that in the German case banking investment policies were determined by market conditions whereas in Spain the rate of return on different industries was distorted by regulation.

Concentration

As can been seen in Table 2.23, the level of concentration of the banking system in Spain was considerable, especially until the mid-1950s. Bank concentration had been higher in Spain than in other countries. In general terms, it appears that the Spanish banking system was less concentrated than the banking sector in the UK – although in this case the diversification of the financial system was higher, similar to the French banking system (in the late 1950s the volume of deposits of the Big Four banks was 55 per cent (Alhadeff 1968: 131)) – and it was more concentrated than the Italian banking system. In Italy the 'Big Six' in 1962 had only 36.5 per cent of total deposits. Moreover, in Italy in 1945 there were 1432 banks, and despite the concentration process promoted by the government in the 1950s and 1960s, in 1965 there were still 1,287 banks. According to Biscani (1979: 117) the Herfindahl Index for the Italian banking industry in 1936 was 0.05, in 1951 it was 0.04 and finally, in 1971 the index was 0.03. The main difference between the five large Spanish banks and their counterparts in Europe was that the 'core' banks in other Western European countries ranked (in size) above the Spanish banks. Moreover, the diversification of the Spanish financial system was narrower than in other more developed financial systems: the only non-banking institutions that developed in this period were savings banks.

Although the level of concentration in Spain was high (Table 2.23), a significant number of small firms remained in the banking industry. The 'waves' of mergers in England in the 1960s, Scotland in the 1950s or Germany in the inter-war period did not take place in Spain, where, although from the end of the Civil

Table 2.23 Concentration in the Spanish banking industry

	Number of banks	Herfindahl Index	Percentage of deposits
1942	114	0.1064	62.97
1944	102	0.1171	66.51
1946	103	0.1145	64.21
1950	139	0.1112	67.53
1055	124	0.1029	64.36
1960	109	0.0982	63.53
1965	126	0.0813	58.17
1970	111	0.0767	56.37
1975	111	0.0636	49.12

Sources: *Balances de la Banca Privada* (SBC) and Pueyo (1998).

War to 1962 there were 52 mergers, there were no mergers among the large banks. It was in the 1980s and 1990s that the restructuring of the Spanish banking system took place.[12] In Spain links between banks were established through the existence of common members on the boards of directors and not through amalgamations.

III. Savings banks

In addition to commercial banks, there was a group of savings institutions (*cajas de ahorro*) which competed with commercial banks. They were non-profit making organisations and they were independent, governed by unpaid directors. The savings banks were under the jurisdiction of the Ministry of Labour and not the Ministry of Finance as in the case of banks, at least until 1957 (Titos 1991: 27). The role of these non-banking institutions in the financing of the economy was very important (around 15 per cent in the 1950s and more than 30 per cent in the 1970s), as Table 2.9 indicates.

Savings banks held about 17–18 per cent of total deposits of the financial institutions in the late 1940s, and around 20–25 per cent in the 1960s (Titos 1991: 29). But 78 per cent of their savings deposits in the 1940s and around 58 per cent in the 1960s were invested (because of regulation) in government securities.

Table 2.24 Savings institutions' investment structure

	1941–46	1947–50	1951–55	1961	1966
1. **Portfolio**	75.5	64.8	68.2	64.0	54.1
public bonds	62.6	54.8	65.4	58.4	32.0
private securities	12.9	10	2.8	5.6	22.1
2. **Loans**	17.8	26.8	22.7	23.3	36.9
free loans	–	26.1	21.1	19.2	22.6
regulated loans	–	0.7	1.6	4.1	14.3
3. **Real assets**	6.7	7.7	7.5	8.6	9.0

Source: Ros Hombravella (1967: 136–42).

Savings institutions were severely regulated. Although these financial institutions developed considerably during the Franco government, the explanation of this expansion is to be found in social and cultural factors. As Caminal, Gual and Vives (1990: 275) indicate, geographical limits on operations, together with higher investment coefficients (they were required to invest a substantial proportion of their deposits in fixed-interest securities, public funds – 60 per cent of their money in 1951 and 41 per cent in 1977 – and in loans at privileged rates) and profit distribution strictly regulated savings institutions. Table 2.24 shows that loans represented around 25 per cent in the 1950s and 37 per cent of total investments; an important share of these loans was regulated by the government (14.3 per cent in 1966). Ninety-nine per cent of these loans were mortgages (Ros Hombravella 1967: 138). Despite this degree of government control, savings banks expanded their activities considerably in this period. Part of the attraction of savings institutions was the 'welfare benefits' of these institutions, for example, the possibility of obtaining a loan for low-cost housing. Another reason for the expansion of these financial intermediaries was the 'psychological' attraction of putting one's money in a non-profit making organisation (Wright 1977: 110).

The Banking Law of 1962 extended the field of operations open to the savings banks and they managed to increase their participation in the whole financial market. Savings banks specialised their activities in small savers, and their main mechanism for taking more deposits was to increase their number of branches. As a consequence of the branching liberalisation which started in the 1960s, savings institutions achieved a higher number of branches than banks and consequently an important market share, despite their volume of deposits being lower.

Considering the asset and liability structure of savings institutions it is very difficult to know how savings institutions competed with banks. Competition was higher on the side of deposits (although until 1973 saving banks were not able to operate in the market for time deposits of more than two years), where the number of branches was the main instrument of competition. Regarding loans, savings institutions had few possibilities for competing with commercial banks for several reasons. First, as indicated above, a large percentage of their resources were regulated. Fornies (1991: 48) considers that from 1962 to 1977 (the period of highest expansion of these institutions), an important proportion of savings bank lending activities were 'controlled' by the government and they were concentrated in 'low-profit' operations; in most cases these investments had been previously rejected by private banks. Saving institutions also had serious geographic limitations in their operations. In this sense, for example, the *La Caja de Pensiones para la Vejez y de Ahorros de Cataluña y Baleares* did not compete with the *Caja de Ahorros de Asturias*, because their activity was limited to their own geographical region (for example, Cataluña and Baleares in the first case and Asturias and Gijón in the second case). Second, an important component of savings bank loans were long-term credits on real estate mortgages, whereas banks were legally forbidden to give loans against mortgages on real estate. For all these reasons, it can be assumed that there was an important segmentation in the loan market.

At the end of 1939 the number of savings institutions according to Titos (1991: 25) was 98. In 1962 the number of savings institutions was 84. The number of branches in 1950 was 1092, in 1956 2058 and in 1962 it was over 3000 (there were 3361 branches in 1965, 5146 in 1970 and 6365 in 1975). The number of branches per inhabitant in 1960 was 0.4. It was therefore clear that the main way savings banks could compete was to increase the number of branches.

IV. Conclusions

At the end of the Civil War, Spain had a relatively small financial system (the ratio 'financial assets/GDP' in 1948 was 94.9 in Spain, in contrast to 154.5 in the UK or 107 in Germany). It experienced an important growth in the 1950s and 1960s but this growth was concentrated in the development of the private banking sector. As a consequence, at the end of the 1960s and the beginning of the 1970s Spain had an important financial sector but one which was less diversified than other more developed financial systems. The Spanish financial system, therefore, grew in size but not in sophistication. This was a direct consequence of a regulatory framework which influenced the development of the banking sector. In Spain, the existence of barriers to entry and other regulatory measures impeded the development of other alternative financial intermediaries. Savings institutions were subject to discriminatory legislation which prevented them competing under equal conditions. As Table 2.7 indicates, other potentially competitive financial intermediaries such as building societies, or finance houses, did not consolidate their position in the Spanish financial system.

The relatively small size of the financial system was conditioned by the low level of savings (Overseas Economic Survey 1956: 4). The low rates of growth in the post-war years and the high rates of inflation (with negative real rates of interest) discouraged (even impeded) people from saving. In 1955 the situation changed and the total volume of deposits in the hands of banks increased substantially. As said before, this growth was not accompanied by diversification: banks remained the major component of the Spanish financial system. In the 1960s the Spanish financial system was comparable with more developed countries in terms of its size, but other characteristics of this financial system show that in many aspects it was closer to underdeveloped countries than industrialised ones: a lack of diversification, small capital market, etc.

From the beginning of the 1960s the Spanish financial system experienced serious transformations. There was a considerable branching expansion (the ratio number of branches per 10,000 inhabitants jumped from 0.8 in 1950 to 2.03 in 1975), there was a decrease in the level of concentration of the banking sector (in 1959 67.5 per cent of total deposits was in the hands of the Big Five banks and in 1975 this percentage was 49.12 per cent), and the discriminatory differences in regulation between banks and saving institutions were reduced (although it was in 1975 that a new trend towards an equal legal treatment for both types of financial institution emerged). Although entry was in theory made more easy for newcomers, in practice there were no essential changes and foreign banks were subjected to various restrictions which remained in place until 1986 (Carbó 1994: 15). There was a substantial increase in competition among banks and between banks and savings institutions although this competition was restricted by regulation, as I will explain in the following chapters.

The main characteristic of Spanish banking was mixed or universal banks. Universal banks possess three instruments (capital shares, proxy rights and membership on supervisory boards) to influence non-bank companies. Two additional characteristics linked to the concept of universal banking are a high proportion of long-term loans and the involvement of banks in the performance of the firms they participate in: 'participating' firms.[13] There are substantial differences between the Spanish and other universal banking systems such as the German one. The low levels of self-financing of Spanish firms show that the proportion of investment financed by loans in this country was higher than in German or Italy. In this sense, we can consider Spain as having a more 'bank-based' system of investment finance than Germany or Italy. However, the characteristics of these loans were very different, because of the lesser importance long-term loans had in the Spanish banking system. Section 12 of the 1946 BSL restricted banks to providing only short-term credit (credit of less than 90 days). In terms of the maturity of loans, the assets structure of Spanish banks was more similar to those of commercial banks (such as in the United Kingdom) than to universal banks.

With respect to the holdings of equity shares and proxy votes, it is evident that Spanish banks' relations with industry were very important. However, the industrial portfolio of Spanish banks is smaller than the German or the Italian ones. As Table 2.16 indicates, Spanish banks' holdings of industrial securities represented only a small percentage of total assets and this percentage decreased continuously from 1943 to 1975. By contrast, public securities' holdings increased substantially, as a consequence of the legal requirement of the government to finance its deficits. In spite of this relatively low investment portfolio, the connections between banks and firms through the existence of common members on their boards of directors was very important. It is very difficult to obtain a concrete conclusion about the 'real influence' of banks on these firms and their power to monitor their participating firms from this information. However, the fact remains that the number of sectors, participating firms and seats increased substantially in this period. Spanish mixed banks concentrated on larger firms and sectors such as electricity, machinery, etc. In Spain the number and importance of small and medium firms in the 1960s was very significant. For example, in 1961 of a sample of 16,117 in the sectors of textiles, food, metal and mechanics, clothing and shoes, wood and furniture, 83.6 per cent had a capital of less than a million pesetas (Report of the Chambers of Commerce about the *Memorandum del Ministerio de Hacienda sobre el Sistema Bancario y Crediticio* 1961: 4). In general, 91.1 per cent of total Spanish firms had 49.6 per cent of paid-in capital and the other 0.9 per cent had 50.4 per cent of paid-in capital. Spanish banks, therefore, participated in a relatively small number of firms and sectors, although, the combined capital of these firms amounted to a very high percentage of the total paid-in capital of Spanish corporations.

The main characteristics of the Spanish financial system are: its relatively large size in comparison to other European countries, a lack of diversification, high concentration and mixed banks, etc. In the following chapters I will concentrate on the relationship between these characteristics and the regulatory framework, and in addition, the influence of regulation on banking behaviour and banking profitability.

Notes

1 Usually the literature made use of the ratio 'financial assets/NI' but I use in my estimates the GDP because this has been the one most recently revised (Prados 1995).

2 As Levine (1997: 704) indicates, Goldsmith's measure of financial development has serious weaknesses. However, this measure is very useful when there is no information about other more sophisticated indicators.

3 There are considerable differences between my estimates of the ratio 'total financial assets/GDP' and Goldsmith's estimates for Spain and the United Kingdom. The main difference is that my estimate of the ratio 'financial assets/GDP' for Spain in 1962 is closer to those of the developed countries than Goldsmith's estimate is.

4 This is not necessarily a characteristic of underdeveloped countries. In fact, in other very developed financial systems such as the Swedish one, banking assets had a very large share of all financial institutions' assets (Sandberg 1978: 678).

5 Collins (1990) considers that the main reasons for this banking decline were: a)

fiscal taxes in favour of assets offered by insurance companies, b) excessive specialisation separated banks from some activities such as mortgages, consumer credits, etc, c) the Government had a discriminatory control over banks because the main instrument of the authorities to control inflation was credit and, only banks had to maintain a coefficient between assets and deposits.

6 In Italy there were six groups of financial institutions: public law banks, banks of national interest, ordinary credit banks, cooperative people's banks, savings banks and special institutions and the participation of the State in the public law banks, banks of national interest and special institutions was very significant.

7 Revell (1987) considers that one of the main differences between Austria, Belgium, Holland, Sweden, the United Kingdom and a second group of countries constituted by France, Germany, Italy, Japan, Switzerland and Spain is that in the first group from 1958 to 1981 some of the most important banks in the country merged ('core banks'). Perhaps the only exception being France where in 1966 the government merged two of the biggest banks in the country: the *Banque Nationale pour le Commmerce et l'Industrie* and the *Comptoir Nationale d'Escompte de Paris*, and both constituted the *Banque Nationale de Paris*, the largest bank in France.

8 The SBC donated their archives to the Bank of Spain in 1996. Unfortunately, the Bank of Spain has not catalogued these archives.

9 For example, Carr (1969: 295) indicates that after the Second World War Spanish banks played a similar role to German banks. In the following pages I will try to analyse the main differences and similarities between Spanish and German banks.

10 According to Ridruejo (1954b: 187), from a practical point of view loans were classified into three groups: credits up to 90 days, credits from 9 to 12 months ('credits for the season'), and loans for longer periods.

11 The important decrease in 1969 is a direct consequence of the forced banking specialisation linked to the 1962 Banking Law and the creation of an industrial corporation.

12 For example, the merger between *Banco Bilbao* and *Banco Vizcaya* in 1988, or between *Banco Central* and *Banco Hispanoamericano* in 1991.

13 The term 'participating firms' refers to those firms in which banks had economic interest (because they own shares of these firms and they have common members in the board of directors of these firms). We will make use of the terms 'subsidiate' firm and 'affiliated' firm with the same meaning.

CHAPTER THREE

Main Regulatory Framework and Regulatory Bodies, 1939–1975

This chapter provides an explanation of the nature of intervention and regulation during the Franco period (1939–1975).

Section I examines the main characteristics of the Spanish banking regulatory framework from the end of the Civil War to 1962. Section II looks at the 1962 Banking Law and subsequent reforms. Section III describes the main regulatory bodies before and after the 1962 Banking Law. Finally, Section IV reviews the main traditional accounts regarding the role of the Spanish banking system in this period. A reinterpretation of most of the traditional assessments of this role is the main objective of the remaining chapters.

I. Banking regulation in Spain, 1939–1962

Before the Spanish Civil War, banking was regulated by the *Ley de Ordenación Bancaria* (BSL of 1921), which guided Spanish banking until 1946. Some authors (Martín Aceña 1985: 126) consider that this law broke with a period of relatively free banking. There were two main objectives of this law: first, to transform the Bank of Spain into a central bank and second, the restructure and regulation of the banking sector. The notion of a bank was defined and the authorities introduced certain controls on banking operations and established close supervision of bank activities. The law created the *Consejo Superior Bancario* (SBC). This institution not only supervised the normal working of the banking sector but also had other functions. It determined, for example, the minimum amount of capital required for the operation of credit institutions, or it could impose certain operating ratios between balance sheet items, such as that between the volume of deposits and the sum of equity capital plus reserve funds.

The Civil War (1936–1939) split the country into two separate and independent financial areas. The Bank of Spain was divided and each part (Republican and Nationalist) issued its own currency (Martín Aceña and Pons 1994: 123). After the Civil War, the first tasks of the new authorities (the Franco regime) were the restoration of the financial system, the control of inflationary pressures and the restructuring of the banking system. As a result, an array of emergency acts were passed. The most important acts were the *Ley de Desbloqueo*,[1] enacted in December 1939, and the *Ley de Reunificación del Banco de España* of March 1942. Both provided the basis for financial reunification, served to regularise the banking system and to cancel an impressive amount of cash balances in the hands of the public (by 'readjusting' the value of money, according to a scale of percentages which had come into being on 18 July 1936). Equally important was the Decree of October 1939, which ratified the so-called status quo by prohibiting the establishment of new banks without prior governmental approval.

In 1946, when the BSL of 1921 expired, it was replaced by a new act: the BSL of 1946. The 1946 Act renewed the note-issuing monopoly of the Bank of Spain, a monopoly that this institution had had from 1874. The Bank of Spain continued to be a private institution although in practice the government gained complete control. The Bank also nominated the Governor, Sub-governor, the Director of the General Directorate of the Banks and Stock Exchanges and four members of its board of directors.

The main regulatory constraints of the 1946 BSL were (see Table 3.1):

1. 'Structural' regulation: barriers to entry. The Act maintained the legal barriers to entry. Although the establishment of barriers to entry started *de facto* with the BSL (B.S.L.) of 1921, it was corroborated *de jure* with the provisional *Ordenes Ministeriales* of 1939, 1940, 1942 and ratified with the BSL of 1946. Financial regulation not only required a set of objective conditions for the potential entrant but it also maintained a large degree of discretion in terms of this entrance. Candidates had to show the need for banking services in a specific geographic area; however, the form that this justification should take was not specified by the authorities and therefore arbitrary. Spanish regulation of barriers to entry was similar to other European legislation, for example, the French or the Italian regulations, although in these financial systems concentration of the banking system was lower than in Spain (see Table 2.22) – the risk of monopolistic behaviour being linked to an increase in concentration.
2. Conduct regulation
   - 2.1 Interest rate controls. Maximum and minimum interest rates were fixed. The authorities fixed a 'ceiling' on the deposit rate. Legal deposit interest rates hardly changed throughout this period. The authorities fixed a 'floor' on the rate of interest on loans. However, this floor had many exceptions; the authorities defined some sectors as 'high-priority' or 'national interest' sectors and they fixed a 'preferential' interest rate for them below the 'floor' rate.

2.2 Other credit controls. Until the 1960s there was no legal requirement which determined the relationship between deposits and loans. Although the BSL of 1946 empowered the Ministry of Finance to require the banks to deposit up to 20 per cent of their total deposit liabilities in cash or unpledged securities with the Bank of Spain, no order was made. Legal requirements, however, had an impact on the ratio of reserves to capital. All private banks which made a net profit in excess of 4 per cent of their paid-up capital plus reserves had to deduct 10 per cent from their profits until they had amassed a reserve fund equal to one-half of their capital. This regulation – and the fact that the BSL prevented banks from distributing a cash dividend of more than 6 per cent on paid-up capital plus reserves – stimulated the accumulation of reserves. Banks were obliged to increase reserves when they issued new shares: this also encouraged the accumulation of reserves. Finally, some banking activities, in particular branch expansion, were linked to the volume of capital and reserves and stimulated the accumulation of reserves still further.

In spite of the lack of a legal ratio, banks maintained a very stable proportion of loans to deposits and of their own resources to total resources. This stability could be an indicator of a possible self-regulation of the Spanish banking sector or a result of a profit-maximising behaviour under uncertainty. From the beginning of the 1960s there was a substitution of 'informal' regulation by formal regulations of cash, liquidity and public debt ratios and reserve requirements.

2.3 State regulation also restricted the banks to providing short-term credit through either discounting self-liquidating commercial bills, or supplying standard commercial credit with a maturity of no greater than 90 days. Only after the Decree-Law 7/1960 could banks provide long-term loans (credits of more than 90 days).

As explained in Chapter 1, the 1950s started with a relative economic and political openness in comparison to the 1940s. However, in the banking area there were no essential changes and interventionism was a main feature of Spanish regulation. Two reasons support this assertion. First, banking regulation in those years 'revitalised' official credit. Second, the main objective of the Law of 26 December 1958 regarding medium and long-term credit was to channel savings towards 'national interest' enterprises. The government had no intention of abandoning its control. The only innovations of the regulation approved in the 1950s were: a) a change in the interest of economic

Table 3.1 Main banking legislation, 1939–1975

1. 'Structural' regulation: BARRIERS TO ENTRY
   - very restrictive, 1939–1962.
   - shy liberalisation, 1962–1975 (barriers to entry for foreign banks were maintained).
2. 'Conduct' regulation:
   2.1. On INTEREST RATES
   - Deposit interest rates:
     - 1939–1969: a maximum deposit interest rate.
     - 1969–1973: a maximum deposit interest rate but free deposit interest rates for more than two-year deposits. From 1969 all interest rates were linked to the Bank of Spain rate of rediscount.
     - 1973: a maximum deposit interest rate in all kind of deposits (including the more than two-year deposits).
     - 1974: deposit interest rates were definitively liberalised.
   - Loan interest rates:
     - 1939–1969: a minimum loan interest rate, with many exceptions ('national interest sectors').
     - 1969–1974: a maximum loan interest rate and 'preferential' interest rates. The more than two-year loan interest rate was liberalised.

   2.2. Other CREDIT CONTROLS
   - preferential interest rates (for 'national interest sectors')
   - investment coefficients:
     - liquidity ratio : 1963–1970
     - cash ratio: 1970–1975
     - investment ratio: 1971–1975
     - reserve coefficient: 1960–1975
     - public bond coefficient:
     - 'informal' regulation or 'moral suasion': 1939–1958
       - 1958–1965: percentage maximum and minimum of public bonds (it was not effective).
       - 1965–1970: legal coefficient (in 1970 it was eliminated).

   2.3. LIMITS TO THE TERM STRUCTURE OF ASSETS AND LIABILITIES
   - 1939–1960: banks were restricted to supply only short-term credit (with a maturity no greater than 90 days).
   - 1960–1975: this restriction was lifted.

   2.4. BRANCHING RESTRICTIONS
   - 1939–1962: more restrictive.
   - 1962–1975: significant liberalisation, especially from 1974.

   2.5. OTHER LEGISLATIVE MEASURES
   - forced specialisation (commercial and industrial banks) in 1962. It was eliminated in 1974.

authorities in controlling inflation, b) the authorities tried to stimulate long-term financing. On 28 December 1958, the legal regulation of the Portfolio Investment Societies was passed and in the same month a law to regulate the performance of medium and long-term credit banks was passed too. Finally, the Decree-Law of 10 August 1960 removed the prohibition of discounting, rediscounting effects and lending money for periods of more than 90 days, and c) the Franco government decided to identify the main problems of the banking system, and the result was the *Ley de Bases* of 1962.

2.4 The BSL of 1946 regulated the expansion of banks through branches. The Bank of Spain authorised a new branch in towns with a population in excess of 10,000 inhabitants, if the number of branches of a bank was no higher than one per 75,000 inhabitants and one per 30,000 current accounts. The Bank of Spain demanded that smaller towns had economic activity that justified the opening of a new branch and lacked other financial intermediaries either in the town or nearby. The Bank of Spain conceded branches to banks with higher ratios of branches per inhabitant and capital plus reserves per inhabitant.

This measure is an important way of reducing competition when interest rates are controlled. The implementation of this regulation tended to favour concentration of branches in the hands of the larger banks which were more able to satisfy the conditions that the Bank of Spain established

II. The Banking Law of 1962 and subsequent reforms

The *Ley de Bases* of 1962 replaced the one of 1946. According to the *Ley de Bases*, the Spanish financial system exhibited a large number of deficiencies.[2] First, the Bank of Spain had insufficient power to operate as a central bank: 'The Bank of Spain must be freed from all those inhibitions which result from its present nature.' Second, banks were restricted to provide only short-term credit despite being the main source of finance for the private sector. Third, the lack of specialisation within the banking system. The authorities believed that 'mixed' banks were unsuitable for industrial promotion and had a discriminatory policy in their granting of credit. Consequently they perceived a need for the creation of a new kind of financial institution: industrial banks, specialised in providing long-term credit. Fourth, the need to reinforce the role of official banks.

The 1962 Banking Law tried to solve these deficiencies, and although the financial reform stimulated competition in some areas, official intervention continued to be a marked characteristic. The main changes of the 1962 Banking Law were:

1. The new legislation nationalised the Bank of Spain.
2. The law imposed some monetary instruments, such as a special deposit requirement, a liquidity ratio and a cash ratio. The main objectives of the creation of these instruments were to secure the solvency and liquidity of the banking firms and to introduce instruments for the management of monetary policy. The main legal requirements were:

   a) The cash ratio. This was not binding until December 1970. The ratio was very high after the Civil War, 18.9 per cent in 1943 and 17 per cent in 1944, but after those years it remained within the range 11.5–9 per cent. From 1965 the cash ratio came down to 7–6 per cent.
   b) The liquidity ratio was officially fixed in 1963 at 10 per cent and the authorities pushed this ratio up to 12 per cent in the same year. It remained at 13 per cent between 1955 and 1970. In Spain the central bank was seriously impeded in its control of liquidity because private banks had the privilege of automatic pledgeability of the long-term public debt. As we indicated before, it was in 1959 that the government decided not to issue more public debt with this characteristic.
   c) The public-debt ratio. Banks were required to invest a certain percentage of their liabilities in public bonds. It was fixed in 1965 at 15 per cent and the government increased this ratio every year to as high as 22 per cent in 1969 to obtain public financing.
   d) Reserve requirements were fixed in 1960. Banks were compelled to hold reserves of up to 10 per cent of their deposits in the Bank of Spain, in the form of cash or public securities. However this power was not exercised.

3. The 1962 Act allowed the establishment of new banks and tried to divide the banking sector into two groups: commercial banks specialising in commercial credit (with a maturity of 18 months or less), and industrial banks concentrating on financing long-term projects and consequently permitted to hold larger amounts of firms' securities (bonds and equities) within their portfolios. The perverse results of this distinction between commercial and industrial banks[3] led to its abrogation in 1974.
4. The law tried 'to make better use of the large resources in the hands of the saving institutions, their widespread network and their altruistic motives in order to promote and assist agricultural investment'.

Despite the stated objectives of the 1962 Law, official intervention continued to be a market characteristic. Interest rates remained under strict government control, although from 1967 the authorities changed the ceilings more frequently. In 1966 the Minister of Finance was given the authority to establish either maximum or minimum loan interest rates, although banks interpreted the new official rates as the only interest they could charge on loans (Lukauskas 1992: 221). In 1969 the Franco government abolished minimum loan interest rates and introduced a ceiling on the rate of interest on loans. It was in 1969 when they liberalised the more than two-year loan interest rate. In 1969 the more than two-year deposit interest rate was liberalised, although in 1973 the authorities fixed a legal maximum again. It was not until 1974 that deposit interest rates were definitively liberalised.

Banks were compelled to maintain the so-called 'investment coefficients' which required that certain proportions of their portfolios consisted of either government bonds or other securities classified as 'special paper'. From the mid-1960s the authorities reinforced their policy of 'investment ratios' and 'preferential' interest rates to 'high' priority sectors. Furthermore, the evolution of the banking sector from the early 1960s does not suggest that liberalisation went too far. Apart from the existing banks, only savings institutions achieved a considerable expansion, although these financial institutions were closely regulated. The law had promised to introduce more facilities through the establishment of new banks (Decree 1312 of 5 June 1963, concerning modification of the status quo, and the Decree 63 of 13 January 1972), but in practice there were no essential changes.

In 1963 the *Central de Información de Riesgos* (Centre for Risk Information) was created. The main objective of this institution was to centralise at the Bank of Spain all information about loans (of more than a certain quantity) and risks assumed by banking customers. This information together with the existence of a register of unpaid sellers (RAI) allowed banks to reduce information problems.

Between 1974 and 1975 the liberalisation process received a major impulse. Branching expansion was the aspect most affected by new regulation, especially from 1974 with the Decree 2245 of 9 August for banks and the Order by the Ministry of Finance on 7 February 1975 for savings banks. Furthermore, in this period many rules which had been used to discriminate between banks and savings institutions were eliminated. In 1978 (Decree 1388 of 23 June) foreign banks were allowed to set up in Spain although with serious restrictions (for example, they could not open more than three offices).

The most important reform of the Spanish banking regulation started in 1978, when the authorities approved new banks, and they allowed more flexible rates of interests. In 1986 the distinction between banks and savings institutions, in terms of ratios to be held, disappeared. This process finished in 1987 with the deregulation of the different rates of interest and commissions and the removing of barriers to entry to foreign banks with the Decree 1144 of 30 September 1988.

III. Main regulatory bodies

As I have already explained, the Spanish banking system was subject to strong controls. But who controlled the banking sector and how? The first responsibility lay with the government. This was not an extraordinary or novel change which had occurred after the Civil War. It had been an observable fact from the early 1930s. The government in turn delegated authority to the Minister of Finance (see Figure 3.1).

1. The Government. Following the 1946 BSL, the general regulations regarding credit policy were enacted by the government, whereas in the previous law (1921 BSL) the matter was the subject of bilateral regulation between the State and the Bank of Spain.

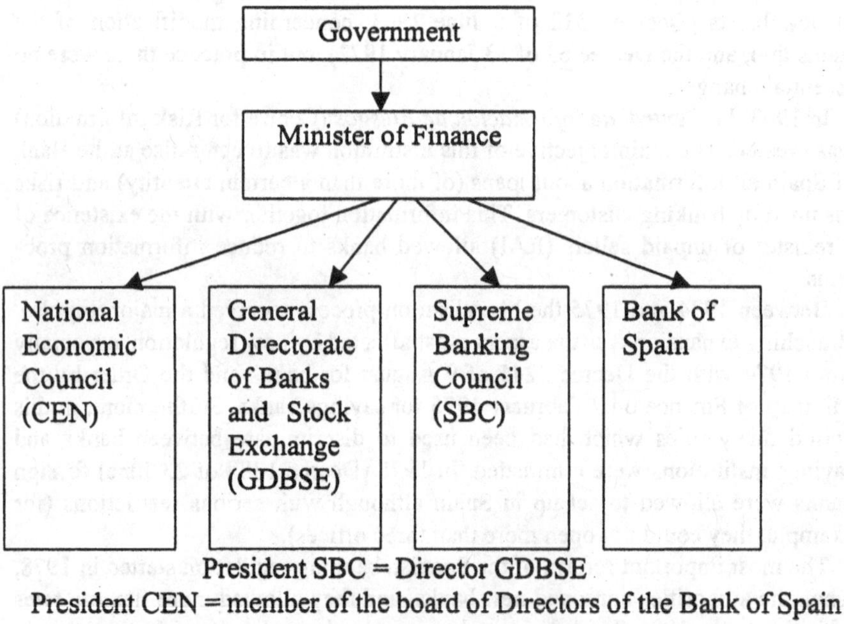

Figure 3.1 The Spanish financial system: main regulatory bodies

2. The Minister of Finance. Following sections 2 and 43 of the BSL, the main functions of the Minister of Finance in relation to the financial system were:

    a) to lay down the general lines of credit policy to be followed by the Bank of Spain, previously advised.
    b) to fix the rate of discount and the rates of interest charged in the rest of operations (to fix the minimum interest rate on loans and the maximum interest rate on deposits).
    c) to supervise the Bank of Spain's function of buying and selling government bonds in the open market.
    d) to give instructions to the Bank of Spain about the 'facility' with which credits should be granted.
    e) to fix minimum capital requirements and a proportion between own resources and total assets.
    f) to establish the way banks had to publish their balance and loss and profit accounts.
    g) to authorise the issues of capital, the agreements among banks about branches, mergers, and so on.

    Although in the control of monetary and banking policy the Minister of Finance had the supreme authority, in the execution of these directives the Minister of Finance relied on the aid of other organs: the Bank of Spain, the General Directorate of Banks and Stock Exchanges and the SBC.

3. The Bank of Spain. Until 1962 the Bank of Spain was a private limited company with private shareholders, although it was under government control. In accordance with section 6 of the 1946 BSL, this control was secured by the right of the government to appoint the Bank's governor and deputy governor and also four other counsellors who were nominated by the Minister of Finance and who 'represented the general interest of national economy' (Sáez de Ibarra 1954: 92). The rest of the members of the general board of directors of the Bank of Spain were: a member chosen by the Minister of Finance from among the directors and high officers of the other official banks, two members designated by the SBC, one designated by the Chambers of Commerce, Industry and Marine, one designated by the Central Committee of the Industry and Services Trade Unions, one appointed by the Agriculture and Farmers Trade Unions, one nominated by the saving institutions, and an employee of the Bank of Spain with at least twenty completed years of service, and finally, twelve members who represented the private shareholders and who were elected by the shareholders at a general meeting by a majority of votes.

In the control of the monetary and banking policy the Bank of Spain was, as Clayton (1962, p.371) indicates: 'only one and not necessarily the most important (executive organ)'. Following Ridruejo (1954: 159): 'the Bank of Spain must be an efficacious instrument at the service of the national economy, and it is incumbent upon the government to dictate the general rules of the credit policy.' The Bank of Spain had no power to fulfil a real central banking function. Its main functions were then: a) the control of the issue of notes, b) to act as government banker (especially, financing its deficits) and c) to grant loans to a number of banks in difficulties.

The power to operate an effective monetary and banking policy was not vested in the Bank of Spain. With the 1946 BSL, the Bank of Spain was exempted from certain rules, for example, foreign exchange policy, which was put into the hands of the new Foreign Exchange Control Institute, called *Instituto Español de Moneda Extranjera.*

4. The SBC (previously called *Comité Central de la Banca Española*). The main function of this institution was to advise the Ministry of Finance. The President of the SBC was the Director of the General Directorate of Banks and Stock Exchanges and the Vice-president of the SBC was the Sub-governor of the Bank of Spain. The main functions of this institution were:

   a) the collection of banking statistics.
   b) to receive all the applications from individual banks (about the opening of new branches, mergers, etc.) and to send them to the Ministry of Finance.
   c) to be consulted by the Ministry of Finance about interest rates and the relationship between liquid assets and deposit liabilities.
   d) to interpret some of the rules approved by the Ministry of Finance and to control the fulfilment of these rules (through the *Junta de Vigilancia*).

   The SBC transmitted to the Ministry of Finance the 'views' of the banking community, which was represented on its governing body.

5. The General Directorate of Banks and Stock Exchanges (*Dirección General de Banca y Bolsa*). This was the technical instrument for examining financial problems and submitting them for the consideration of the Minister of Finance. Following section 47 of the 1946 SBL, the main function of the General Directorate of Banks and Stock Exchanges were:

   a) to give suggestions to a bank or banker about its credit policy.
   b) to give suggestions to a bank or banker about its dividend policy.
   c) the inspection of banks.

d) to control that the banks followed the general requirements of credit policy.
e) to register banks and bankers.
f) to authorise banks and bankers to change or buy shares of other banks.

As indicated above, there was a close liaison between the SBC and the General Directorate of Banks and Stock Exchanges: the President of the SBC was the Director of the General Directorate of Banks and Stock Exchanges. The Vice-president of the SBC was the Sub-governor of the Bank of Spain (see Table 3.2). The remaining members of this institution were: five representatives of the national banks, three of the regional banks, two of the local banks, and two representatives of the banking employees' organisations.

In 1957 there was a reorganisation of the General Directorate of Banks and Stock Exchanges. It was merged with the Directorate of Insurance and it was called General Directorate of Banks, Stock Exchanges and Investments (*Dirección General de Banca, Bolsa e Inversiones*). As of that year this institution controlled the functioning of the savings institutions which had previously been in the hands of the Ministry of Labour.

After the *Ley de Bases* of 1962, the monetary and credit authorities continued to be in hands of the Minister of Finance. In fact, the 1962 Banking Law (section 1, regarding the conduct of monetary and credit policy) reproduced the same words as the 1946 BSL:

> The authority in matters of money and credit shall belong to the government, which shall indicate to the Bank of Spain and to the different credit organisations, through the Minister of Finance, the directives which they are to follow at each stage, and shall finally guide monetary and credit policy in such a manner as may best suit the country's interest.

The Bank of Spain was nationalised and it was under the control of the Minister of Finance. In fact, the 1962 Banking Law (section 2 (c)) considered that the Bank of Spain was 'an instrument of the Government monetary policy'.

The government created the Institute for Medium and Long Term Credit (*Instituto de Crédito a Medio y Largo Plazo*), which was the organ for relations between the Government and the official banks and the Credit Institution for the Savings Banks (*Instituto de Crédito para las Cajas de Ahorro*), to direct, coordinate and inspect savings banks. Although the Foreign Exchange Control Institute was maintained, section 2(g) of the 1962 Banking Law established that the movement of foreign payments and the centralisation of gold and foreign exchange reserves should be assigned to the Bank of Spain. This was the first step towards ending the separation between foreign and internal monetary policy.

In 1973 this institution disappeared and its functions were transferred to the Bank of Spain and the Minister of Finance (Decree-Law 6/1973 of 17 July) to reinforce the Bank of Spain's rights and to ensure closer co-operation between the central bank and the private banks.

As we can see, there were no essential changes in the regulatory bodies after the 1962 Banking Law with the exception of the nationalisation and the reinforcement of the Bank of Spain and the creation of two agencies, the Institute for Medium and Long Term Credit and the Credit Institution for the Savings Banks. In this period the Ministry of Finance continued to be the main regulatory body of the financial system.

At the top of this solid regulatory structure was the Minister of Finance (and then, the government). But, what were the interrelationships among the agencies? It is evident that Franco's government adopted the necessary measures to avoid conflicts of interest among the different regulatory bodies. The main evidence of this is the liaison among agencies. The President of the SBC was the Director of the General Directorate of Banks and Stock Exchanges, the Vice-president of the SBC was the Sub-governor of the Bank of Spain and the President of the CEN was a member of the board of directors of the Bank of Spain. In spite of this it is possible to find some conflicts of interest among these institutions. For example, at the Bank of Spain, the most important conflicts between the government (or the Minister of Finance) and the bank took place in the 1940s. Although the 1946 BSL did not nationalise the Bank of Spain, the increase in interventionism in the central bank was clear. The Directors' Minutes of the Bank of Spain in 1946 and 1947 show the main differences between the representative of private shareholders and the State. For example, the 3 January 1947 (Bank of Spain Archives, *Actas del Banco de España (Secretaría)* 1947, file 2785) the *Conde de Limpias* (a representative at the Bank of Spain of private shareholders) showed its serious disagreement with the 1946 BSL, especially with reference to the Bank of Spain legislation and the high degree of interventionism of the Minister of Finance in this institution. For the same period, there are other examples of the conflicts between the representatives of the private shareholders and the rest of the members of the board of directors of the Bank of Spain (the representatives of the State) such as the Directors' Minutes of 26 November and 6 December 1946 (Bank of Spain Archives, *Actas del Banco de España (Secretaría)* 1946, file 2784), where the *Conde de Vallellano* and the *Conde de Limpias* protested about the use by the government of the reserves of silver of the Bank of Spain (which, in their opinion, was the rightful proprietor of these reserves in contrast to the opinion of the Governor of the Bank of Spain and the Minister of Finance who considered the State to be the proprietor of these silver reserves). From the beginning of the 1950s the Directors' Minutes of the Bank of Spain are more 'opaque' and it is not possible to find any reference to the opinions of the members of its board of directors. It is true that some of the most 'belligerent' members were not at that moment at the Bank of Spain, such as, for example, the *Conde de Vallellano* who left the Bank of Spain in 1955 because he had been nominated Minister (Bank of Spain Archives, *Actas del Banco de España (Secretaría)* 1955, file 3248).

Moreover, in the Bank of Spain Directors' Minutes of 10 June 1947 (Bank of Spain Archives, *Actas del Banco de España (Secretaría)* 1947, file 2785) and in different journals (Olariaga 1947), Olariaga (who was President of the SBC and member of the board of directors of the Bank of Spain as a representative of the government)[4] showed his disagreement with some aspects of the 1946 BSL, in particular with those related to the Bank of Spain and the control of interest rates. Olariaga supported, for example, more independence of the Bank of Spain and the introduction of more instruments to control inflation.

The Report of the Bank of Spain (1946, D-6421) introduced some 'reservations' about the monetary policy of the government and its inflationary risks. These criticisms were even stronger in the reports of the late 1960s, for example, the Report of the Bank of Spain about the situation of the Spanish economy in the 1950s and 1960s (D-6824, undated 20–21), where the Bank of Spain considers the policy of public financing of the Franco government as one of the main reasons for inflation.

What about the rest of the agencies? The only information available is from the Superior Banking Council. The Reports of the SBC and the *Banco de Vizcaya* about the 1946 BSL (Bank of Spain Archives, *Informe del Consejo Superior Bancario sobre el Proyecto de Ley de Ordenación Bancaria de 1946* and *Informe del Banco de Vizcaya sobre el Proyecto de Ley de Ordenación Bancaria de 1946*) show that there were some important discrepancies between the private banks (represented by the SBC) and the government. Some of these differences were solved in the final version of the 1946 BSL, when the government passed some of the SBC amendments, but others were not. However, as I will explain in Chapter 4, the government tried to minimise these conflicts of interest and it did not make use of some of the 'powers' considered in the 1946 BSL.

IV. Traditional views about the role of the Spanish banking sector during the Franco regime

As I explained in Chapter 1, the evolution of the Spanish economy from the end of the Civil War to 1975 has different sub-periods: the immediate post-war years, the slow recovery in the 1950s, the economic growth of the 1960s and the crisis of the 1970s. An important aspect of the analysis of the Spanish economy during the Franco regime is what the role of the Spanish banking system was and how it contributed to or retarded this economic transformation. The most widespread claims about the Spanish banking performance during the Franco regime were: 1) the financial system failed to provide the capital required in some sectors. Conservative lending practices of banks – their predilection for short-term loans and credit discrimination – supposedly delayed the recovery of the Spanish economy in the 1940s and 1950s, 2) banks discriminated in favour of those sectors in which they were involved: oil, electricity or the iron and steel industry, 3) banks behaved monopolistically in setting deposits and lending rates and 4) the dominance of banks was ensured by regulation and reinforced by interlocking directorates of the largest banks. The following paragraphs are an attempt to re-evaluate these views.

Chapter 2 showed that Spain had a very low level of self-financing in comparison with other European countries. The principal source of finance for Spanish firms was borrowing (mainly, short-term credits) and the evolution of capital investment was closely linked to credit conditions. A large provision of funds is not a sufficient condition in itself to ensure a high rate of investment but it is an essential prerequisite. For this reason, many authors consider that the inadequacy of Spanish banks as long-term lending institutions is an explanation of the lateness in the process of industrialisation in Spain (Lieberman 1982: 246 or *Informe del Consejo Superior de Cámaras de Comercio, Industria y Navegación para contestar al Memorandum del Ministerio de Hacienda de 12/9/1961 sobre el sistema bancario y crediticio, Ministerio de Hacienda,* 1961: 4). There are several aspects that we must examine before we can evaluate this claim.

The existence of market failures apart, it seems incredible that an unsatisfied demand (the long-term loan demand) would not have provoked a response on the supply side of the market. If the origin of this problem was the lack of effectiveness of competitive forces, we must look for the origin of this inefficiency. It is necessary for those who allege market failures to explain why financial intermediaries did not respond to demands. Furthermore, Lluch's figures (Table 2.15) clearly suggest that there did exist a very important response from the supply side.

A first explanation might be the role of legislation. As shown in Section I, regulation affected banking lending conditions. Banks were not allowed to make long-term loans and to take long-term deposits. Furthermore, restrictions of entry, and legal discrimination against non-banking institutions, reduced the level of competition. Banks were not forced to improve credit conditions because they held a dominant position as suppliers of funds. In this sense the monopolistic power exercised by the Spanish banks thanks to regulation helped to prevent a response in loan supply to demand changes. Moreover, regulation also controlled the term structure of liabilities. As seen in Table 2.16, in Spain a large part of all borrowed capital was obtained from short-term deposits. A great percentage of assets in the form of long-term investments was only possible thanks to the sizeable balances banks were able to obtain from the central bank. These were acquired through the so-called mechanism of *pignoración* (the pledging of public paper and other comparable securities). It is possible that banks looked to a ratio of liquid assets to liabilities – and made a low volume of long-term loans – where asset characteristics were restricted to the time conditions of liabilities. This banking behaviour can be interpreted as a 'prudential' measure to control liquidity in a financial system where regulation did not introduce the necessary measures to allow this end. Furthermore, Spanish banks contributed to the financing of the public sector in a larger measure than in other more developed countries. The peculiarities of the public debt and the role of regulation must be taken into account to understand banking behaviour.

If we accept that banking behaviour was closely circumscribed by regulation, we must take into account the responsibility of the government in this possible 'failure' of the banking sector in the financing of Spanish industry. The allegations of the insufficiency of long-term funds and the lack of adequate finance for small firms was not merely a Spanish, but a universal problem. As Collins (1991: 9–12) indicates, economists and historians have criticised the role played by British monetary institutions in providing financial services – especially in the provision of long-term finance – essential for the development of a modern industrial system. In Spain we cannot claim that banks were not involved in industry. Spanish banks were essential in the process of financing industrial activity. Lluch's figures indicate that the banks provided 70 per cent of industrial finance. However, it is argued that some particular sectors, such as agriculture – in spite of the existence of the Agriculture Credit Service – had special difficulties in obtaining financial resources in comparison with other sectors such as electricity, where banks had economic interests. If government intervention – with the definition of 'privileged sectors' and the establishment of measures to finance these sectors – did not manage to solve these financing problems, then we cannot consider the banks alone as being entirely responsible.

As explained in Chapter 2, Spanish banks were 'mixed' financial institutions, commercial banks with strong links with the industrial sector. However, the expected yields on investments were distorted by regulation through a policy of 'privileged sectors' and other measures and banks took advantage of these market conditions. Banks did not see themselves as an instrument for improving resource allocation; they were simply like other firms seeking profit from their activities. However, unlike the others, they could influence regulation or take advantage of existing regulation to increase profits. This problem is discussed in more detail in Chapters 4 and 6.

Claims about the failure of Spanish banks in the financing of industry do not take into account what happened on the demand side of the market. Referring to the Spanish lending conditions in the 1960s and 1970s Wright (1977: 48) wrote: 'In common with procedures in allocating credit to the agriculture sector, loans for industrial projects are more often granted on the basis of the collateral than on the merits of the specific project.' But this is not necessarily unsatisfactory behaviour. When banks maximise profits they must consider different factors such as the viability of the investment, the capacity of the firm to repay or what is the collateral offered as guarantee to the loan. From a bank's point of view, the small scale of most Spanish enterprises meant that the probability of repayment of the loan would be too low. Banks are profit-maximising firms but a cautious approach can ensure a more stable banking system.

To understand the role of the banking system in financing the process of industrialisation in Spain we must consider the influence of two elements: the consequences of the war (in terms of physical destruction and low income) and the impact of inflation on the demand for loans and the supply of deposits.

It is very difficult to provide a general conclusion as to how inflation affects the decisions of savers and borrowers. In general, inflationary pressures raise the demand for loans because inflation diminishes the real rate of returns individuals have to pay for loans. However, there are two factors we must consider before accepting this claim. First, this positive relationship between demand for loans and inflation depends on the assumption that these changes in prices are not cancelled out by an increase in the loan interest rate. Hence, this claim is only true in a free market when inflation is unanticipated. Second, the demand for loans depends on how inflation affects other ways of obtaining resources (Capie and Collins 1991: 60–61). This aspect is very important when we analyse firm behaviour. Inflation makes equity more attractive than bonds. When inflation rises, if firms' costs and revenues increase in line with inflation, dividends can be maintained in real terms but the opposite applies to bonds. When inflation increases, bond prices fall. Thus, the final effect that these partial consequences of the evolution of prices have on the demand for loans and other alternative financial effects is not yet clear. Other factors such as taxation can also affect the final outcome.

Quite a different aspect is how very low levels of income affect the nature of the demand for loans. We must take into consideration how the difficult post-war situation affected risk, and the probability of default. The demand for loans depends on the expected rate of return on investment and investment conditions were affected by the war.

High inflation can discourage saving. However, there are other factors which affect this decision. For example, in times of high inflation people could have an incentive for saving to maintain the real value of assets. When the rate of inflation falls, the need for such saving decisions declines. It is very important to consider the effects of war on saving decisions. As explained in Chapter 1, in the post-war years Spain had low rates of economic growth and savings.[5] This evolution of savings was a direct consequence of the difficulties of the Spanish economy in the post-war years and of Franco's economic programme. The authorities fixed a maximum interest rate on deposits. Taking into account the evolution of prices, the main result was that the real return on deposits was negative throughout most of this period and the incentives for saving were low. However, Spain achieved an increase in industrial production at the expense of the consumer goods sector. Real wages decreased in the 1940s and the possibilities of saving for a very important percentage of the Spanish population were very low (Morella 1992: 137). However, in the mid-1950s the economic situation in Spain changed and the ratio 'deposits/GDP' rose (see Table 2.5).

Therefore, in the 1940s with a very low level of savings in the hands of financial intermediaries and a weak and risky demand for loans as a consequence of the situation of the Spanish economy, it is difficult to consider the banking sector as being solely responsible for the possible lack of financial resources of Spanish industry. In the 1950s and 1960s the volume of savings in the hands of financial intermediaries was very significant and it increased at a faster rate than national income. Moreover, the low levels of self-financing of Spanish firms leads us to believe that banks did play an important role in the financing of the Spanish economy. Finally, we cannot affirm that a greater supply of loans would have had a positive effect on Spanish economic growth. As Lluch (1974: 57) indicates, the role of the banking system in industrial finance has been lower in more industrialised countries than in less developed countries and so, we cannot establish a causal relationship between the supply of loans and economic growth.

Another aspect is not simply the amount but also the characteristics of loans and the influence these credit conditions have on investment. Table 2.16 shows that German and Italian banks assigned a larger share of their funds to long-term credit that Spanish banks. These credit conditions forced Spanish firms to finance long-term investment with short-term credit; this situation increased risk (firms worked under a very high level of uncertainty because they did not know if a loan would be renewed or not) and strengthened the firm's dependence on banking decisions. For example, as Antolín (1996: 251) affirms, the main means of financing capital investment of *Hidroeléctrica Ibérica* were short-term loans and bonds. This financing strategy imposed very high financial costs on this firm (around 55 per cent of total costs) and increased the dependence of the firm with respect to the *Banco de Vizcaya*. Comín and Martín Aceña (1996: 25) consider that this financing strategy (to finance long-term investments with short-term credits) limited the expansion of the firms.

The conclusion I have reached is that more research in this area is required before a clear nature of the relationship between banks and industry is established and it is for this reason that the remaining chapters will concentrate on the effects of regulation on banking behaviour.

V. Conclusions

The new regulatory conditions existing after the Civil War in the finance and banking sector were established by the provisions of the 1946 BSL. This BSL ratified most of the provisional measures or *Órdenes Ministeriales* passed in the immediate post-war years and the BSL supported the governmental tendency to intervene in the economy. The legislation regarding the Bank of Spain, and the criticism of the private shareholders are an example of this. The Bank of Spain was transformed into an instrument at the service of government policy, and it was the government who dictated the general rules of credit policy. Another example of the interventionist orientation of this law was the creation and reinforcement of official banks.

With respect to private banks, the BSL of 1946 maintained barriers to entry, controlled branching expansion, interest rates and other banking operations. Discriminatory legislation between banks and savings institutions was also maintained. Consequently, this law contributed to maintaining the so-called status quo, in which the main Spanish banks (especially, the Big Five banks) consolidated their position in the Spanish financial system.

In spite of the theoretical plurality of the institutions which constituted the regulatory body of the Spanish financial system, the control of the Minister of Finance was very important. The other bodies which helped the Minister of Finance in banking matters were: the General Directorate for Banks and Stock Exchanges, the SBC and the Bank of Spain. As will be explained in the following chapter we cannot affirm that the interests of these different institutions were identical. The joint stock company nature of the Bank of Spain meant that the interests of the private shareholders and the rest of the members of the board of directors of the Bank (who represented the State interests) were different. However, the government adopted the necessary measures to ensure its control of this institution and at least the *Actas del Banco de España* (Directors' Minutes) from the beginning of the 1950s do not reflect disagreements between representatives of the government and representatives of the private shareholders (probably because after the 1946 BSL, private shareholders were conscious of the fact that it was a 'lost battle').

The SBC was an association of banks and bankers and for this reason they represented the interests of private banks (although some representatives of the official banks were also members of this institution). As I will explain in more detail in Chapter 4, there is no coinciding of bank and State interests. The *Informe sobre el Proyecto de Ley de Ordenación Bancaria de 1946* is an example of these disagreements.

In 1962 a new Banking Act was passed. Despite the stated objectives of the *Ley de Bases* of 1962, there were few liberalising measures contained in this law. Barriers to entry were maintained, and controls on banking operations (through 'investment coefficients') were even reinforced. The only area where the 1962 Banking Law introduced important changes was in branching. I will go on to show later how the relative liberalisation of the number of branches was an important instrument to increase competition and how it had a very important influence on the increase in competition between banks and savings institutions.

Notes

1 During the War, the National government set up a 'blocking procedure' whereby certain obligations for the payment of money, which had originated in the Republican territory, were suspended. The Law of 1939, called of *Desbloqueo* or 'Unfrozen Procedure' recognised the current account balances of 18 July 1936 and for the current account generated after that date the law established a scale of percentages of conversion.

2 In September 1961 the Minister of Finance, Mariano Navarro Rubio, wrote a Memorandum about the main problems of the Spanish banking system. This Memorandum was sent to seven Spanish institutions (such as, for example, the Bank of Spain and the SBC, among others) and it laid the foundations for the *Ley de Bases* passed on 14 July 1962.

3 In the sense that the main banks were the owners of the new created industrial banks.

4 Olariaga was one of the first Spanish neo-classical economists. According to Almenar (1999: 201), in numerous articles in the journal *Moneda y Crédito* and in his book 'El Dinero' he incorporates the monetary theses of traditional English literature (Robertson, Sayers, etc).

5 There is no reliable estimate of the evolution of savings in Spain in the 1940s and 1950s. Plaza Prieto (1971: 243), estimated a series of savings, but the analysis of this series has many difficulties. He obtained savings as a difference between gross national product and consumption; the main problem is that he obtained these two

series (product and consumption) as a residual of other estimations. At the end he obtained a series of savings with serious ups and downs, especially in the 1940s, which are very difficult to explain. It is in the mid-1950s when the quality of this series improves.

CHAPTER FOUR

The Reasons for Regulating the Banking Sector in Spain, 1939–1975

This chapter analyses the political and economic foundations of the Spanish banking regulatory framework after the Civil War. Section I examines the main theoretical interpretations of the causes of regulation in the banking sector. This section is divided into two parts. Part 1 examines the 'public interest' theories of regulation. Economists have traditionally justified regulation on the basis of market failures and as banks play an essential role in economic performance, regulation is often seen as a means of avoiding market failures and of improving efficiency. Part 2 discusses the 'capture theories' for regulating the banking sector where regulation appears as a set of government favours demanded and controlled by industrial and other interest groups. It also examines the supply of favours by the government. Section II analyses possible explanations for the emergence of the Spanish banking regulatory framework and its development from 1939–40 to the mid-1970s. Here, I discuss whether in fact the Franco government used regulation to offset market failures or whether regulation was a means of using State power in the interests of the regulated sector: the banking industry.

I. The causes of banking regulation: some theoretical considerations

Public interest theories of banking regulation

It is a common feature of all countries that the financial sector is more closely regulated than any other sector in the private economy. Some authors consider that the main reasons for regulating the banking industry lie in the key role that banks play in the efficient functioning of the economy and in the implementation of monetary policy.[1] There are four main functions of financial intermediaries:

1. Expenditure and income flows between different sectors of the economy may be such that some sectors are in surplus when others are in deficit. Banks (and other financial institutions) intermediate between these sectors. They accept money in the form of deposits from the group of people who

are in surplus and lend it to those who are in deficit. Although in principle it would be possible for surplus and deficit units to channel financial resources directly, there are communication problems between the sectors which financial intermediaries help to solve.

2. Financial intermediaries provide liquidity to the economy by transforming non-convertible assets into liquid assets. Banks provide a bridge between the surplus and deficit agents by offering the depositors a different type of asset, in terms of liquidity, security, divisibility and other inducements to hold assets, from that acquired by the financial intermediary. For example, people who have money want to lend it but they want to get it back whenever they wish. On the other hand, there are people who want to borrow but who want to repay the money in several years. Thus, the function of the bank is to convert short-term deposits into longer-term loans.
3. Banks provide special services to business, for example, specialist information services, or support for exports and imports. In some instances banks supply initiative and enterprise because they are directly involved in industrial activity. Furthermore, banks may be actively involved in the management of firms which have been financed by them.
4. Banks are an integral part of the payment system and hence, an important function of the financial intermediaries is to provide an efficient payment mechanism. For this reason, financial intermediaries are an essential element used by the monetary authorities to carry out their macroeconomic policy.

The fundamental reason why financial intermediaries can provide the above-mentioned services is specialisation. Thanks to specialisation and the scale of their operations, banks can obtain better and cheaper information, they can reconcile the needs of different agents and they are able to spread the risk among a larger number of them.

The major influence of financial intermediaries on economic growth stems from four distinct roles: a) they increase the rate of saving by producing incentives to save. They are able to combine the payments of interest with other services to appeal to savers of different preferences and circumstances, b) financial intermediaries are not only concerned with the mobilisation of resources but they can facilitate the accumulation of capital by stimulating saving, c) they facilitate the necessary funds to finance capital formation. For many investors the availability of funds as a result of the performance of financial intermediaries and the access to them on reasonable terms probably have favourable effects on their investment decisions, and d) they allow an efficient allocation of resources for investment purposes. As Levine (1997: 695) notes, many firms and entrepreneurs will solicit capital, but financial intermediaries will select those entrepreneurs with the best chances of successfully initiating new goods and production processes. Financial intermediaries will thus induce a more efficient allocation of capital.

As we have seen above, financial intermediaries play an important role in the efficient functioning of the economy. Under certain conditions allocation of resources by a free market produces a *Pareto* optimal outcome, however, when these conditions are not fulfilled, there is market failure. The most important market failures are:

a) The need to control monopoly power. This type of failure arises when there are scale and scope economies in the banking industry or barriers to entry.[2] When scale economies in any one industry are so great that the number of firms operating in this sector is very small, firms can increase their profits by restricting output and charging higher prices. The small number of firms decreases the costs of collusion. In this case, regulation tries to capture the benefits of size while avoiding monopolistic behaviour.
b) Information problems. In the banking system there may be asymmetric information between the bank and its customers (borrowers and lenders). Depositors are said to be unable to adequately judge the quality of bank assets and thus the default probability associated with these banks. The same situation arises when banks lend money: banks are not fully informed of the quality of the agent who is in need of a loan. This lack of information between depositors and banks and banks and borrowers increases the probability of a banking crisis. Regulation is a possible means of increasing the information available or of insuring depositors against bank failures.
c) Another justification for regulation has been the existence of externalities. We define externalities as a situation where an agent is directly affected by the actions of another without a direct transaction between them having taken place. In the financial system, this problem appears when the failure of a 'bad' bank may cause a run on 'good' banks. There is a 'contagion effect' of one individual failure on the banking system as a whole. Glasner (1989: 181) considers that banks are more vulnerable than other industries because of the nature of banking activity: when a bank creates a deposit, it is then obliged to redeem this deposit at a fixed rate. However, the value of a bank's assets can never be known with certainty. Banks have largely fixed value liabilities in the form of deposits, while their assets can vary in value due to market fluctuations or default. In markets with imperfect information, if the public begins to doubt the solvency of a bank, many people raise

Capture theory of regulation

Regulation is not always seen to be in the public interest. The second interpretation of the origins of regulation is the 'capture theory'.[3] Capture theory has two different approaches. The first claims that regulation is a means by which the regulated firms (in this case banks) can use the coercive power of the State to benefit their own interests. Even regulation, which originally begins in the public interest, can later be 'captured' to serve the interests of regulated firms. Regulation is viewed as a means of avoiding competition and increasing profits. When the benefits of regulation are concentrated, the beneficiary group has a strong incentive to organise and exercise political pressure. Interest groups influence government to the extent that the marginal benefit from such pressure is equal to the marginal cost.

The second approach of the 'capture theory' focuses mainly on the capture of politicians. Peltzman (1976: 213) considers the possibility that the regulatory process is the result of a political calculus. Politicians seek to maximise majority support and they make use of regulation to maximise their expected voting majority. This political support is a function of the number benefited by regulation and the probability that they will support the politician, the number harmed by regulation and the probability that they will vote against the politician. There are other elements which affect this process such as the relationship between the benefits of the gaining group and the cost of lobbying and organising a cohesive group of beneficiaries. The importance of this second approach is to underline government interest in regulating any given sector.

According to regulatory capture theory, regulation has important costs: a) moral hazard problems – when regulation is designed to introduce insurance mechanisms it can lead banks and customers to reduce the normal standards of prudence and therefore to incur more risk, b) it interferes with allocation efficiency, c) losses in economic welfare – when agents execute fewer transactions than they otherwise would have, d) it increases the cost of supplying financial services, e) it reduces the opportunity of banks to react to changes in market conditions, and f) it may entail high administrative and other costs.

All these problems make it difficult to define the 'optimal' level of regulation. If we accept the existence of regulation costs – in terms of rent-seeking behaviour, losses in efficiency and so on – we must evaluate whether these costs are higher than, equal to or lower than the benefits of intervention.[4] If the costs from regulation are higher than the benefits, the main objective of the government must be to reduce intervention and to introduce measures which allow the correction of market failures. It is possible that regulation serves a specific purpose in one particular area but it may cause inefficiency in other dimensions.

sions about the convenience of accepting a new bank, without this concept ever being defined.

The authorities did not state whether these restrictions to entry were a permanent or temporary measure. However, the measures remained until the mid-1960s (regulation was less restrictive after 1962 although it still discriminated against foreign banks) and this fact makes it difficult to accept that they were passed as a temporary regulation in the unstable post-war years.[6] The existence of barriers to entry does not mean that the number of banks remained unaltered in this period (Table 2.1), however, after this law was passed only regional and local banks were established. The small size of these financial institutions and the legal restrictions on their abilities to compete – for example, for branching expansion – meant that the structure of the Spanish banking system was not affected by their entry.

Spanish regulation of barriers to entry was similar to other European legislation. Under the Banking Law of 1946 the *Conseil National du Credit* in France was granted the authority to regulate banking entry and the Bank of Italy acquired full power to control bank mergers and the opening of new banks and branches. But the market structure of these banking systems was very different. For example, Italy was a country where concentration was quite moderate by European standards. There the authorities justified the existence of barriers to entry as a means of increasing concentration in a financial system where in 1946 there were 1432 banks, 6889 branches and where the six largest banks held 35.5 per cent of total deposits. In comparison, in the same year there were 100 Spanish banks, with 2000 branches and the six largest Spanish banks held 63 per cent of total deposits. However, not all European countries maintained barriers to entry. The main difference between the UK and other European banking legislation was that the British financial system lacked entry barriers.

Nevertheless, Alhadeff (1968: 189) insists that the absence of legal barriers to entry is not necessarily a substantial difference as the situation does not prevent banks from introducing anti-competitive devices. In the UK, banks formed a powerful cartel which regulated the conditions of banking competitiveness. Alhadeff claims that the UK cartel was even more successful in restraining competition than other countries with elaborate and detailed regulations.

However, having compared the two cases, the UK financial system with 'informal' regulation (a private agreement or cartel) and Spain with legal regulation, there appears to be one important difference. In Spain, regulation restrained competition through barriers to entry and price controls, and caused the incentives to improve efficiency to disappear. There were no other alternative financial institutions, and savings banks were subject to discriminatory legislation which prevented these institutions from competing with banks under equal conditions.

There were no formal agreements among the main banks, although some banks eventually established accords[7] to collaborate in their activities. It is true that in the UK the cartel was very successful (Aldaheff 1968: 190 or Collins 1990: 111), but in the UK case the improvements in efficiency appeared outside the banking system. As Collins (1990: 448) indicates: 'Banks had to pay more attention to their own competitiveness if they were to slow-down the loss of retail deposits to institutions such as the building societies.'

This then was the main difference. In a financial system with state regulation, as in the Spanish case, competition cannot work except outside the system in the black market. However, in a non-regulated financial system, as in the British case, it is possible that other institutions try to compete and they force banks to become more competitive. In other countries such as France, regulation favoured a high degree of specialisation in the banking system and all credit institutions were subject to the same rules – the same liquidity ratio, solvency ratio, etc. As explained in Chapter 2, in Spain savings institutions were subject to discriminatory legislation and other potentially competitive financial intermediaries did not consolidate their position within the Spanish financial system (see Table 2.2).

The argument of increasing size used by other European governments to regulate entry – regardless of its validity[8] – is not applicable to Spain. Although concentration of deposits increased from 1939 to the late 1950s, an important number of small banks managed to hold their ground in the market. There was no substantial increase in the average size of banks and from the end of the Civil War to the 1980s there were no mergers among the 'core banks'. In fact, Spanish commercial banks were small by European banking standards.

Financial regulation limited the development of bond and equity markets, too. The *Junta de Inversiones* (Investment Board) of the Ministry of Finance had to approve bond and stock issues and it regulated bond yields; the final effect of these measures was to discourage most companies from using direct financial markets to access funds. Moreover, the Ministry of Finance required investors to report all their purchases of bonds and securities to fiscal authorities, but did not require them to report their banking deposits. As maintained by Lukauskas (1992: 172), the Franco government had important reasons for impeding the development of direct financial markets. First, financial authorities can more easily control the allocation of credit when direct financial markets do not perform. Second, it is more difficult to extract seigniorage from direct financial markets than from the banking system. Lastly, banks opposed the development of these alternative financial markets because the lack of modernisation of bond and equity markets meant that banks had complete control over them. This regulation encouraged savers to maintain their wealth in the form of deposits.

One of the most important steps of the Banking Law of 1962 was that, in theory, the banking sector was to be made more accessible to newcomers. What were the main reasons for this change and what influence did it have? From the questionnaire that the Minister of Finance sent in 1961 to the Bank of Spain, the SBC, the Chambers of Commerce, the Institute of Political Studies, the CEN, Savings Institutions and Trade Unions (Ministry of Finance, 1961, *Memorandum del Ministerio de Hacienda sobre el sistema bancario y crediticio e Informes sobre el mismo de los siguientes organismos: Banco de España, Consejo Superior bancario, Organización Sindical, Instituto de Estudios Políticos, Cámaras de Comercio, Industria y Navegación, CECA y Consejo de Economía Nacional*), it is possible to ascertain the opinion of these different institutions regarding the removal of barriers to entry and other questions. In general, all of them favoured removing barriers to entry with the exception of the Chambers of Commerce and the SBC. Both these institutions remarked on the necessity of maintaining some Spanish banking 'historical privileges' and restricting the entry of foreign banks (Report of the Chambers of Commerce 1961: 4 and Report of the SBC 1961: 29). Other institutions such as the Trade Union Central Committee or the Institute of Political Studies were completely in favour of removing barriers to entry and increasing competition (Report of the Trade Union Central Committee 1961: 5 and Report of the Institute of Political Studies 1961: 18).

In the 1962 Banking Law, regulators shared the view that banks enjoyed a privileged position and that the main results of this lack of competition were inefficiency and supernormal profits. The *Ley de Bases* of 1962 (Section 7) was intended to be the main instrument of change in this situation. As explained in Chapter 1, the role of international pressures in this regulatory change (*Informe del Comité Económico sobre la Ejecución del Plan de Estabilización*, D-1191, 1960, art. 8 or Perez 1997) must also be taken into account. The Reports of the Bank of England of 1962 about the Spanish banking system made continuous references to the external pressures the Bank of England authorities exerted on the Bank of Spain (Bank of England Archives, OV61, 21 November 1962: 1). The 1960s were a period of financial liberalisation in many European countries and the Franco government followed, although very cautiously, this liberalisation process.

In spite of the declared official intentions, there were no essential changes made. The number of banks in 1962 was 109, rising in 1965 to 126 and falling in 1970 to 111. The new banks created during those years were a result of the obligatory specialisation of the BSL of 1962 (section 6). There was no agreement as to the convenience of industrial banks. For example, the SBC and the Chambers of Commerce remarked on the important role that mixed banks played in the Spanish economy and they were in favour of maintaining the universal character of Spanish Banks (Report of the Chambers of Commerce: 4 and Report of the SBC: 11–23). The Bank of Spain was very cautious about the convenience of forced specialisation (Report of the Bank of Spain: 14). By contrast, the Trade Union Central Committee and the Institute of Political Studies were in favour of the separation of commercial and industrial banks (Report of the Central Committee of the Syndicates 1961: 5 and Report of the Institute of Political Studies, 1961: 17).

Fifteen 'industrial' banks were established in the 1960s, but ten of these had powerful connections with existing commercial banks which had been forced by the Banking Law of 1962 (section 6), the Decree Law 56 of 6 December 1962 (concerning portfolios and ratios for private banks), and the Decree Law 53 of 29 November 1962 (concerning industrial banks and banks d'affaires) to open an industrial bank. According to the Decree Law 56 of 6 December 1962, the law tried 'to create sufficient incentives to make the present mixed banks tend to specialise without abruptly changing their organisation or disturbing the capital market', and, as Section 2 above indicated, 'the banks and bankers operating on the date when this Decree Law is published must not acquire further industrial securities without the Finance Minister's express and definite authorisation.' To avoid these difficulties, most of the existing banks opened a new industrial bank. Therefore, we cannot say that after the *Ley de Bases* of 1962 differences were substantial. As a special correspondent indicated in *The Economist* (1962, 12 May: 586): 'The bankers have known for two years that reform was inevitable and do not appear depressed . . . They [banks] believe that if they play ball their present holdings will continue to prosper.'

In short, the BSL of 1946 not only introduced barriers to entry but also controlled the expansion of banks through branches. In the immediate post-war years, the main private banks were very critical of this measure (Annual Reports *Banco Vizcaya* 1943 and *Banco Bilbao*). The SBC in a report about the bill of the 1946 BSL (Bank of Spain Archives, *Informe sobre el Proyecto de Ley de Ordenación Bancaria de 1946*: 14), deemed that the law imposed serious restrictions on branch expansion and demanded the removal of these branching controls. These restrictions, in their opinion, should only be a transitory measure in the unstable post-war years; they made no sense after this period. In spite of this, branching restrictions were maintained until the 1962 reform.

After analysing 193 applications to open branches in the period 1945–1956,[9] it would seem that the Bank of Spain applied the same criteria to large and small banks alike (Bank of Spain Archives, Reports for the opening of branches 1945–1956). Although the Bank of Spain could exercise its discretion, this was not normally done. In spite of this lack of discrimination in the Bank of Spain's behaviour, regulation tended to favour the concentration of branches in the hands of larger banks (see Table 2.15), which were more able to satisfy the necessary requirements.

The only field where the new legislation of 1962 altered the pattern of evolution of Spanish banking was in branching (see Tables 2.13 and 2.14). After reducing branching restrictions, banks used branching expansion as an instrument to compete, increasing the volume of deposits by location and advertising. This increase in the number of branches in the 1960s is of prime importance as the huge network of branches which has its origin in the Banking Law of 1962 was the main 'natural' barrier – although not the only one[10] – to entry into the banking industry for new banks. With respect to savings banks, these institutions specialised their activity in small savers, and their main mechanism to take more deposits was to increase the number of branches. As a consequence of the branching liberalisation which started in the 1960s, savings institutions achieved a higher number of branches than banks and an important market share, although their volume of deposits was lower.

Other 'prudential' measures There were relatively few bank failures or bankruptcies in the period 1940–1975. Two factors explain this 'good' result.[11] First, mergers and absorption took place in the face of anticipated possible failures. This period saw numerous mergers (see Table 2.5) which avoided failures and bankruptcies. Mergers were also a typical strategy used by the national banks to increase in size in a market where branching expansion was restricted. Second, the Bank of Spain intervened and gave help to banks in financial difficulty (Clayton 1962: 358).

Regulation also allowed banks to perform in a relatively 'peaceful' environment. However, the cost of this stability was high: first, efficiency suffered as banks were not forced to compete or modernise their structures.[12] Second, this lack of competition coupled with the 'paternalistic' attitude of the state increased moral hazard. Banks made use of risky and 'bad' banking practices and was one of the reasons for the banking crisis between 1978 and 1982 (Rodríguez 1989: 1035 and López Roa 1983: 111).[13] This crisis affected 51 banks of a total of 111, although the Deposit Guarantee Fund (*Fondo de Garantía de Depósitos*) only intervened in 29 cases.[14] The crisis led to the dismissal of 27.19 per cent of workers in the banking sector (Cuervo 1988: 83–4).

Although the BSL of 1946 empowered the Minister of Finance to require the banks to deposit up to 20 per cent of their total deposit liabilities in cash or unpledged securities with the Bank of Spain, no such order was ever made. The cash reserves that banks held with the Bank of Spain were in fact the result of convention, self-regulation, convenience, or profit-maximising behaviour. There was a very serious discussion about this legal requirement between private banks (represented by the SBC) and the Minister of Finance. In the Report of the SBC regarding the Bill of the 1946 BSL, this institution expressed its criticisms of this legal requirement (Bank of Spain Archives, *Informe sobre el Proyecto de Ley de Ordenación Bancaria de 1946*: 8–9). In a similar report written by the *Banco Vizcaya* (Bank of Spain Archives, *Informe del Banco de Vizcaya sobre el Proyecto de Ley de Ordenación Bancaria de 1946*), the removal of this section of the law was also called for. This institution was even more critical of this section (being 'indignant about this requirement') probably because this was a private report sent to the SBC about the Bill of the 1946 BSL and the report of the SBC was the final report sent to the Minister of Finance. The Report of the SBC (Bank of Spain Archives, *Informe del Consejo Superior Bancario sobre el Proyecto de Ley de Ordenación Bancaria de 1946*: 8) considered that this legal requirement was a measure used by the government to ensure the 'collaboration' of the banking sector in the financing of its deficits and its public bond policy. They indicated to the Minister of Finance their 'voluntary' collaboration. However, in spite of criticism from private banks, the government decided to maintain this power, although it was never exercised. The government maintained this regulatory measure to secure an element of pressure in its public deficit financing policy. In fact, as seen in Chapter 2, although the public bond holdings were not subject to any legal limit, from 1946 to 1975 the bulk of public bond issues were taken up by the banking sector.

The Bank of Spain continually sent commercial banks 'recommendations' about the optimal level of loans these credit institutions should lend. However, it did not transform these 'recommendations' into legal requirements.[15] The only perceptible means of control took the form of mere 'requests' which the Bank of Spain made to commercial banks in an attempt to reduce their advances, appealing to the bankers' sense of responsibility and introducing some economic incentives to those banks which followed the Bank of Spain's recommendations.[16]

Monetary stability Achieving accelerated industrialisation demanded the sacrifice of this goal of monetary stability. In order to attain monetary stability, the *Ley de Desbloqueo* of December 1939 aimed to combine the two wartime monetary systems, while avoiding inflationary pressures. The *Ley de Desbloqueo* stabilised the monetary system and avoided a greater increase in prices (Sardá 1968: 449). Martín Aceña's estimate (1991: 13–31) shows that this law allowed the cancellation of 13,251 million pesetas in legal money and 10,258 million pesetas in banking money. To control inflation, the government passed other complementary measures involving: a) a new corporate taxes collection plan, b) a decision that only 25 per cent of unfrozen banking assets and liabilities could

drove up prices. To understand the growth of prices and money in this period it is necessary to consider the role of credit in Franco economic programme. After the Civil War the Bank of Spain (1946, D-6421) published a report about the Spanish economy, stressing credit's importance in the task of reconstruction. According to this report, the Civil War had significantly reduced production and NI and the Bank of Spain (1946, D-6421: 6) was conscious that in the short term the only way to obtain credit was by increasing the issue of money.

A strategy of reconstruction based upon credit expansion has two main risks: inflation and speculation, but the report considered that these 'dangers' could be avoided if the government increased the stock of money at the same rate as the volume of production. Unfortunately, inflation was not accompanied by stimulating effects on production and employment (see Table 4.1).[21] As the 'Private and Confidential' circular of 5 February 1951 to bank managers from Luis Sáez de Ibarra, President of the SBC, indicates (Bank of England Archives, 1951, OV61/4, 12 March: 4):

> This expansion of credit, given the conditions in which the Spanish economy operates today, has not been reflected fundamentally either in a larger and quicker turnover of produce, or in a productive expansion of industry to merit larger working capital investments therein; but in prices since the volume of production has been, in recent times, practically the same, only achieving higher costs and which could as should have been financed satisfactorily by a volume of credit inferior to that which has been received.

Some authors consider that the Franco authorities were not conscious of the seriousness of inflationary problems associated with the industrialisation programme (González 1979: 45). However, the Bank of Spain Report D-6421 of 1945 emphasised the grave effects of inflation on the Spanish economy. Paris Eguilaz (1947: 188–90) also remarked on the serious consequences of the lack of inflationary control measures in the 1946 BSL. Furthermore, there was an interesting debate among the main contemporary economists – Paris Eguilaz, Olariaga and Figueroa, among others – about whether inflation was or was not a priority problem of the Spanish economy (Velarde 1988: 58). Nevertheless, the official approach considered that the top priority was the increase in production, especially industrial production, and inflation was the price that Spain had to pay for its industrialisation. The Overseas Economic Surveys for Spain (1956: 5) admits that: 'Some inflation there must be as the price of development in conditions of scarce resources.' Although again in these reports, the main reasons for the problem of rising prices were identified as Franco's programme of industrialisation and the way in which this programme was financed (Overseas Economic Surveys 1951: 17).

Taking into account all of these circumstances, some authors consider that from the end of the Civil War to the late 1950s there was no monetary policy in Spain to speak of.[22] Yet this is no different from the experience of other European countries. The influence of Keynesian economic theory in those years determined that fiscal policies occupied a central position in those employed by the governments of developed countries. It is difficult to believe that the Spanish government could have been greatly interested in avoiding inflation if in the United Kingdom 'monetary policy remained something of a Cinderella' (Collins 1990: 329). In spite of this, Paris Eguilaz (1947: 186–87) made reference to a letter that Keynes sent to him where the author indicated the dangers of an uncontrolled increase in the amount of money in circulation.

There were special Spanish circumstances explaining the differences between the policy of Franco government's policy and other European countries' experiences. First and foremost, there was the massive use of inflationary methods of public financing (Overseas Economic Survey 1948: 15–16). When banks pledged some of their government securities at the Bank of Spain, the central bank opened a loan account on their behalf. Banks had the right to draw against this account up to a limit fixed between 80 and 90 per cent of the current value of these securities. Banks paid interest on the amount borrowed but also received interest on all the pledged securities. The consequence was that government paper was equivalent to cash in terms of liquidity but it also yielded interest. The result of financing public sector deficits by issuing government securities which were monetised at the Bank of Spain in the manner already described was that the Bank of Spain had no power to control the amount of money within the economy (Overseas Economic Surveys 1951: 17), and so inflation was greater than in other more developed countries (see Table 4.1).

Second, Spain was exceptional in the length of time when monetary policy remained passive. The first serious attempt to reconsider the role of monetary policy was only made in 1959 and, even then, monetary policy did not become very active. Some legal ratios were created to regulate liquidity: the government agreed not to issue more public debt that could be automatically pledged with the Bank of Spain while automatic recourse of public agencies to the central bank was also limited.

Third, banks, as we have seen, held a privileged position in financing firms and the majority of these loans were short term. Consequently, firms were very vulnerable to the changes in the level of liquidity within the banking system. That is why financial authorities encountered very serious difficulties when establishing a more restrictive monetary policy without reducing many firms' level of liquidity.

Table 4.1 Money supply (notes + coins), industrial production and inflation in Spain and the UK, 1940–1958 (rates of growth, in %)

	Spain			UK	
	IPI	Money Supply	Price Inflation	Money Supply	Price Inflation
1940–1958	4.7	12.1	8.74	5.84	3.5
1940–1950	2.2	10.4	11.47	9.2	2.4
1950–1958	7.9	14.0	5.43	1.8	4.3
1940–1945	0.8	8.2	8.99	14.6	2.1
1945–1950	3.6	12.2	13.99	3.9	2.6
1950–1955	7.7	12.4	2.80	1.9	5.5
1955–1958	8.2	16.6	9.96	1.6	3.7

Sources: Spain: Martín Aceña (1988: 109–18), Morella (1991: 129) and Carreras, ed. (1989: 522). United Kingdom: Liesner (1985: 32) and Capie and Weber (1985: 529).

As explained in Chapter 3, after the Stabilisation Plan and the Banking Law of 1962, the Bank of Spain was technically equipped to execute monetary policy, in comparison with the monetary instruments that other European countries employed. However, the authorities failed to resolve some problems:

1. A conversion of the existing public debt that would also abolish the bank's privilege of automatic pledgeability. At the end of the 1960s 90 billion pesetas of public debt which could be automatically pledged with the Bank of Spain were outstanding, the greater part being in the hands of private banks.
2. A liberalisation of the rate of interest. From the mid-1950s most European countries employed a more active discount-rate policy but the Spanish government lost an opportunity of bringing the fixed rate of interest to a market clearing level.
3. The government did not achieve the revitalisation of the stock market, open market operations and other institutions and mechanisms that in a more industrialised and complex economy would have been necessary. In fact, the steps taken by the government to control prices comprised rather hesitant exhortation. The fundamental concept of the Banking Reform Law was not expressed clearly as a concrete policy but rather it was stated that

monetary policy was determined by the government 'in such a way as will best serve the national interest'. The results of the Banking Reform Law according to the Report of the Bank of England about Spanish banks (Bank of England Archives, 1963, OV/61/8: 4–6), were clear:

> This nebulous policy (the lack of a concrete monetary policy) is to be given effect by the Ministry of Finance acting through the Bank of Spain and the other credit authorities. As has already been seen the number of separate authorities created (the Bank of Spain, the Institute of Medium and Long term Credit, and the Institute for Savings Banks) and their opposing interests do not make for an effective handling of the problems arising. It is also the case, that there are too many theoreticians and amateurs involved. The former conceived the Banking Reform Law and ancillary arrangements and the latter are operating the mechanism. This is, unfortunately, especially true of the Bank of Spain itself where three new Deputy Governors without the necessary practical experience have replaced one experienced and distinguished professional banker. Indeed, instead of the Bank of Spain having become, as was intended, the supreme monetary authority, its prestige has never been so low as it is now . . . To put it crudely, whatever the government and its amateur advisers do, they cannot dispel the impression that they do not know what they are doing.

Monopolistic behaviour

Paris Eguilaz (1947: 43), who was the Chairman of the CEN, considered that one of the main reasons for regulating the banking sector was to use regulation as a means of avoiding 'monopolistic behaviour'. In a market structure with barriers to entry banks could adopt cartel agreements and fix prices thanks to their monopolistic power. Here, the role of regulation would be to avoid this behaviour by holding prices close to the competitive equilibrium level. In Spain the Franco government restricted the rate of interest, fixing a maximum rate of interest on deposits and a minimum rate of interest on loans.[23] To assess the consequences of these measures we must consider: a) whether the statutory rates of interest avoided monopolistic pressures and b) the possible negative effects of these interest controls in terms of a reduction in the level of savings, a misallocation of resources or an incentive for black markets.

Paris Eguilaz (1947: 222–23) considered that the BSL of 1946, in comparison with previous legislation, introduced some useful instruments for reducing the monopolistic influence of Spanish banks on the economy. However, he recognised that the regulatory measures concerning interest rates failed to solve completely the problem of monopolistic behaviour. His opinion is very relevant if we take into account that the Ministry of Finance fixed interest rates after consultation with the CEN. Eguilaz claimed that some of the main problems of the performance of the banking sector were not solved with the BSL of 1946.[24] Nonetheless, he did believe that the main objective of the government with this reform was to secure the collaboration of the banking sector in the application of the political economy 'whatever the means we use' (Paris Eguilaz 1947: 197).

The Bill of the 1946 BSL established that the Minister of Finance fix interest rates and banking commissions. However, the banking sector was very critical of this measure. In the Report of the SBC about the Bill of the 1946 BSL the banking sector claimed that this measure was an 'error'. They felt it was impossible that the intention of the Minister of Finance was to introduce this high degree of interventionism (Bank of Spain Archives, *Informe Sobre el Proyecto de Ley de Ordenación Bancaria de 1946*: 7). They suggested the introduction of an amendment to the Bill and they proposed that the Minister of Finance fix the minimum loan interest rate and the maximum deposit interest rate. According to the SBC, there were two main reasons for this amendment. First, they considered that 'excessive' competition among banks to take more deposits would increase interest rates too much, when the government should be promoting a

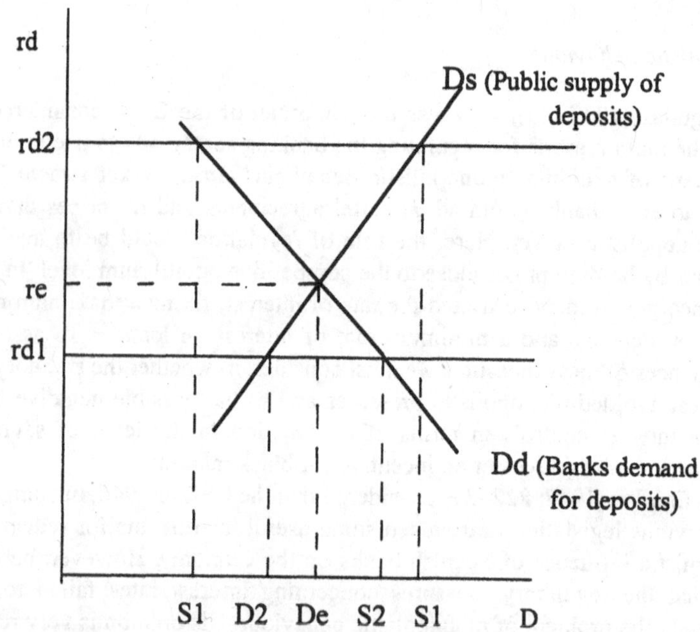

Figure 4.1 Control deposit interest rate (competition)

cheap money policy. Second, the SBC considered that an increase in competition to provide more loans would encourage 'bad banking practices', reducing interest rates to levels which would not allow banks to cover costs, and causing serious problems in banking institutions. The pressures of private banks were reflected in the final version of the 1946 BSL.

To avoid monopolistic behaviour by banks the authorities should have fixed a binding minimum rate of interest on deposits (or a floor) higher than the monopolistic deposit interest rate and a maximum loan interest rate (or a ceiling) lower than the monopolistic interest rate. However, as noted above, the Franco authorities did the opposite: they fixed a maximum on the rate of interest on deposits and a minimum on the rate of deposits on loans.

In a situation of perfect competition interest controls may cause a 'market disequilibrium' (a gap between the desired supply and demand for loans and deposits). With a 'ceiling' on the deposit interest rate and a 'floor' on the loan interest rate the total amount of deposits and loans may be lower than the equilibrium levels. In Figure 4.1, the public willingness to make savings deposits is assumed to be positively related to the rate of interest. *Ds* is the supply of deposits by the public and *Dd* is the demand for deposits from the banks. The public will supply more deposits when the remuneration they obtain on these deposits is higher. When the ceiling on the deposit rate, or *rd1*, is below the equilibrium rate *re*, banks would accept more deposits *D1*, but *S1* is the quantity of deposits that the public supplies at the existing rate. When the ceiling on the deposit rate, or *rd2*, is above the equilibrium interest rate *re*, the actual rate of interest on deposits would be *re*:

if *rd1* < *re* then — (*S1* < *D1*)
if *rd2* > *re* then — (*D2* < *S2*)

Banks are willing to advance more loans when they receive higher returns. The public will demand fewer loans as the interest charged increases. When the authorities fix a minimum on the loan interest rate, if the 'floor' on the rate of interest on loans is below the equilibrium rate of interest (*rl1* < *re*), the actual loan interest rate would be the equilibrium interest rate *re*. When the minimum interest rate is above the equilibrium interest rate (*rl2* > *re*), at this rate the amount of loans that banks would make is *S2*, but *D2* is the amount of loans the public demand (see Figure 4.2). In short, in a model of perfect competition when the authorities introduce a ceiling (a floor) on the rate of interest, the total amount of deposits (loans) may be lower than the equilibrium one.

Results, however, are different in a monopolistic situation. If banks have monopoly power,[25] they will maximise profits when they set the rate of interest

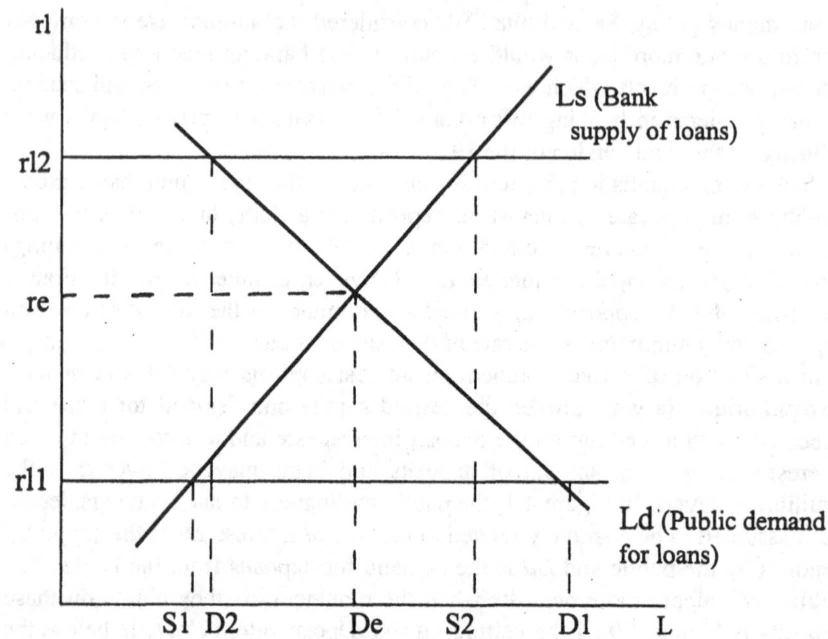

Figure 4.2 Control loan interest rate (competition)

on deposits (rm) below the equilibrium competitive interest rate (re). Monopolistic banks drive up the interest rates they will have to pay on deposits, the more deposits they take. They therefore accept fewer deposits than competitive banks. With this market structure, the consequences of interest rate regulation depend on those restrictions the government introduces: a) a binding rate of interest, b) a 'floor' on the rate of interest on deposits (or loans) and c) 'a ceiling' on the rate of interest on deposits (or loans) (Courakis 1984: 341–70).

As we can see in Figure 4.3, if the authorities introduce a binding ceiling deposit interest rate and this fixed rate of interest on deposits *rd2* is below the monopolistic rate of interest *rm*, the total amount of deposits demanded for the banks *D2* is lower than both the equilibrium *De* and the monopolistic *Dm* volume of deposits. In this case, government intervention is the worst situation. However, in a market structure with monopoly on the demand side of deposits by banks we cannot say that constraints are always undesirable. In a monopolistic banking structure a binding rate of interest (or a floor on the rate of interest on deposits paid by banks) can result in a lower volume of deposits than in competition but higher than in monopoly (*De* > *D1* > *Dm*). In Spain,

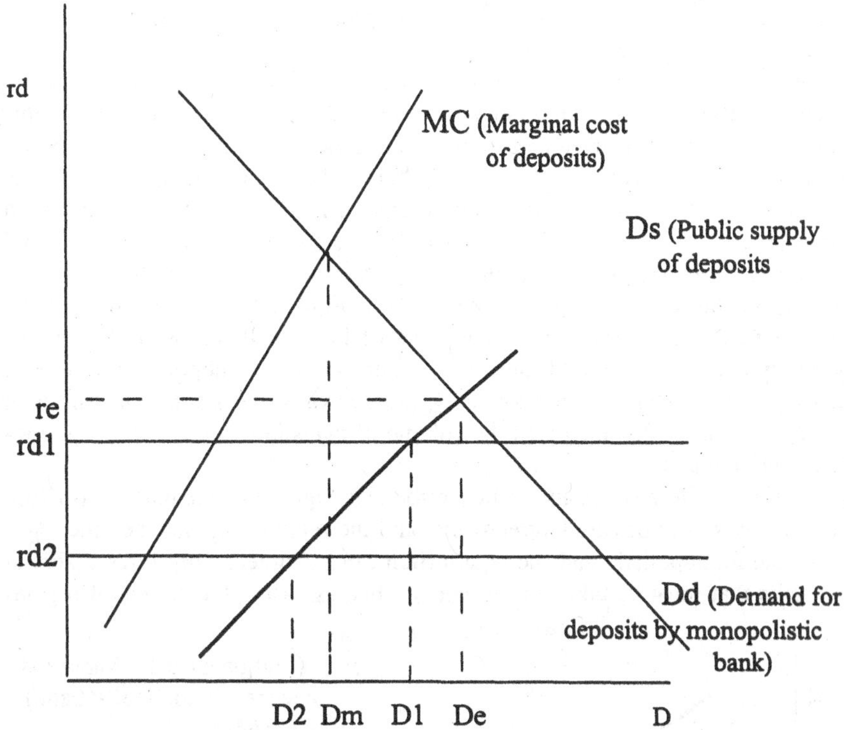

Figure 4.3 Control deposit interest rate (monopoly)

where the authorities fixed a 'ceiling' on the rate of interest on deposits, banks chose the rate of interest subject to the restriction that the chosen rate of interest *rdi* must be lower than or equal to the ceiling *rd*: *rd* > *rdi* > *rm*. In this case, the total amount of deposits in comparison with the equilibrium would depend on the decisions of the banking industry about where to fix the rate of interest on deposits. However, with a 'ceiling' on the deposit interest rate, the authorities did not avoid monopolistic behaviour no matter where the ceiling was set.

Regarding loans, the analysis of the Spanish banking industry is more complex. Although the authorities introduced a 'floor' on the rate of interest on loans, other complementary credit controls were instituted in order to direct the flow of bank funds to 'high-priority' areas. That is why some industries had a 'preferential' rate of interest – that is to say, the authorities fixed a binding interest rate for loans in these privileged sectors below the general floor. It is therefore very difficult to reach a clear and precise conclusion as to the consequences of loan interest controls.

Generally, however, when the authorities fix a binding rate of interest on loans, the effect on the total volume of loans will depend on where they fix this binding loan rate. When the authorities fix a floor on the rate of interest on loans, if the minimum rate of interest is below the monopolist rate (*rl1* < *rm*), banks would choose *rm* and the total volume of loans would be the same as in the monopolistic case (see Figure 4.4). This regulation, then, does not avoid monopolistic behaviour. The situation is different when the authorities fix a ceiling on the loan interest rate. When the ceiling is below the monopolistic interest rate (*rl1* < *rm*), the total volume of loans will be lower than at the perfectly competitive equilibrium, but higher than the monopolistic volume of loans (*Le* > *L1* > *Lm*). With monopoly, there always exists some binding loan rate (or a ceiling) that increases the volume of loans in relation to the monopolistic loan volume.

To sum up, the way the authorities introduced regulation, the market structure (and the existence of cartel agreements) and the relationship between the regulated, the monopolistic and the equilibrium rates of interest are three essential elements that must be taken into account when assessing the effects of regula-

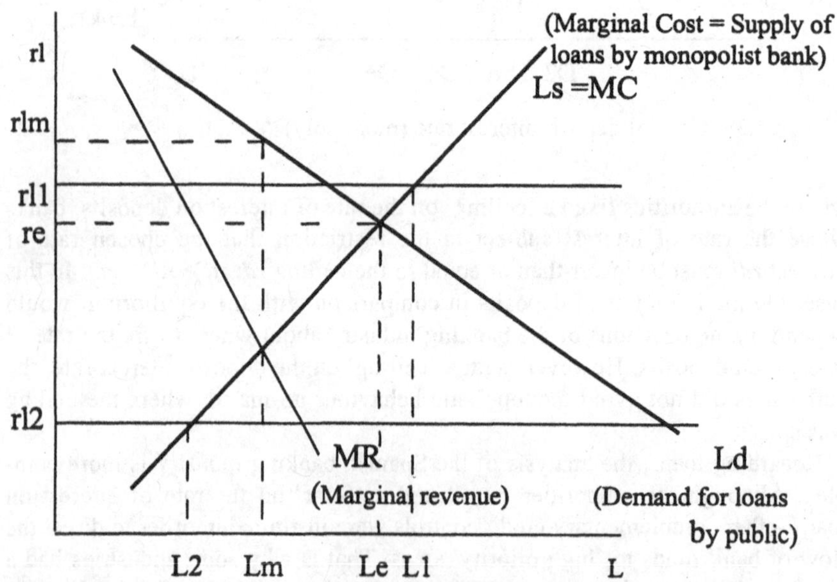

Figure 4.4 Control loan interest rate (monopoly)

tion. Although the following chapter will discuss this problem in depth, the foregoing analysis shows that Spanish banking regulations could not remedy monopoly behaviour. The existence of several cartel agreements among banks to fix banking conditions confirms this fact[26] as we will see.

Thus, interest controls do not only affect deposit and loan decisions. Although the main activity of banks is to transform deposits into loans, banks can make profits from deposits through other, different, activities such as industrial or public debt investments. Interest controls have an important effect on these alternative activities also. In Spain, the government introduced some 'preferential' loan interest rates to stimulate the economic growth of these favoured sectors. Low loan interest rates reduce the willingness of banks to take risks. They hold banks back from supplying funds in the form of loans (in part this is the reason why the Franco authorities introduced other complementary credit controls to guarantee banking funds to some sectors) and are an incentive for direct investment. The main problem of this industrial investment is that its real return was completely distorted by regulation.

Interest controls are essential for understanding the 'mixed' nature of Spanish banks. As loan rates were controlled, banks tried to increase their profitability through direct investments. As Tortella and García (1993: 21) indicate, in the post-war years banks could obtain high levels of profits if they adapted their behaviour to the new circumstances. In this sense, banks had good returns if they invested in 'protected' industries.

The existence of a policy of privileged sectors (known as '*circuitos privilegiados de financiación*') naturally influenced the investment decisions of banks. The problem is whether banks invested in 'priority sectors' to take advantage of regulation, or whether the definition of 'priority sectors' by the Franco government was the result of banking pressures, as the 'capture theory' would suggest. It is to this problem that we turn our attention in the following section.

Allocation purposes

As Paris Eguilaz (1947: 196–7) explains, the main justification for interventionism in the banking system was 'allocation' objectives. As explained above, after the Spanish Civil War and because of the economic recession that this caused, the Franco government introduced many measures to accelerate industrialisation. The Civil War had caused an important reduction in the level of production and national income and there was a lack of resources to start the task of reconstruction. Spain had a low level of savings (Overseas Economic Surveys 1956: 77) and it was isolated from the rest of the world – both as a consequence of the diplomatic and economic boycott imposed by most countries, and as a matter of choice. In these circumstances the government established an economic programme based on credit expansion.

In general, by holding down interest rates in some 'priority' sectors the government tried to stimulate private investment and to obtain cheaper financing of the state budget. The Spanish authorities adopted several measures to achieve this regulatory aim:

1. As explained before, they introduced mechanisms to obtain privileged financing for 'priority sectors'. These industries were considered very important not only for their influence on income but also for their influence as suppliers of essential inputs to other industries. So the authorities required banks to maintain 'compulsory ratios' to provide loans to specific sectors.
2. The Franco government introduced the concept of '*acciones concertadas*'. The idea was that when a firm was incorporated into this plan of '*acciones concertadas*' the government gave it financial, fiscal and other advantages. In return the firm agreed to achieve certain levels of production and productivity and other goals.

According to Cuadrado Roura (1977: 124), at the beginning of the 1960s the percentage of the total resources provided by the financial system and controlled by the government – through compulsory coefficients and other additional controls – was around 25 per cent. At the end of the 1960s this percentage was about 40 per cent. There is insufficient information on the sectors which benefited by this policy but the main 'privileged sectors' in the 1960s were capital goods, exports and shipbuilding.

The analysis of the effects of state interventionism for allocation purposes involves serious difficulties. This problem is related to the definition of a 'priority' sector. It is very difficult to evaluate empirically, however, what the costs and benefits of this intervention were. According to the capture theory, intervention results from pressure brought to bear upon politicians and government officials by organised interests. Even if regulation began as a measure to be used in the public interest, eventually in the end regulators served the interests of the regulated. González (1979) maintained that the policy of 'privileged sectors' established a serious imbalance between regulated and unregulated areas which helped discretion and stimulated a 'rent-seeking' competition. In the words of González (1979: 321): 'it is evident that entrepreneurs competed, at times in terms of prices and quality; but in general they competed to obtain official rewards.' However, the origin of regulation was more complex than this and we must consider other factors.

Table 4.3 Relationship between 'top' public officials and the board of directors of banks

	1935	1945	1955	1965
(1)	22	145	167	210
(2)	1.3	8.9	10.3	12.9
(3)	16	83	91	106
(4)	7	36	45	53
(5)	9	47	56	53

Notes: (1) Number of top public officials who were members of the board of directors of a bank, (2) Percentage of top public officials who were members of the board of directors of a bank with respect to the total number of top public officials, (3) Total number of top public officials with banking links, (4) Total number of top public officials who were members of the board of directors of a public bank, (5) Total number of top public officials who were members of the board of directors of a private bank.

Source: Viver Pi Sunyer (1978: 274 and 280).

directors who were also 'top' public officials of the Regime. The number of 'top' public officials who were members of the boards of directors of banks (public and private banks) can be seen in Table 4.3.

Lukauskus (1992: 138) affirms that Spanish banks were able to 'capture' the policy-making apparatus and obtained extremely favourable financial regulation. Thanks to this regulatory framework banks earned high and risk-free profits. He recognises that the government was gradually able to use financial regulatory policies in its own interests, but he considers that the regime lacked a 'well though-out economic doctrine or plan'; rather it sought political survival.

Politicians and bankers had strong reasons for regulating the banking sector and legislation was the result of these two interest groups' pressures. Even if the extraordinary influence of the main banking and industrial groups upon the financial regulatory framework is accepted, the politicians' incentives for regulating the banking system cannot be forgotten. The most important regulatory measures to achieve industrialisation under state direction were passed and many firms were declared to be of 'national interest' in the first years of the Franco regime, when the links between banks and government were less important or at least less 'formal'. These laws[28] reflected the Franco regime's economic ideology in the same way as other measures, such as the creation of the INI did. For this reason, political ideology (based on nationalism, interventionism and autarky) must be considered as being essential to the origins of financial legislation. Furthermore, several financial policies did not in fact benefit the banking system. For example, the Annual Reports of the *Banco Vizcaya* and *Banco Bilbao* during the 1940s contain continuous references to the problems associated with branching control and the need to remove such regulation. The same criticisms appeared in the Report of the SBC about the Bill of the 1946 BSL (Bank of Spain Archives, *Informe del Consejo Superior Bancario Sobre el Proyecto de Ley de Ordenación Bancaria de 1946*: 14). The limit on dividends is yet another example.[29] Moreover, it must be remembered that some of the regime's most influential economists discussed the convenience of nationalising the banking system,[30] although it is difficult to believe that this economic measure was actually in government plans. One final but important point is that many bankers were liberals and did not support the Franco dictatorship. García and Tortella (1994: 29–30) take as an example Villalonga, the President of the *Banco Central*, 'an admirer of the extreme economic liberalism of the Vienna school, and an old liberal-conservative and Valencian-regionalist politician, who, on finding his way into politics barred after the civil war, had become a full-time banker'. Another of their examples is Jose Llado, 'a left-of-centre liberal who had spent some time in prison after the Civil War, before joining the *Banco Urquijo*'. They concluded that 'the attitudes of the other big banks varied, but it is fair to say that in general they viewed the Franco dictatorship as a "lesser evil", but did not show any enthusiasm for it.'

There is another example of this lack of coincidence between government and banking interests. Spanish banks were involved in industrial activity. In 1941 the *Banco Urquijo* – with the collaboration of other banking institutions such as the *Banco Hispanoamericano*, the *Banco Español de Crédito*, the *Banco de Aragón*, and Fiat and other firms – applied to the government to open the first Spanish automobile firm: SIAT. The Franco government, however, did not approve of the creation of this business. In 1947 the *Banco Urquijo* and FIAT made a new application. Later, in 1949 the Franco government made use of the Report of the *Banco Urquijo* to open a state automobile industry: SEAT. The *Banco Urquijo* was very upset over this decision and, thereafter, it was clear that Suanzes, the president of the INI for over more than two decades and a very close friend of Franco, was hostile towards the bank (San Román 1995: 88). Although the contemporary newspapers wrote about the strong collaboration between the INI and private banks (ARRIBA, 10-5 1950), *Banco Urquijo* considered itself seriously damaged by this decision and requested compensation for damages.

Neither must we forget the differences between the SBC and the Minister of Finance. As explained in Chapter 3, in some areas, such as the control of interest rates, the government was 'captured' by the interests of the banks. Nevertheless, regulation could also be explained by the regime's need for cheap financing of the budget deficit and cheap investment funds for the privileged sectors. In other areas, such as the legal requirement to deposit up to 20 per cent of their total liabilities with the Bank of Spain, the Minister of Finance did not pass the bankers' amendment to pressure them in its public deficit financing policy, as the SBC indicates. The result of these pressures was, as Table 2.16 indicates, a very important contribution of the banking sector to the financing of the public sector.

Regulation was also affected by the government's interest in protecting the traditional social and economic élite. This fact is clearly evident in the 1960s. It is in this period when the reinforcement of intervention for allocation purposes (*circuitos privilegiados de financiación*) coincided with the strengthening of links between banks and government. As explained in Chapter 1, a period of relative liberalisation of the Spanish economy began at the end of the 1950s. However, in the area of allocation controls the government reinforced interventionism. The government strengthened the mechanism of financing 'national interest industries' by increasing private banks and saving institutions controls as well as the role played by public credit.

The changes in the political and economic environment from 1959 could well indicate that liberalisation of the Spanish market started in the late 1950s but, as explained in Chapter 3, in the banking sector nothing could have been further from the truth. Allocation purposes were again an essential reason for regulating the banking system and they were a basic element of the *Ley de Bases* of 1962.

There is an important difference between the systems of altering the allocation of resources before and after 1962. The Law of 1939 had extended privileges to 'national interest enterprises' but Law 152/1963 substituted the concept of 'industry' (a selected sector or a geographical area) for 'enterprise'. The purpose of this change was to avoid discretion in the choice of the selected firms. However, the government reserved the power to concede preferential treatment to firms located in these sectors or geographical areas. In the end, the scope of discretion was enlarged and the government rejected the introduction of a free market system. The main problem with this law is that it was ambiguous. The law remarked on the lack of financing of small and medium-sized firms and the bad performance of the capital market. However, the sectors that the authorities considered of 'national interest' were areas where firms had the biggest average size.[31]

In the area of intervention to solve problems of allocation of resources, there were no great transformations in the Spanish policy. The Stabilisation Plan had not created a market economy. The changes of financial regulation in this period do not suggest that the idea of liberalisation was in practice very influential. Financial institutions, especially savings banks, were required to put a high proportion of their deposits in government securities and other industrial bonds. Commercial and industrial banks were also required to invest a proportion of their deposits in public debt and various forms of medium-term credit. The establishment of a higher investment ratio in savings institutions than that of banks, reducing the formers' possibilities of competing, provides evidence of the fact that the liberalising intent behind the 1962 law was not very influential.

It is not possible to separate the 1962 Banking Law from the rest of the political and economic changes that took place in Spain in the late 1950s. These transformations had several origins. First, there were the limitations of autarky. As explained in Chapter 1, economic and political problems forced the Franco regime to introduce many reforms. Lukauskas (1992: 240–49) deems that economic liberalisation was politically motivated. During the 1960s social instability grew: there was an increase in the number of strikes, student protests, etc. The Franco authorities and, in particular, Carrero Blanco (the closest Franco subordinate) considered that strong economic growth was the best means of defusing political opposition and ensuring the stability of the regime. As Lukauskas (1992: 241) affirms: 'Prosperity would create a depoliticised majority which was willing to accept an increased standard of living in lieu of political liberties.' And the authorities believed that the main instrument to promote economic growth was liberalisation. Not all the Franco authorities agreed with this liberalisation process. The prime proponents were the Bank of Spain and the Minister of Finance (the *tecnócratas*). The main criticisms came from the Ministers of Industry and Agriculture. The banking sector was also conscious of the urgency of this liberalisation process. As Perez (1997: 79) indicates: 'As the most important investors in the Spanish economy, the banks also stood the profit from a shift in economic policy that would tie the Spanish economy to the blooming post-war economy.' Second, it is necessary to take into account international pressures. The reports from different international institutions Spain joined in the late 1950s (OEEC, IMF) were severely critical of the Spanish financial structure and they recommended a reform of the regulatory framework (*Informe del Comité Económico sobre la ejecución del Programa de Estabilización*, Report D-1191 Bank of Spain, 1960, section 8). In 1961, the Minister of Finance wrote a memorandum where the main problems of the Spanish financial system were explained. He sent the Memorandum to seven institutions: the Bank of Spain, the SBC, (CECA), *Consejo Superior de Cámaras de Comercio, Organización Sindical, Instituto de Estudios Políticos* and CEN). After some changes to the initial Memorandum, on 14 April 1962 the *Ley de Bases sobre la Ordenación del Crédito y la Banca* (1962 Banking Law, concerning provisions for regulation of credit and banking) was approved. As Almenar (1999: 194–230) indicates, the economic and political difficulties, the coordinated action of most of the main economists who were in key advisory posts (academic economists and experts such as Sardá, Fuentes Quintana or Sampedro), plus the support of foreign economists of international agencies (the IMF[32] and the OEEC) explain this transformation. Finally, we must not forget that the 1960s were a period of financial liberalisation in other European countries. As Anderson (1970: 164–67) indicates, many of the technocrats' actions were based on a direct and almost complete importation of regulatory institutions from Spain's immediate neighbour to the north, France. In France the first shock of deregulation came in 1966–1967 (De Boissieu 1993: 194) during which time very similar forms of financial regulation were also adopted in countries with very different political regimes from the Spanish, not just France, but also Norway or Sweden (Perez 1997: 69).

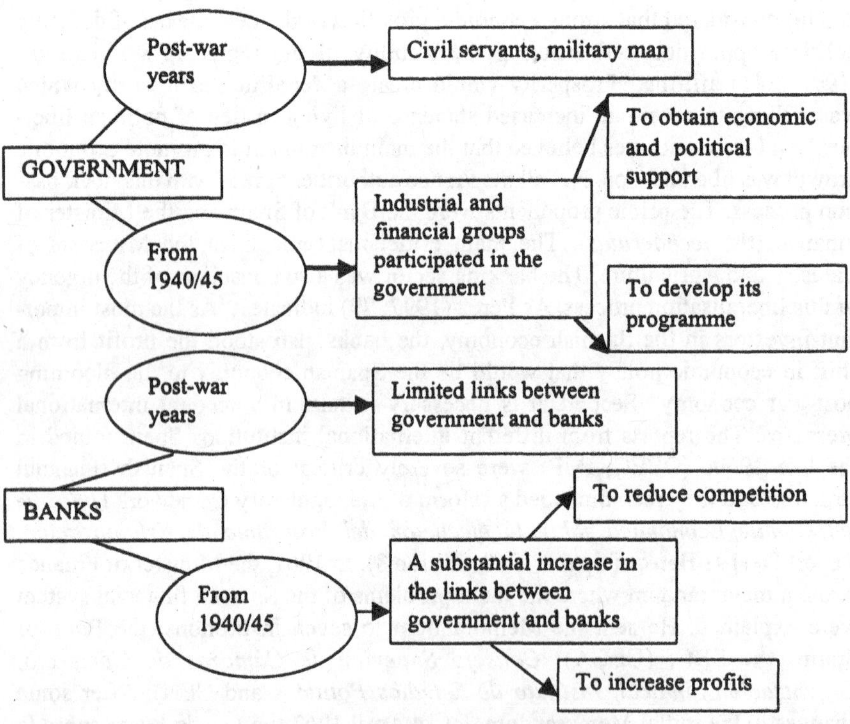

Figure 4.5 Government and bank regulatory objectives

To sum up, in spite of the efforts at liberalisation which started in 1962, Spain had a restricted financial system until the late 1970s. The Franco authorities started a timid process of liberalisation in 1962 because politicians believed that a more market-oriented economy could contribute towards greater economic growth and political stability and also because of international pressures. However, this financial reform had many contradictions. It was in the mid-1970s, with the transition from a dictatorship to a democratic system, that the interest of politicians in liberalising the financial sector became clear (Lukauskas 1992: 515).

III. Conclusions

There are two theoretical interpretations of the causes of regulation. The 'public interest' theory claims that the main objective of regulation is to compensate the effects of market failures. The 'capture theory' suggests that regulation is a means used by different interest groups – the regulated firms, politicians, and so on – to use state power to their own benefit. The Franco government justified regulation in terms of 'public interests'. However, as already explained in this chapter, many of the official reasons for regulating the financial system were not achieved. Contradictions have also been found with regard to the official reasons for regulating the banking system and the kind of instruments the government used to achieve these ends.

As we have seen, the Franco authorities justified financial regulatory measures as the means to achieving three objectives: a) to achieve stability (monetary stability and banking stability or 'prudential regulation'), b) to avoid monopolistic pressures and c) for allocation purposes. The main conclusion I have come to is that we cannot accept that the 'real' reasons for regulating the banking sector – with the exception of allocation purposes – coincided with these 'official' arguments. We have also been able to link the origins of the Spanish regulatory framework with the 'capture' theory.

Monetary stability At the end of the Civil War, the government adopted some measures to control inflation, for example, the *Ley de Desbloqueo*, the restrictions on the process of the unfreezing of deposits, or an increase in government borrowing to use up monetary funds. However, these monetary objectives were not achieved and prices rose rapidly.

The top priority of the Franco regime was industrialisation and they viewed inflation as the price that had to be paid. Although this policy can be criticised as inflationary, it is 'understandable' in the context of government motives. We cannot say that the economic authorities were not conscious of the seriousness of the inflationary problems associated with their industrialisation programme. But in an autarkic economy, lacking savings – as a result of the low rates of growth of the Spanish economy and of the lack of incentives to stimulate savings – and without foreign aid – imposed by the exclusion of Spain from the world trade community but as a matter of choice – they did not have many alternatives. The only alternative would have been to change the strategy of development, an option rejected by the government.

Furthermore, the influence of the post-war economic policy and Keynesian theory in those years determined that the emphasis on fiscal policy was a common experience in many European countries. However, other European policy makers were more sensitive to the risks of inflation. Following the example of the UK after the World War, the Labour government tried to control inflation through: a) an increase in taxes b) direct controls (price and income constraints) and c) transforming a budget deficit into a surplus (Cairncross 1992: 67–74). In both countries – Spain and the UK – the government authorities' attitude towards interest rates was similar: rates were kept as low as possible, to minimise government interest payments and to stimulate investment. In general terms, these measures coincided with the Spanish instruments of controlling inflation, but differences were substantial. The volume of the budget deficit and the way of financing this deficit determined an increase in inflation greater than in other, more developed, European countries.

Thus, the main conclusion I have reached is that until the end of the 1950s we cannot accept that monetary stability was a reason for which the Franco government regulated the banking system.

Banking stability ('Prudential regulation' to reduce the risk of bankruptcy and a banking crisis). The Franco authorities justified the establishment of barriers to entry and branching restrictions as measures to achieve the 'stability' of the banking system. Although it is true that in this period there were few failures and bankruptcies, there are two important aspects I must remark on. First, this relative 'stability' of the banking sector was not a consequence of the existence of barriers to entry and other controls. The main reason for the lack of bankruptcies was the role of the Bank of Spain. This institution intervened when banks had problems – for example, liquidity shortages and a good indicator of this 'protective' attitude was the banking crisis at the beginning of the 1980s, when the Bank of Spain decided to reduce intervention. Second, it is necessary to evaluate the usefulness of this relative 'stability'. We must take into account what the possible cost of these controls were (lack of competition and diversification of the financial system, among others).

Then, if one of the reasons of Spanish banking regulation was to avoid failures, the question is why the government did not consider other alternative measures to achieve this end – avoiding the high costs of barriers to entry and other controls – such as deposit insurance, or legal requirements.

Monopolistic pressures It is obvious that the declared 'official' intention of avoiding monopolistic behaviour on the banking system was not a 'real' intention. The kind of instruments the government used to control interest rates not only did not avoid monopolistic pressures but in fact reinforced them in some areas, at least in the 1940s. In those years regulation allowed banks to use monopoly power to exploit depositors. The differences between the initial intention of the government in the Bill of 1946 BSL and the final measures passed in the law, is good evidence of the 'capture' of the authorities by private banks. The authorities said that only low deposit interest rates allowed low loan interest rates to encourage investment. However, there are several questions we must consider:

1. If the real intention of the government was to maintain low interest rates, they should have introduced other alternative measures to achieve this end, while avoiding possible monopolistic pressures. For example, the government should have replaced the floor on the rate of interest on deposits with a ceiling on the rate of interest on deposits.
2. If the deposit interest rate was below the monopolistic interest rate – and as Chapter 6 will show, this is possible from the beginning of the 1950s – the effect of this regulation would have been worse than the profit-maximising monopolistic behaviour.

So, financial regulation not only did not avoid monopolistic pressures but had other costs for the evolution of the banking system that allow us to consider that this official approach – the necessity of avoiding monopolistic pressures – was false.

Allocation purposes This was the main reason for regulating the banking system. Chapter 1 showed how the Franco government chose a strategy of development based on accelerated industrialisation. The Franco authorities tried to involve banks in this industrialisation programme. It was in the immediate post-war years – from 1939 to 1942 – when the government passed the main regulatory measures to achieve industrialisation and they defined the 'national interest' sectors. The role of 'ideology' – independently of other factors – in this initial legislative work was essential. Another different aspect is that of the influence of interest groups on this regulation. Many scholars (Muñoz 1969 or

Brasa, Buesa and Molero 1984) affirm that the main beneficiaries of banking and other regulatory measures were banks themselves and other industrial groups. It is true that the number of 'top' official men (*altos cargos*) linked to the banking sector increased substantially in the 1940s and 1950s. If we consider that banks had strong links with the main industrial sectors such as electricity, iron or steel, and that these industrial sectors were the main beneficiaries of financial regulation – in terms of preferential interest rates and investment ratios to finance these sectors – (Braña, Buesa and Molero 1984: 170), the main conclusion we are drawn to is that it is necessary to include banking and industrial pressures as a reason for regulating the financial sector. However, there is an important difference between these traditional conclusions and my own interpretation of the origin of the Spanish regulatory framework.

This chapter shows that financial regulatory legislation was the result of two pressures. There was the interest of the Franco government in involving the banking sector in their industrialisation programme. In this sense, banks were used as an instrument of forced industrialisation. They were also used as a means of obtaining cheap public financing. However, the government offered some advantages to the banking sector to secure their collaboration. It is evident that banks and other industrial groups tried to take advantage of this regulatory framework and in fact banks which followed a strategy of growth based on investment in these protected industries – mixed banks – achieved better results than commercial banks (Tortella and García 1994: 22–7).

Bringing together the demand and the supply side of regulation, we appreciate that the legal framework was the result of pressure from multiple interest groups. There was a market for regulatory decisions and the final result reflected the power of these different interest groups. We cannot assume – as these other scholars did – that there is a coincidence between government and industrial (including banking) interests.[33]

Notes

1 See Gowland (1990), Balternsperger and Dermine (1987), or Balternsperger (1990).
2 The most important criticism is that empirical research does not show conclusive results on the existence of scale economies of the banking sector. See, for example, Balternsperger (1972), Lawrence (1989), Revell (1989), or Vives (1988).
3 This idea of 'regulatory capture' is especially associated with Downs (1957), Stigler (1964, 1971) and Stigler and Friedland (1962).
4 As Lukauskas (1992: 30–33) explains, 'the government must play an active role in minimizing the microeconomic problems identified above – adverse selection, the incentive effect, and moral hazard – throughout the liberalization process.' He

speaks even about 'the current consensus on the optimal composition and timing of financial liberalization' and the need to adapt a general strategy to the particular circumstances of each country.

5 Sáez de Ibarra (1954b: 156) considered barriers to entry as a necessary condition for 'reconstruction'. According to him: 'Reconstruction, from the banks' point of view, meant to recover assets; to justify the possession of securities; to make good the illegitimate withdrawals of funds, to reconstruct book records; and in a higher order, to bring the money market back to a sound condition; to normalize the trade in securities; and, above all, it meant to make a supreme effort to bring together, and this is a just manner, the funds proceeding from two monetary communities quite different from each other.'

6 Lukauskas (1992: 177–78) affirms that the decision to close the banking sector to new entities was politically motivated. The Franco government restricted competition because it believed that it was a necessary condition to ensure political stability.

7 For example, the *Banco Urquijo* and the *Banco Hispanoamericano* signed the *Pacto de Jarillas* to collaborate in their activities and the *Banco Central, Hispano Colonial, Banco de Valencia* and *Crédito de Zaragoza* created the association *Bancor*.

8 As indicated before, there is no agreement about the existence of scale economies in the banking sector and when the scale diseconomies appear. See Revell (1985), or Lawrence (1989: 368–79).

9 The Bank of Spain only allows the consultation of private information until 1952.

10 New banks faced other difficulties in entering and competing in the Spanish banking sector: legal barriers to entry over a period of more than twenty years gave banks that worked in the Spanish banking system during this period substantial advantages in terms of customer loyalty.

11 We can speak about a 'good' result because bank failures impose serious costs on depositors and bank shareholders.

12 Chapter 6 examines the influence of regulation on banking efficiency and profitability.

13 We cannot consider that risky and bad banking practices were the only reasons for the Spanish banking crisis. Other variables such as the oil crisis, or the links between banks and industry must be taken into account too. However, it is a fact that these causes were further aggravated by the 'lack of prudence' of certain banking directors.

14 The *Fondo de Garantía de Depósitos* was instituted in response to the crisis with two functions: a) insurance of deposits of up to 1.5 million pesetas and b) intervention in cases of emergency (Caminal, Gual and Vives 1993: 278).

15 Some contemporary authors consider that this 'indirect' way of controlling money was effective (Prados Arrarte 1958: 97). However, it is a fact that this 'moral suasion' did not manage achieve to control inflation.

16 For example, Circular 509 (22/12/1953) of the Superior Banking Council indicates that the Bank of Spain conceded some economic advantages to all private banks which had 35 per cent of their total deposits invested in public bonds.

17 Banks were permitted to pledge all government paper with the Bank of Spain in return for loans which could amount to between 80 and 90 per cent of the market value of public securities and bear the same rate of interest. Thus, they were able to obtain cash against the security of public funds.

18 This note-issue system backed by gold and silver was established in the Banking Law of 1929.

19 Gold reserves were spent by the Republic to finance the Civil War. The Law of 13 March 1942 tried to determine the bank statement of the Bank of Spain after merging the balance sheet of the Republican and the National Banks of Spain. Viñas (1976: 239–59) explains that the item of gold and silver reserves was completely fictitious because 72.64 per cent of the nation's gold reserves was sent to the Soviet Union between October and November of 1936. 25.4 per cent of reserves was spent on the purchase of weapons, 9 per cent was retained by Russia as charges for shipments, insurance and other services and 65.6 per cent was sent to Paris to help the Republic.

20 For example, Great Britain suspended the gold standard in 1931.

21 We are not talking about causality but of correlation.

22 See for example, Poveda Anadón (1981: 43), Fanjul, Fernández and Rodríguez (1987), or Rojo (1963: 98).

23 The Law of 15 October 1940 fixed the maximum deposit interest rate at 3.71 per cent. Credits with industrial securities guarantees had a minimum rate of interest of 4.25 per cent, credits with commercial assets and merchandises had a floor on the rate of interest of 4.5 per cent, and finally personal credits had a minimum rate of interest of 4.75 per cent.

24 We must be aware about the existence of discrepancies among the collaborators of Franco. As San Roman (1997: 27) indicates, it is necessary to break with a 'homogeneous image' of the Franco regime. The continuous problems between the President of INI (Suanzes) and other members of the cabinet tend to support this.

25 As Chapter 6 will explain, because of the small number of competing banks and other conditions, the Spanish banking sector does not conform to the classical description of competitive markets.

26 In addition to the existence of several agreements among the private banks to fix interest rate conditions reported by the SBC, some banks adopted temporal pacts. For example, as said before in 1944 the *Banco Urquijo* and *Hispanoamericano* signed the *Pacto de Jarillas* to collaborate in their activities. In the same way, the *Banco Valencia, Banco Central, Banco Hispano Colonial and Crédito Zaragozano* created the banking association *Bancor*. Unfortunately, the text of these agreements was never published and it is difficult to evaluate the real influence of these pacts.

27 In non-democratic regimes, the authorities do not have an incentive to supply collective goods but to supply particularistic benefits – those which benefit the groups which support the regime.

28 The Law of Protection and Development of National Industry of 24 October 1939 and the Law of Regulation and Defense of National Industry of 24 November 1939.

29 According to Lukauskus (1992: 180), the limit on dividends was politically and economically motivated. On the one hand, it was a concession to an important family within the regime, the Falangists, who were pressuring Franco to limit the dominant position of banks and to control profits. On the other hand, it was an indirect mechanism to encourage banks to invest their profits.

30 See, for example, Sáez de Ibarra (1961). As Tortella and García (1994: 29) indicate, 'many Falangists agreed wholeheartedly, seeing the banks as bulwarks of international capitalism, and thinking that the regime had gone soft on plutocrats and forgotten the social revolution, a vague concept that figures prominently in the

Falange's program and that the regime had supposedly embraced.' That is why, many Falangists agreed with the nationalization of the Spanish banking sector.

31 The Order of December 1966 about the regulation of industrial banks declared as 'preferential sectors': capital goods – the government extended the advantages of this sector with the Order of September 1967 and December 1969, exports and shipbuilding.

32 Muns (1986: 30) explains the main recommendations of the IMF in 1959 in the financial field. He shows how from 1960 some economists who were advisers to the state or the Bank of Spain attended courses and seminars of the IMF and they were very influenced by the 'guidelines' of this institution. In spite of this, the flow of Spanish economists to the IMF represented a small proportion of the potential opportunities (Muns 1986: 224–6).

33 Although Lukauskas (1992) considers that the Spanish regulatory framework reflected the strong bargaining power of the banking sector, his work offers a very similar picture to the one this chapter shows. He recognized that banks were not able to control financial policy as some writers have suggested.

CHAPTER FIVE

Banking Regulation Theory

In Chapter 4 a simple model was employed to explain the causes of banking regulation under Franco. The present chapter extends the theoretical analysis to provide an understanding of the effects of Spanish banking regulation. Economic analysis proceeds by a process of simplification. This approach abstracts the simplest but key elements of a problem in order to understand their implications. Only after this abstraction has been done is the model made more realistic by the introduction of additional terms. The first stage of this chapter is to provide an understanding of the simple behaviour of a monopoly bank in the absence of regulation. The effects of the character of 'mixed' banks on this banking behaviour is discussed, in particular with reference to the differences between the profit function of a commercial bank and a universal bank. This analysis of banking behaviour occurs in two steps. The first, assuming that all deposits are loaned out, and the second step allowing the ratio between loans and deposits to be a prudential choice variable for the bank. It is in Section II that regulation is introduced. First, I discuss the cost and benefits of legal barriers to entry. Second, I analyse the effects of other regulatory measures: the first is rate of interest regulation and the second deals with compulsory reserve requirements that constrain the 'loan/deposit' ratio. Both steps include the discussion of non-price competition consequences such as an increase in the number of branches to extend business when regulatory constraints are binding. The effect of dividend controls and a public bond ratio is also analysed. Only at the end of Section II is the complication of oligopolistic bank competition introduced.

To make the logic of the model more comprehensible, I will rely on diagrams. I will make use of Courakis' work (1984) although to a different end. The main purpose of Courakis' paper was to analyse the effect of regulatory constraints on the evolution of deposits and loans in less developed countries. In this chapter I concentrate my attention on the effect of regulation on banking profits, a problem of lesser importance in Courakis' work.

I. A model of banking behaviour without regulation

Banks provide two kinds of services. First, services connected with the liabilities of accepting funds, especially in the form of deposits. Second, services related to asset operations. Banking is a two-stage process, producing the necessary services to take deposits and transforming them into loans and other profitable assets.[1]

We shall begin with a model where the supply of deposits (by depositors) depends positively on the rate of interest on deposits.[2] In a more complex model, other deposit supply determinants such as the rate of interest on other alternative financial assets (government bonds and equities), the NI and the level of risk will be considered. The supply of deposits depends positively on the level of income and the rate of interest on deposits and negatively on the rate of return on alternative assets:

$$Ds = \mathrm{f}(\underset{+}{rd}, \underset{-}{rb}, \underset{-}{ra}, \underset{+}{Y}) \tag{5.1}$$

where *rd* is deposit interest rate, *rb* and *ra* are the return on alternative assets (government bonds and equities, respectively) and *Y* is *NI*.

With respect to the demand for deposits (from banks), the volume of deposits a bank takes depends positively on the yield of financial assets (loans, equities and bonds) and negatively on the costs of deposits. Backus, Brainard, Smith and Tobin (1980: 265), assume that banks accept all deposits the public supplied at the existing rate. This is quite a reasonable assumption. However, banks are not 'passive' in the determination of the total volume of deposits. They not only affect the supply of deposits through the rate of interest on deposits but through other means such as advertising or branches.

The analysis of the loan market is more complex. To simplify, we can consider that the demand for loans depends negatively on the loan interest rate:

$$Ld = \mathrm{f}(\underset{-}{rl}) \tag{5.2}$$

and the supply of loans is positively related to the rate of interest on loans:

$$Ls = \mathrm{f}(\underset{+}{rl}) \tag{5.3}$$

This last relationship is an extreme simplification as the volume of loans a bank gives depends not only on the rate of interest on loans but on the following variables: a) it depends positively on the total volume of funds they take in the form of deposits, b) the cost of deposits. When financial costs increase, the incentives to lend decreases – *ceteris paribus*, c) the yield on alternative bank assets (bonds and equities). When the return on alternative assets rises, banks prefer bonds or equities to loans, d) the possibility of obtaining credit from the central bank or other alternative financial intermediaries to face a 'run' and the cost of these resources and e) the risk.

In the loan market there are 'honest' and 'dishonest' borrowers but because of the existence of imperfect information banks may not distinguish between these two kinds of individuals. Following Stiglitz and Weiss (1981: 393), the rate of interest a bank charges affects the riskiness of loans. The interest rate an individual is willing to pay is an indicator of the 'quality' of this borrower. Those willing to pay higher loan interest rates are, on average, a worse risk because their willingness to borrow at higher interest rates reflects that these borrowers perceive their probability of repaying the loan to be low. Furthermore, a higher rate of interest induces individuals to undertake riskier projects. For this reason, at the loan interest rate rl^* banks might not raise the rate of interest they charge on loans, even if there is an excess demand for credit, because to do so might lower the return they receive (see Figure 5.1). The probability of default is defined as p and it depends positively upon the rate of interest on loans: p =

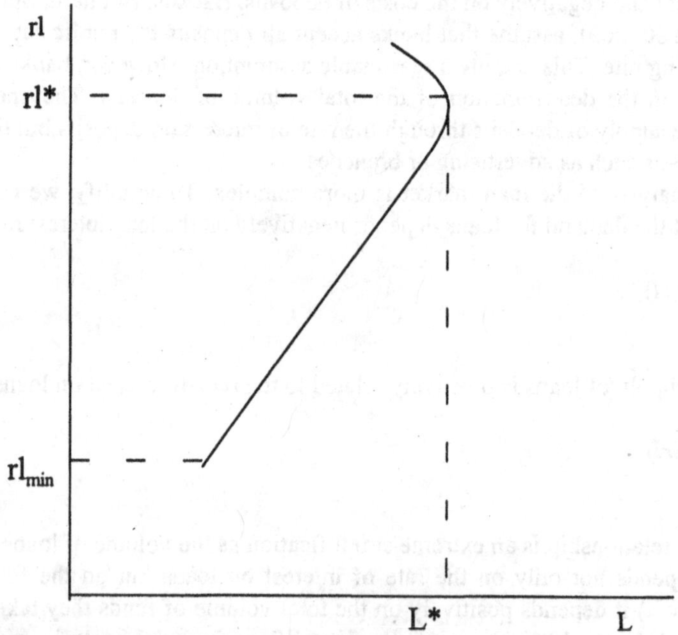

Figure 5.1 Loan supply

f(rl). Thus, if we define rl^* as the interest rate at which the expected return to the bank is maximised, the bank would not lend to an individual who offered to pay more than rl^* and the positive relationship between loan supply and loan interest rate disappears (Stiglitz and Weiss 1981: 393–410).

Moreover, there may be a minimum interest rate for lending (rl_{mim} in Figure 5.1). Loan interest rates below this minimum interest rate would not allow banks to cover costs, and so they would, therefore, not supply loans when interest rates are below rl_{mim}.

The main problem of this analysis of the loan market is that it assumes that all borrowers are inherently dishonest and they will default if it is to their benefit without considering the future. In a one-period model this result could be right but in a multiperiod model we must consider the penalties that lenders can impose on defaulting, especially the possibility of obtaining a loan in the future (the role of 'reputation'). Then, an effective threat of cutting off credit could be an important means of influencing borrower behaviour. Furthermore, banks can protect themselves from risk in a number of ways, for example, with the adoption of collateral requirements. Banks will pursue three courses of action to minimise risk. First, they will increase information. The level of information available to banks depends on the banking structure, especially on the degree of centralisation or decentralisation of banking activity,[3] and on how directly banks are involved in industrial business, among other factors. Second, banks will set penalties or collateral requirements and third, they might introduce monitoring mechanisms to control the customer's activity. When the bank is able to control the borrower's activity the possibility the borrower will act to his or her detriment is lower.

There is an important question about whether a bank can diminish risk by introducing collateral requirements in the loan contract. As Stiglitz and Weiss (1986: 106) indicate, increasing the collateral requirements can induce individuals to undertake safer projects. But the literature about collateral and other ways of increasing certainty has important shortcomings. Although an increase in collateral requirements may reduce the risk of default, they could also have adverse selection effects: borrowers who are willing to accept more collateral requirements will undertake riskier projects. That is why, even with collateral, there may still be credit rationing.

To sum up, there is no clear relationship between the probability of default and the rate of interest on loans, especially if collateral is effective. I will therefore assume that the probability of default is an exogenous variable and it depends on variables such as the level of information obtained.

In modern banking systems, we can distinguish between specialised banks (mainly commercial and investment banks) and universal banks. Commercial banking consists of wholesale and retail banking activities. Investment banks are banks which provide long-term fixed capital for industry. Additionally, they may exercise many merchant bank functions such as merger making, commodity trading, advising on investments, etc. Finally, as Chapter 2 explained, universal banks combine investment, wholesale and retail banking services. Saunders and Walters (1994) identified four different types of universal banks: a) the 'fully integrated' universal bank, which supplies the complete range of financial services from one institutional entity, b) the 'partially integrated' financial conglomerate, where several services are provided through wholly-owned or partially-owned subsidiaries, c) the 'bank subsidiary structure', where the bank focuses essentially on commercial banking and other functions, including investment banking and insurance carried out through legally separate subsidiaries of the bank and d) the 'bank holding company structure', where a financial holding company owns both banking and non-financial firms. In the Spanish case, we can consider that the largest banks adopted this last structure.

The main function of commercial banks is to take deposits and transform them into loans. The profit function of a commercial bank is:

$$\pi_i = L_i.rl - D_i.\ rd - C(L_i, D_i) \tag{5.4}$$

where π_i are profits, L_i loans, *rl* the rate of interest on loans, *rd* the rate of interest on deposits, D_i deposits, and $C(D_i, L_i)$ the non-financial costs of producing deposits and loans (for example, wages, advertising, and so on). These non-financial costs are most conveniently assumed to depend upon the level of deposits and loans.

In the case of universal banks and industrial corporations, banks do not only give loans but also participate in other activities, mainly direct investments. In this case, the profit equation for the *ith* bank is defined as:

$$\pi_i = (L_i.rl + O_i.ro) - D_i.rd - C(D_i, L_i, O_i) \tag{5.5}$$

where $L_i.\ rl$ are revenues from loans, O_i other alternative investments such as equities or public bonds, *ro* the rate of return on these alternative investments, $rd.D_i$ the costs of deposits and $C(D_i, L_i, O_i)$ the non-financial costs of producing deposits, loans and other investments.[4] To simplify, it is assumed that *Oi.ro* includes not only the revenues from other alternative investments but also other profits derived from the issues of capital (of the banks and the participating firms).

It is assumed that the main objective of a firm is to maximise profits.[5] Then, the objective of financial corporate groupings must be to maximise the profitability, individually or collectively, of the member firms. If there is complete independence between the bank and the participating firms, the objective function of the bank is to maximise its own profits because:

$$\text{max (profits bank + profits firm 1 + … + profits firm n)} = \text{max (profits bank) + max (profits firm 1) + … + max (profits firm n)} \quad (5.7)$$

However, if there is interdependence between the bank and the affiliated firms, the objective function will be to maximise the conglomerate profits.[6] In this second case, the maximisation of the conglomerate profits does not imply the maximisation of the individual firm profits:[7]

$$\max (\pi_b + \pi_{f1} + \pi_{f2} + ... + \pi_{fn}) \neq \max \pi_b + \max \pi_{f1} + \ldots + \max \pi_{fn} \quad (5.8)$$

where π_b are the profits of the bank and π_{fi} are the profits of the subsidiary firms (1, 2, … n).

The banking profits and the profits of the participating firms are related because the output of the bank (in this case loans) is an input for the subsidiary firms. Thus, a conflict of interests is possible between the bank (which *ceteris paribus* will obtain higher profits the higher the loan interest rate it charges) and the firms (which obtain higher profits the cheaper loans are) (Kroszner and Strahan 1999). There are other possible conflicts of interest between the bank and the affiliated firms. For example, Aoki (1983: 219) considers that banks want firms to rely upon debt financing to a greater degree than warranted by share-price optimisation of the firm. The banks' shareholdings may be then interpreted as a means of influencing the participating firms and realising this preference. There are also other positive interdependencies or 'synergies' between the bank and the affiliated firms. For example, these 'synergies' may appear because of the possibility of sharing 'information' about common customers or the creation of an 'internal' capital market among the firms of the group (Canals 1995: 136). In this case:

$$\pi_{cong} > \pi_b + \pi_{f1} + \pi_{f2} + ... + \pi_{fn} \quad (5.9)$$

where π_{cong} are the profits of the conglomerate.

The question is: do mixed banks provide loans to the participating firms at market prices or subsidised prices? Do universal banks show preferential credit treatment towards its affiliated firms? If banks give loans to the participating firms at a subsidised loan interest rate, a reduction in the costs of subsidiary firms implies a reduction in banking profits. In this case, the maximisation of conglomerate profits is different from the maximisation of individual firm profits.

Figure 5.2 considers a hypothetical model where bank i holds shares of two firms (firm 1 and firm 2). This bank lends L_1 and L_2 to the firms 1 and 2, L_3 to the public and L_4 to the rest of firms (non-participating firms). The bank may charge different loan interest rates to these four different customers (rl_1, rl_2, rl_3, rl_4, respectively). If the bank charges a subsidised loan interest rate to the affiliated firms, it does not maximise its own profits. However, it is possible that those banks which maximise their own profits will charge a lower loan interest rate to the subsidiary firms. Edward and Fischer (1994: 22–48) demonstrate that it is possible to provide a solid analytical basis for the view that the existence of proxy voting rights and representation on supervisory boards allows banks to exploit economies of scale and scope in information-collection. Then, the existence of lower financial costs for bank-affiliated firms may be the result of lesser risk (because mixed banks are better at dealing with asymmetric problems) and, consequently, of profit maximising behaviour.

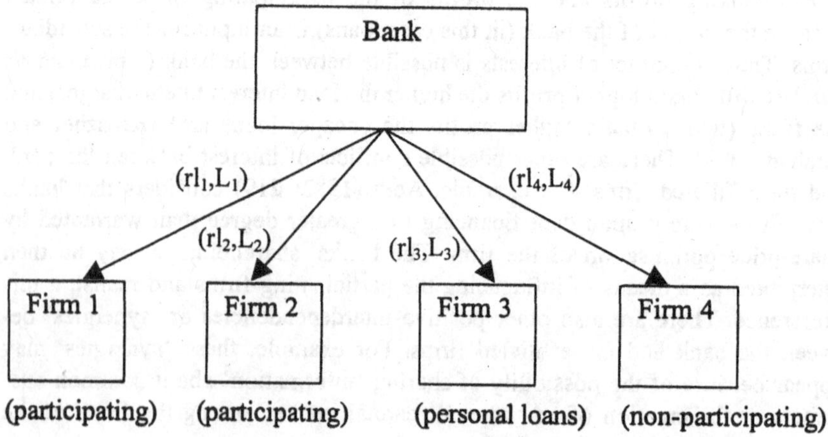

Figure 5.2 Loan activity of a bank holding structure

When the profit maximisation hypothesis cannot be used, the literature considers other alternative profit functions. For example, Aoki (1994) considers that banks fix their mixed strategy of investment (as lenders and shareholders) so that they maximise net income. Monti (1971, 1972) considers that banks maximise the total volume of deposits. In other cases, such as Sklivas (1987: 453) or Barcena-Ruiz and Espinosa (1994), they assume that banks maximise a linear combination of profits and revenues:

$$g_i = \gamma i.\pi_i + (1 - \gamma_i).RV_i \qquad (5.10)$$

where πi and RVi are profits and revenues, respectively, and γi is the incentives parameter chosen by the owner of the firm i.

The main problem is that there is weak theoretical support for choosing among different profit functions. To opt for one of these profit functions we must rely on empirical evidence. Can it be assumed that the main objective of Spanish banks was to maximise profits? Would it be more suitable to consider that 'mixed' banks tried to maximise the conglomerate profits? Did Spanish banks charge subsidised loan interest rates to their participating firms? What was the degree of intervention of Spanish banks in their affiliated firms? What was the influence of loan interest controls in banking objectives? The following chapter considers all these variables and it analyses whether profit-maximising behaviour is an appropriate assumption for the Spanish banks in this period or not.

To simplify, it is assumed that the only interdependence between the bank and its non-banking firm affiliates is the existence of subsidised loan interest rates. There are other possible relationships or conflicts of interest between the bank and these firms such as making loans to a failing commercial firm affiliate to keep it in business, or giving 'more facilities' to the participating firms to obtain a loan (i.e. not using normal credit evaluation criteria in the application for loans) reducing prudence and threatening the safety of the bank itself (Saunders and Walter 1994: 239–41). If the only interdependence between the bank and its subsidiary firms is the existence of subsidised loan interest rates, the profit function will be:

$$\pi_i = (Lnp_i.rlnp + Lp_i.rlp + O_i.ro) - D_i.rd - C(D_i, L_i, O_i) \qquad (5.11)$$

where *Lnp* is the volume of loans the bank lends to customers and non-participating firms, *rlnp* the interest rate the bank charges on loans to non-participating firms, *Lp* the volume of loans the bank lends to its affiliated firms and *rlp* the interest rate the bank charges on loans to its subsidiary firms. In this case, the bank will maximise π_i subject to:

$$rlp < rlnp$$

or the bank subsidises loan interest rates to its affiliated firms. This is not necessarily a constraint to the bank because, as explained above, the bank may charge a lower loan interest rate to participating firms because of the existence of lesser risk.

about the same output response from its rival. Then each firm knows that if, for example, it raises output the other will do likewise. In this case, the results for both the firm and the industry are equivalent to the result for a monopolist.

Because of the extreme complexity of the analysis of an oligopolistic model, this section starts with the simplest model, where the oligopolistic firms adopt an agreement about prices. When banks adopt a cartel agreement we have the monopolist solution. This model is very useful in understanding the Spanish banking sector, especially in the first years of the Franco regime. Later, I will consider an oligopoly without collusion. In this case the solution (and the interest rates that banks fix) could be anywhere between the monopolistic and the competitive price.

The monopoly model

The following assumptions have been made:

a) it is assumed that the rate of inflation is known with complete certainty. Then, the bank's choice of a nominal deposit rate determines the real deposit rate.
b) it is considered that, because of the existence of a legal coefficient or prudential behaviour, the amount of loans banks make depends on the amount of deposits they take. For simplicity's sake, we can assume that this relationship is linear: $L_i \leq ai.D_i$, where $0 \leq a_i \leq 1$. In this general model without regulation, this assumption reflects prudential behaviour on the part of banks and the relationship between loans and deposits a_i is chosen by the bank. To obtain the most simple model, the simplifying assumption that $a_i =$ 1 has been made: therefore, $L_i = D_i$. In this case, when bank i chooses the volume of deposits it takes (or, alternatively, it fixes the deposit interest rate), simultaneously it also chooses to lend an equal volume of loans. Later on, this assumption will be altered.
c) only two assets are considered: deposits and loans. For this reason, we do not consider other determinants of the demand for and the supply of deposits and loans such as the yield on alternative assets (government bonds and loans). After analysing the simplest case, a more complex model such as the one described in equation (5.11) will be considered.
d) it is assumed that the objective function of the bank is to maximise banking profits.

Under these conditions we have the following profit function,

$$\pi i = rl.\ L_i - rd.D_i - C(D_i) \tag{5.12}$$

and considering $L_i{=}D_i : \pi_i = D_i.\ (rl - rd) - C(D_i)$ (5.12′)

where the deposit supply function may be written as:

$$Ds_i = \text{f}(rd) \text{ and } \partial Ds_i/\partial rd > 0 \tag{5.1′}$$

Banking behaviour will be analysed diagrammatically. In Figure 5.3 *Ld* describes the demand for loans by the public and *Ds* the supply of deposits from the public. *MC* is the marginal cost and *MR* the marginal revenue. In a monopoly, equilibrium is defined by the intersection of *MR* and *MC* (Shaw 1973: 82–4). In this simplified model where $ai = 1$, the volume of deposits and loans is equal $L_m = D_m$. That is why the loan supply curve L_s coincides with the deposit supply curve D_s: the supply of loans by the bank is equal to the supply of deposits by the public. As Figure 5.3 shows, the rate of interest charged on loans is rl_m (the monopolistic loan interest rate) and the interest rate paid on deposits rd_m (the monopolistic deposit interest rate). Banking profits are determined by the volume of loans and the spread between the monopolistic loan interest rate and the monopolistic deposit interest rate. The spread between rl_m and rd_m depends not only on the costs of loans being converted from deposits but it also depends on the elasticities of the demand for loans and supply of deposits.

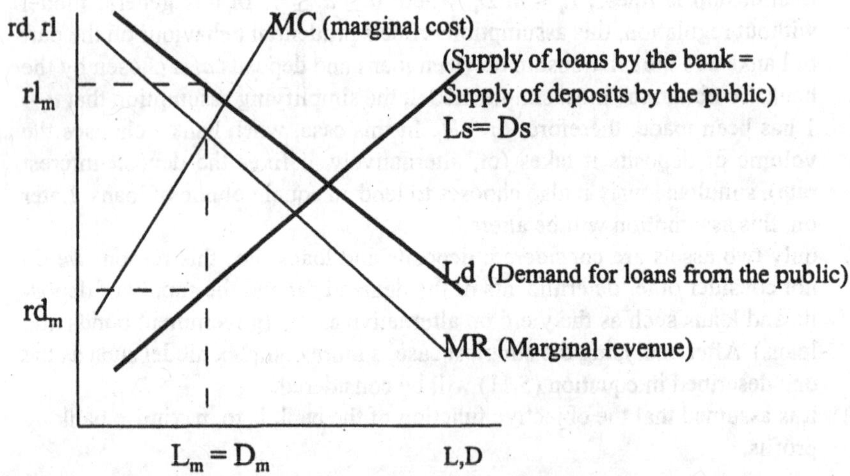

Figure 5.3 Equilibrium with monopoly when L = D

A strong assumption is being made about the relationship between deposits and loans when we consider that the amount of loans the bank lends is equal to the volume of deposits it takes: $Li = Di$. Thus, we can modify this assumption and consider that $L_i \leq D_i$. The main determinants of the ratio 'loans/deposits' are:

a) the probability of default p. It is assumed that the probability of default is determined exogenously,
b) what the probability of depositors' demand for liquidity is (or demand for withdrawals). Depositors' liquidity demands are uncertain although there are different factors which affect this variable, for example: the number of depositors, the average size of deposit accounts and the maturity of deposits (short-term or long-term deposits),
c) the possibility of obtaining resources to face a run (the existence of an open market or a lender of last resort, for example) and the cost of these resources.

If we consider that loans are a proportion of deposits, the profit function is

$$\pi_i = a_i.D_i.rl_i - D_i.rd_i\ C(D_i) \tag{5.13}$$

where the supply of deposits depends positively on the deposit interest rate, Ds_i = f(rd), and the proportion between loans and deposits, or a_i depends positively on the loan interest rate and negatively on the probability of default, ai = f(rl, p).

Figure 5.4 shows the solution to this second model where the volume of loans is lower than the volume of deposits. In this case the supply of deposits to the banking system Dm is larger than the supply of loans by the banks Lm: $Dm > Lm$. This implies that the cost per unit of deposits is not equal to the cost per unit of loans and the marginal revenue per unit of loans is not equal to the marginal revenue per unit of deposits. When the volume of loans the bank lends is only a percentage of the total volume of deposits it takes, the marginal cost curve on loans shifts to the left (as now to lend the same amount of loans as in the case where $L_i = D_i$, the bank has to take more deposits), also reducing its slope (Courakis 1984: 346); and the marginal curve on deposits shifts to the right (as now only a percentage of the total volume of deposits can be made profitable). As we can see in Figure 5.4 in this case the volume of deposits the bank takes is Dm' at rdm' deposit interest rate and the volume of loans it lends is Lm' at rlm' loan interest rate.

To sum up, when $L_i < D_i$ the monopolistic profits π_m' are lower than in the case where $L_i = D_i$. We can therefore say that banks sacrifice a part of their profits to achieve higher stability.

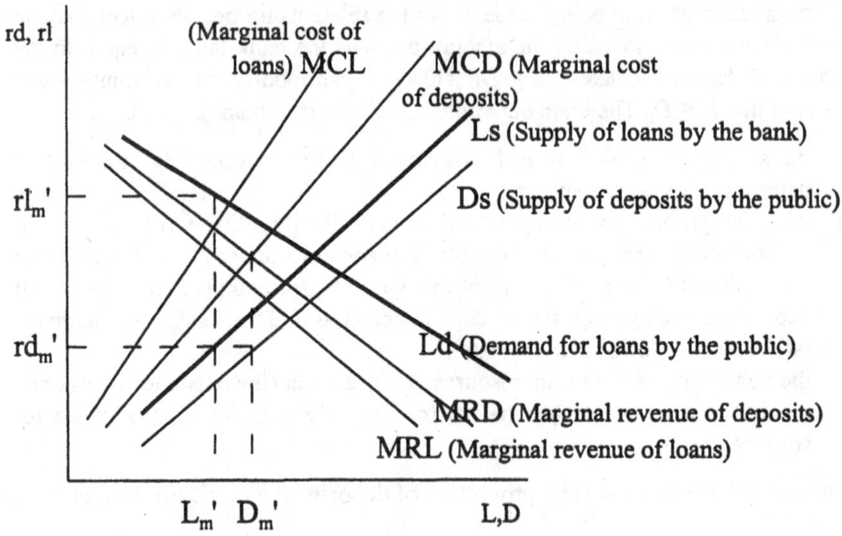

Figure 5.4 Equilibrium with monopoly when $L_i = a.D_i$

If we consider a more complex model where there are loans (to the participating firms *Lp* and the non-participating firms *Lnp*) and other assets (bonds and equities), the total volume of assets $(Ln + Lnp + O)$ must be lower than the total volume of deposits (D): $(Lnp + Lp + O) < D$.

When we include this restriction $(Lp + Lnp + O < D)$, the total volume of profits is lower than when $(Lnp + Lp + O = D)$.

As indicated above, this monopoly model can be useful to understand Spanish banking behaviour, principally in the first years of the Franco regime. However, from the mid-1950s onwards it is very difficult to accept the existence of a collusive agreement among banks or at least a 'successful' cartel agreement. In the next section, the effects of regulation in a model with and without collusion are analysed.

II. The effects of regulatory constraints on banking behaviour

This section analyses the effects on banking behaviour of different regulatory measures. In particular, it considers: a) the existence of legal barriers to entry and b) other regulatory measures such as interest rate controls, reserve requirements and dividend controls.

Legal barriers to entry

The main purpose of this section is to discuss whether free entry is desirable or not for social efficiency. Some authors (Mankiw and Whinston 1986, or Di Battista and Grillo 1988) consider that under certain conditions the number of entrants in a 'free entry equilibrium' is excessive. As explained in Chapter 4, the public interest theory considers that when there are scale economies in an industry, the optimal number of firms has to be regulated. The theoretical concept of scale economies refers to the relationship between the cost of production and the size of a firm. In a scale economy industry, when the output increases the firm will operate under conditions of increasing returns. For this reason, when we restrict the number of firms in the market, the level of output increases, the average cost per unit of output decreases and there is an increase in efficiency due to the better exploitation of scale economies.

Di Battista and Grillo (1988) offer an alternative interpretation of the necessity of establishing legal barriers to entry. They affirm that when there are very high costs of exit in an industry, it could benefit a firm to reach an agreement with the rest of the firms in the market in order to reduce competition and 'survive'. They consider that a collusive agreement would be more inefficient without barriers to entry than with barriers to entry because in the case without barriers the agreement would be among a higher number of firms.

To analyse the veracity of these assertions we must look at two different aspects: the existence of scale economies and the cost of barriers to entry.

From a theoretical point of view, there are several reasons for accepting the existence of scale economies in the banking sector. Following Revell (1988: 69), there are some areas of banking operations in which economies of scale are important. First, advantages in terms of management. It is sometimes said that large banks have economies of scale in managerial staff, enabling employment of the best managers. However, an increase in the size of a bank is usually accompanied by diseconomies in the administration. The bureaucracy makes managing a bigger bank more costly than smaller banks.

Second, marketing is an aspect of banking operations that benefit from scale economies. The economies of scale in marketing derive from the fact that marketing costs do not depend on the size of the bank. Then, the increase in size of a bank would not raise marketing costs proportionally.

Third, risk is subject to considerable scale economies. Risk can be classified into different groups: liquidity risk, credit risk and concentration risk. A big bank has a larger number of accounts on both sides of the balance sheet, and it has less relative need for resources of liquidity than a smaller bank because there is a greater chance that movements on the accounts will offset each other.

In a big bank the portfolio of loans and credits is larger than in a small bank and, as a consequence of the greater diversification, the credit risk is lower. There are two important criticisms to this claim. Big banks are more concerned with large customers and therefore, the concentration of risk is higher. Carnevali (1993) considers that an increase in the size of banks has serious diseconomies in terms of information, and indirectly affects credit risk. The probability of loan default depends on the level of information the bank has about its customers and the activities they are going to undertake with these loans. A small bank has better knowledge about individual customers (because it has personal knowledge of the person involved), the sectors where its customers are working and their environment, that is to say, the economy of the region and the local business activity (because the bank's profits depend narrowly on the local business activity). That is why when the bank increases in size, the level of information it has about its customers decreases and the risk rises. There are reasonable doubts, then, about the existence of scale economies in terms of risk.

The process of automation in the banking sector has introduced scale economies into many parts of the payment system. However, there is still a long way to go in this area and this argument is not very useful in understanding the evolution of the Spanish banking system from 1939 to 1975 due to the lack of modernisation in this sector until the beginning of the 1970s. The final argument for accepting scale economies in the banking sector is that banks need to be large in size to participate in international operations. However, international banking is very risky. There is no central bank to control international banking activity, there is no lender of last resort and it involves risks intrinsic to its nature (political risks, currency risks and so on). For these reasons, the argument that banks have to increase in size to participate in international business is not a very persuasive one.

To summarise this discussion, it could be said that: 'The economies of scale that are advanced as one of the main justifications for regulation seems rather elusive' (Revell 1988: 68). Empirical evidence is not conclusive. There have been many studies of US banking and the general finding of these studies is that economies of scale are exhausted at a relatively small size of bank. Humphrey (1992) suggests that there are slight economies of scale for small US banks, but slight diseconomies for larger US banks. Unfortunately there are not many studies in Europe and other developed countries. Altunbas and Molyneux (1993) examined the cost structure of the banking sectors in France, Germany, Italy and Spain. They found overall scale economies in all four countries, but in most cases the coefficients were not statistically significant. For example, Italy showed significant scale economies over all levels of output but in Spain scale economies were present only for the smallest banks.

Scale economies, therefore, seem to be a poor justification for legal barriers to entry in the banking sector.

Even if we do accept the existence of scale economies in the banking sector, the second element we must take into consideration, when evaluating the justification for regulating entry, is the consequences of this intervention or the costs of barriers to entry. The main effect of the establishment of legal barriers to entry is to reduce the number of firms in the market. With a small number of firms the costs of collusion are lower and the probability of the market organising as a monopolistic industry increases. The effects of a monopoly are well known:

a. In a monopolistic situation prices rise above the competitive level. Consumers who purchase the seller product at the new higher price (in a monopolistic banking sector, borrowers pay a higher loan interest rate and depositors receive a lower deposit interest rate than in a competitive one) suffer a loss exactly offset by the additional revenue that the seller (the bank) obtains at a higher price. The first consequence of monopoly is thus a transfer of wealth from consumers (depositors and borrowers) to the owner of the monopoly firm (the bank).
b. As a consequence of these new higher prices, some consumers decide to stop buying the product (the deposit or the loan). The second consequence of monopoly, then, is to reduce the quantity of the product (deposits and loans).
c. The possibility of obtaining monopoly profits will attract resources into efforts to obtain monopolies. Prospective entrants will have an incentive to spend resources on persuading the government or the regulatory body to their own advantage. Furthermore, the 'fortunate' banks which operate in the market will have an incentive to persuade the government to maintain the barriers to entry and their privileged position. This rent-seeking behaviour must be considered as an additional social cost of monopoly.
d. The privileged position of a monopoly reduces its incentives to innovate.

To sum up, the establishment of barriers to entry increases the probability of banks organising as a monopolistic industry, with all the costs of this industrial organisation (higher prices, less product, rent-seeking behaviour and a lack of innovations). However, barriers to entry could promote an increase in the size of firms and generate scale economies. Unfortunately, there is no general consensus about the advantages of increasing size. For this reason, it is extremely difficult to measure the costs and benefits of this intervention. As indicated above, Di Battista and Grillo (1988, pp. 423–31) consider that a collusive agreement is less inefficient with legal barriers to entry because the number of firms in this last situation is lower and they can utilise scale economies in size. However, there is an important criticism to this claim. The government does not have enough information to determine the 'socially efficient' number of firms. So, we cannot affirm that the result of state intervention will be the determination of the efficient number of firms, but that, with the establishment of legal barriers to entry, the government does establish an 'institutional monopoly' with the social costs that this industrial organisation involves. A cartel agreement without regulation is more unstable than a cartel agreement in a regulated market, because in the first case banks always have the threat of new entrants. For this same reason, in a non-regulated market, the incentives for increasing efficiency are higher.

As we have seen, there are many doubts as to the existence of scale economies in the banking sector. We cannot accept, therefore, this argument as the main justification for regulating entry. Moreover, if the main reason for establishing barriers to entry is the existence of high costs of exit, we must look at the means to reduce these costs more than to regulate entry. Overall, the justification for the regulation of entry into the banking sector is weak.

Other regulatory measures: interest rate controls, compulsory coefficients and dividend controls

Interest rate controls Table 5.1 summarises the main interest rate regulations and whether these regulatory measures avoid monopolistic behaviour or not.

To analyse the consequences of government intervention it is necessary to consider the effects of regulation on banking behaviour and then, on the 'strategy' variables that banks choose to maximise profits. This section presents a model of banking behaviour and it examines the effects of regulation on bank balance sheet decisions.

Deposit interest rate controls

Case A When the authorities fix a binding deposit interest rate, we can consider two different situations:

A.1 The legal deposit interest rate (*rd**) is higher than the monopolistic interest rate (*rdm*). In this case, the main objective of regulation is to avoid monopolistic situations, because to maximise profits monopolistic banks will try to minimise the rates of interest they pay on deposits. The main effects of this interest constraint are (see Figure 5.5):

a) if we assume that at this interest rate *rd** banks accept all deposits the public supplied at this rate (Backus, Brainard, Smith and Tobin 1980: 256), the new

Table 5.1 Interest rate regulation

Regulation	Case	Outcome
Deposit interest rate regulation	Case A. A binding deposit interest rate (*rd**)	A.1. $rd^* > rdm$: Regulation avoids monopolistic behaviour
		A.2. $rd^* < rdm$: Regulation does not avoid monopolistic behaviour
	Case B. A ceiling or a floor on the deposit interest rate (*rd**)	B.1. max $rd^* > rdm$: Regulation does not avoid monopolistic behaviour
		B.2. max $rd^* < rdm$: non-price strategies to compete
		B3. min $rd^* > rdm$: Regulation avoids monopolistic behaviour
		B4. min $rd^* < rdm$: Regulation does not avoid monopolistic behaviour
Loan interest rate regulation	Case A. A binding loan interest rate (*rl**)	A.1. $rl^* < rlm$: Regulation avoids monopolistic behaviour
		A.2. $rl^* > rle$: Regulation does not avoid monopolistic behaviour.
	Case B. A ceiling or a floor on the loan interest rate (*rl**)	B.1. min rl^*: Regulation does not avoid monopolistic behaviour
		B.2. max rl^* < rle: Regulation avoids monopolistic behaviour

Notes: 'rd*' and 'rl*': legal deposit and loan interest rate, respectively, 'rdm': monopolistic deposit interest rate, 'rde': deposit interest rate in equilibrium, 'rlm': monopolistic loan interest rate, 'rle': loan interest rate in equilibrium.

equilibrium will be an increase in the total volume of deposits and loans $((L^* = D^*) > (Lm = Dm))$, and a decrease in the loan interest rate $(rl^* < rlm)$.

b) only if we assume that the bank does not accept all deposits, will the main

controls are enforced, we can assume that banks tend to respond to government-decreed ceilings on explicit interest rates by engaging in non-price competition for deposits. This type of non-price competition could take the form of an over-expansion of bank offices, the guarantee of obtaining loans ('tie-ins'), free services, lottery or raffle tickets, gifts and so on. Some authors regard the payment of these bank payments such as lottery or raffle tickets, gifts, etc, as a form of price competition and they define such remuneration as an 'implicit interest rate' (Burkett 1986, Spellman 1980 or Startz 1979). As the main objective of this research is to identify the main effects of regulation, and some of these generally defined 'implicit interest remunerations' could be controlled, we will differentiate between: a) the 'extra' costs (in addition to the explicit deposit interest rate) banks incur to increase the volume of deposits as a consequence of interest regulation (lottery tickets, free services and so on) defined as 'implicit' interest rate remuneration, b) branching costs (a way of increasing customers' remuneration in terms of services) and c) advertising. Some of them imply an increase in customers' remuneration or services (for example, more branches or free services), and others do not (for example, advertising). For simplicity, it is assumed that the implicit rate of interest on deposits, the costs of branches and the advertising costs are completely separable from other costs.

When the authorities control rates of interest, banks have the following profit function:

$$\pi_i = L_i.rl_i - D_i.rd_i. - m_i.D_i - C(A_i) - C(B_i) - C(D_i, L_i) \tag{5.14}$$

where π_i is profit, L_i loans, rl_i the rate of return on loans, rdi the rate of interest on deposits, D_i deposits, $C(D_i, L_i)$ the non-interest cost of producing deposits and loans, mi the implicit rate of interest, $C(A_i)$ the costs of advertising and $C(B_i)$ the cost of branches.

We start with a very simple model where $L_i = D_i$. When the monopolistic deposit rate is above the regulatory controlled rate of interest on deposits, the firm maximises profits with respect to the implicit rate of interest m_i, the number of branches $C(B_i)$ or the costs of advertising $C(A_i)$ as they are the only variables at its discretion. Then,

$$\pi_i = L_i.rl - D_i.rd - m_i.D_i - C(B_i) - C(A_i) - C(D_i, L_i) \tag{5.14'}$$

where $L_i \leq D_i$ and the supply of deposits by the public depends on the legal deposit interest rate, the implicit remuneration, the number of branches and the advertising policy,

$$Ds_i = f(rd^*, m_i, B_i, A_i) \tag{5.15}$$

As Figure 5.6 describes, the main effect of a binding deposit interest rate *rd** below the monopolistic deposit interest rate *rdm* is to reduce the volume of deposits and loans ($D^* = L^*$) < ($Dm = Lm$). As the total volume of deposits the bank takes is equal to the volume of loans it lends, the chosen loan interest rate would be rl^*. Consequently, although profits may fall, the rate of return on loans rl^* will rise. But when the authorities fix a binding deposit interest rate, banks can respond to these regulatory measures by: a) paying implicit remunerations, b) increasing the number of branches and c) with an advertising campaign. As a consequence of these alternative ways of remuneration to increase deposits the marginal cost rises. When the marginal cost curve shifts above (MC'), the return on loans $rl^{*\prime}$ will decrease and the depositor remuneration will be the binding deposit interest rate plus the non-interest rate remuneration $rd^* + m$ (see Figure 5.6).

If more branches, advertising and so on are effective, the demand for banking services (in terms of the public supplying more deposits and demanding more loans) will increase. Therefore, the demand for loans curve and the supply of deposits curve shift rightwards, with an increase in the loan interest rate, a

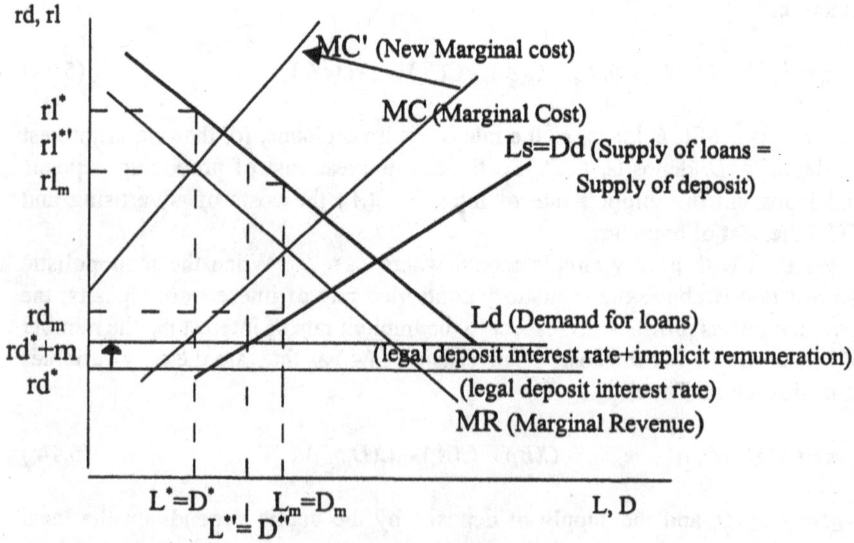

Figure 5.6 The effects of implicit remuneration in monopoly (a binding deposit interest rate below the monopolistic deposit interest rate)

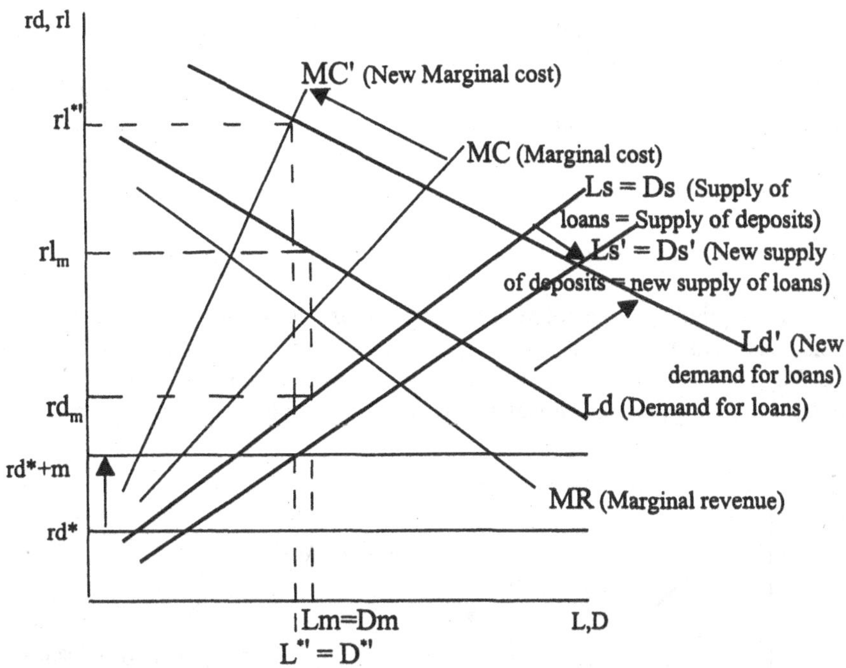

Figure 5.7 A binding deposit interest rate below the monopolistic interest rate (the effects of implicit remuneration)

decrease in the deposit interest rates and an increase in the volume of deposits and loans (see Figure 5.7). In this case, the volume of profits may rise.

Case B A ceiling or a floor on the rate of interest on deposits. In a monopolistic model banks will attempt to fix the rate of interest on deposits below the equilibrium one. When the authorities establish a maximum rate of interest on deposits (or a 'ceiling') equal or above the equilibrium interest rate they do not avoid the adoption of monopolistic agreements (the only case is when the legal ceiling is below the monopolistic deposit rate). In this case, deposit interest regulations do not affect banking profits. Only when the legal ceiling is below the monopolistic deposit interest rate, can banks develop non-price strategies to compete for deposits, and in the short term, deposit interest constraints will have a negative effect on profits.

The establishment of a minimum on the rate of interest on deposits equal or above the equilibrium deposit rate can avoid monopolistic behaviour. In this case, the final effect of deposit interest rate regulation on profits depends on the elasticities of the demand for loans and the supply of deposits. If the volume of deposits and loans increases sufficiently to compensate for the reduction in the spread between the loan and the deposit interest rates resulting from the deposit interest rate constraints, profits will rise. If not, the final result of regulation will be a decrease in banking profits.

Loan interest rate controls

Case A A binding loan interest rate. The most usual situation is when the authorities introduce a binding loan interest rate below the monopolistic interest rate. Figure 5.8 shows the main results of this intervention in the most simple model where deposits are equal to loans $L_i = D_i$. When the authorities fix a

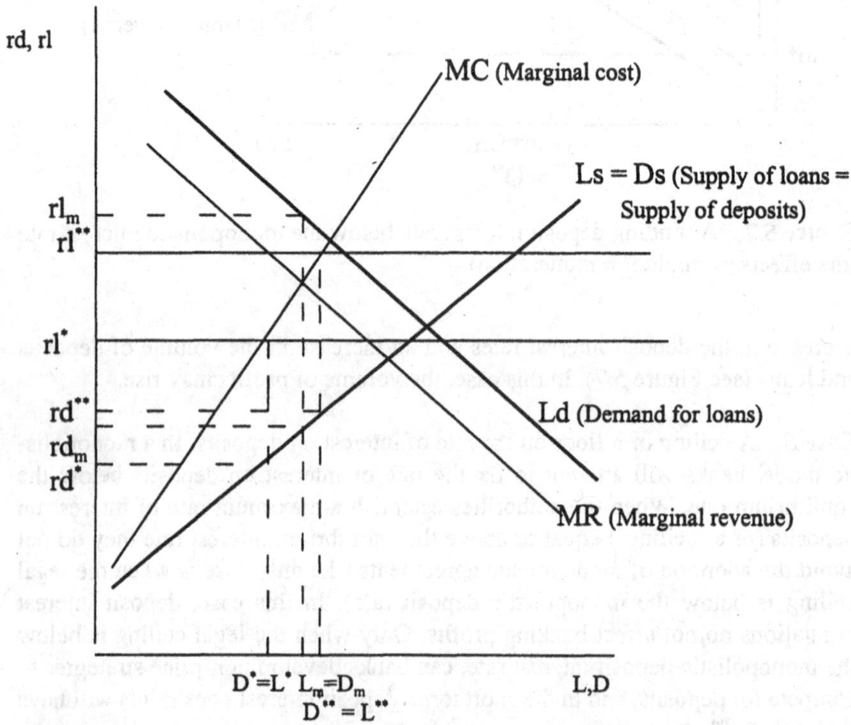

Figure 5.8 The effects of a binding loan interest rate below the monopolistic loan interest rate (monopoly)

binding loan interest rate *rl** below the monopolistic loan interest rate (*rl** < *rlm*), there is a decrease in the volume of deposit and loans (*D** > *Dm* and *L** > *Lm*) and a decrease in the deposit interest rate. However, as Figure 5.8 indicates, it is possible to fix a loan interest rate *rl*** which increases the total volume of deposits and loans ((*L*** = *D***) > (*Lm* = *Dm*)).

In a more complex model where banks have a compulsory coefficient, the final outcome is more difficult to obtain. In a monopolist model it is possible that the combined effect of a compulsory coefficient and a binding loan interest rate would be to increase the number of deposits and loans with respect to a situation with only a compulsory coefficient. As Figure 5.9 shows, the volume of deposits and loans with a compulsory coefficient and a binding loan interest rate is higher than the volume of loans only with a compulsory coefficient:

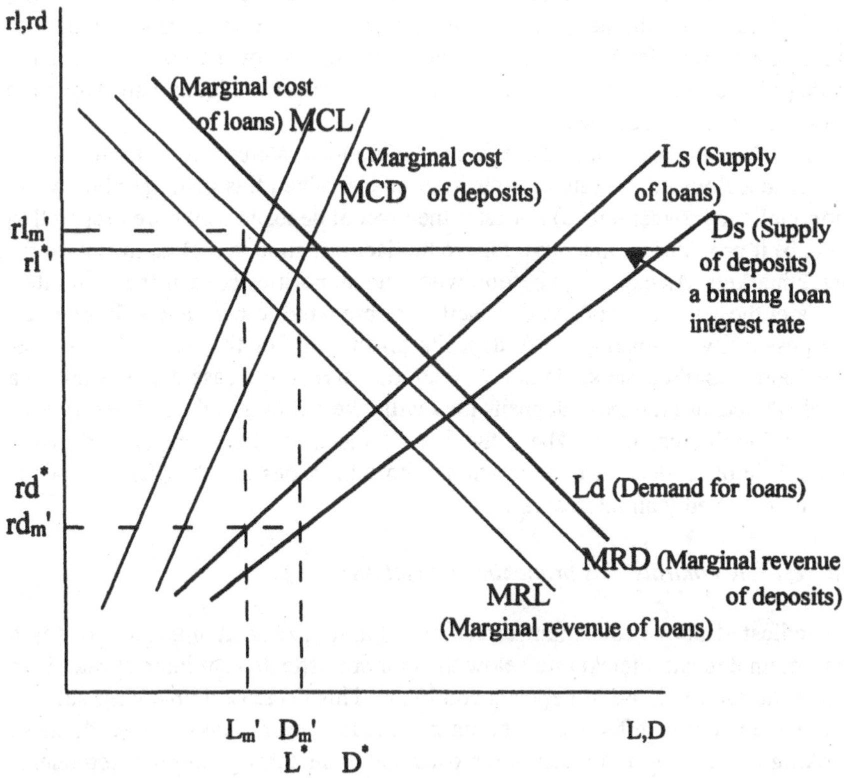

Figure 5.9 A binding loan interest rate and a compulsory reserve coefficient (monopoly)

$L^* > L_m$ and $D^* > D_m$. In this case, the final effect on profits depends on whether banks can compensate for the reduction in the spread ($rl^* - rd^*$) (with respect to a situation with a compulsory coefficient) with an increase in the volume of loans.

Loan interest controls have important effects on universal banks. If there is a legal ceiling on the loan interest rate, the bank could reorient its resources towards other more profitable investments (buying, for example, equities or public bonds). If the authorities establish 'preferential' rates to 'high-priority' sectors, the bank may change its investment policy towards these sectors.

Case B A ceiling or a floor on the loan interest rate. In an oligopolistic market banks will try to fix the rate of interest on loans above the equilibrium rate. When the authorities introduce a minimum rate of interest on loans (or a 'floor') they do not avoid the adoption of monopolistic agreements because banks can fix a rate of interest higher than the equilibrium rate of interest and near the monopolistic rate. Only a maximum rate of interest on loans can avoid the adoption of collusive agreements.

Therefore, the existence of a legal maximum loan interest rate is more restrictive than a floor on the rate of interest on loans. When this ceiling is below the monopolistic interest rate: a) it affects the level of deposits banks are prepared to take, b) it provides an incentive for credit discrimination and c) an incentive for black markets. As explained before, when the authorities control the loan interest rate, the level of deposits that banks are prepared to take is conditioned by the possibility of making these deposits profitable. For this reason, in a rate-constrained market, banks do not have an incentive to increase deposits above a level D^* because the extra deposits they will take represent idle cash reserves or non-profitable resources. Then, the bank's incentive for increasing deposits through implicit deposit remunerations, more branches or advertising depends on the regulated loan interest rate.

Interest rate controls plus branching restrictions

As indicated above, the main effect of a binding deposit interest rate (or a maximum deposit interest rate below the monopolistic deposit interest rate) is to lower the total volume of deposits and loans. This decrease in banking activity may have negative effects on banking profits. However, banks can evade these banking restrictions and increase deposits and loans through implicit remunerations, more branches and advertising campaigns. Thanks to these mechanisms banks can recover part of the profits they had lost initially as a consequence of regulation. If the authorities control these mechanisms, in particular, branching expansion, they restrict the capacity of banks to recover a part of the profits they have lost because of regulation.

Interest rate controls plus dividend controls

It is important to remark on the effect of deposit interest rate controls when there is an additional regulation: the existence of dividend controls. As indicated above, when there is a binding constraint on the deposit rate the loan interest rate rises (rl^*). In this case, returns on capital increase although profits may rise or fall. If profits rise and the authorities fix a dividend control, since larger profits cannot be paid out, these may be spent on more branches, advertising, and so on. Some of these expenditures will provide implicit remuneration for depositors but others will not – for example, these larger profits which cannot be paid out will be spent on more sumptuous branches or 'gold plating'. If banks transfer these retained dividends to reserves, the main effect of this regulation will be to sacrifice profits in order to increase banking stability. However, if these non-paid out dividends are expended in 'gold plating', it is more difficult to find a reason for dividend control regulations.

A compulsory coefficient

When the bank chooses the deposit remuneration, the number of branches or its advertising policy, it determines the volume of deposits. When the authorities introduce a compulsory coefficient, a_i is determined and the only variables at the bank's discretion are m_i, B_i or A_i. Figures 5.10.A and 5.10.B show the effect of a compulsory ratio on deposits and loans.

Regarding loans, when the authorities fix a_i, then $L_i < D_i$. This compulsory ratio leaves the marginal revenue on loans *MR* and the demand for loans *Ld* unchanged but shifts the marginal cost on loans to the left. The effect of a compulsory reserve ratio is to reduce the volume of loans *L* and to increase the interest rate charged on loans *rl*. Regarding deposits, the compulsory ratio shifts the marginal revenue from *MR* to *MR'* (making it 'flatter'), while the marginal cost on deposits remains unchanged (Courakis 1984: 348). Following Courakis (1984: 346), the shift in the marginal revenue curve reflects the fact that 'with any downward sloping demand for loans the introduction of a cash ratio (in this case a reserve ratio) implies that the average ratio at any particular volume of deposits D_j does not depend on the rate on loans that can be charged were the whole of D_j free to be granted as loans, but on the higher market clearing loan rate that $L_j = (1 - k).D_j$ implies.' Figure 5.10.B indicates that the effects of a compulsory ratio are: a) an increase in the deposit rate rd', b) an increase in the

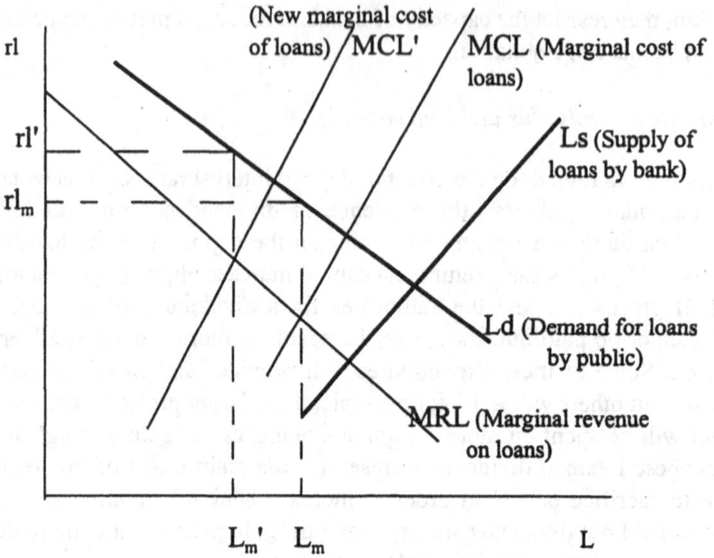

Figure 5.10.A The effect of a compulsory reserve requirement on loans (monopoly)

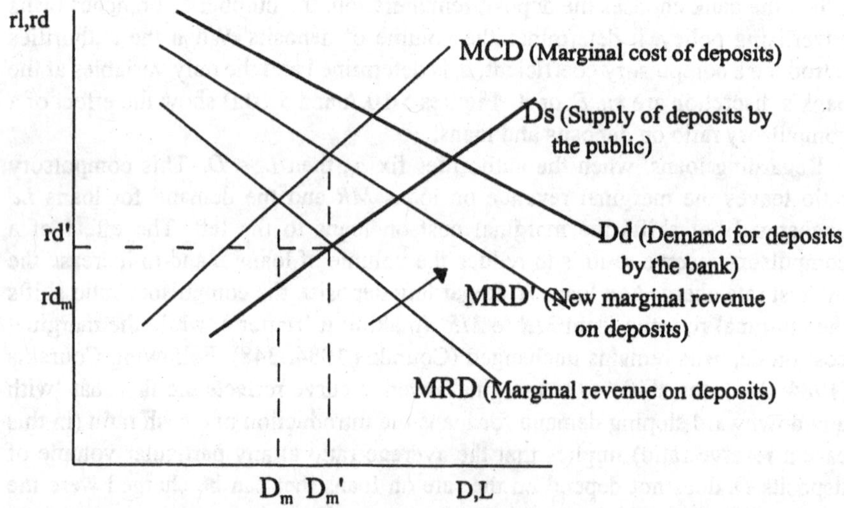

Figure 5.10.B The effect of a compulsory reserve requirement on deposits (monopoly)

volume of deposits D_m', with respect to a situation without compulsory coefficients, c) an increase in the loan interest rate rl' and d) a decrease in the volume of loans in comparison with a situation without compulsory coefficients ($L_m' < L_{m'}$).

The establishment of a compulsory coefficient may have a significant effect in the case of a universal bank. A possible link between the universal bank and its participating firms is the guarantee of obtaining loans. When the authorities introduce a compulsory coefficient (and the total volume of resources the bank can lend is lower than in the case without regulation), the bank may ration the supply of loans to the public and the non-participating firms (to guarantee the volume of loans it can lend to the firms of the group). The final effect on profits will depend on whether the bank subsidises loans or not.

An important question is: what is the effect on deposits, loans and profits of a combination of deposit interest rate constraints and a compulsory coefficient? As indicated above, when the authorities fix a compulsory coefficient, the supply of deposits (by the public) Ds is not equal to the supply of loans by the bank Ls because there is a percentage of deposits that is not transformed into loans. The main effect of lending only a part of the total volume of deposits is to raise the loan and deposit interest rates in comparison with a situation where $Ls = Ds$. The final effect of a combination of deposit interest rate controls and a compulsory coefficient on profits depends on the elasticity of the supply of deposits and the demand for loans and it also depends on the magnitude of the compulsory coefficient.

Other banking regulations: a public bond coefficient

If we consider a banking model where there are different financial assets (loans, public bonds, securities, and so on), the government can fix certain legal requirements such as, for example, the proportion of government bonds banks have to hold. When the authorities require a proportion of bank assets be held as bonds (and we assume that the return on these public bonds is lower than the rate of return on other alternative assets), this shifts the marginal costs (MC') to the left, raises the loan interest rate (rl^*) and reduces the volume of deposits and loans ($L^* = D^*$). If the authorities fix this public bond coefficient and simultaneously a binding loan interest rate, banks cannot transfer the loss in the rate of return on assets to the loan interest rate. In this case, the negative effect on banking profits is clear.

The oligopolistic model

Until now we have assumed that banks have organised as a monopolistic industry. However, the model changes if we assume that the banking industry is organised as an oligopolistic industry. It usually makes sense to consider that oligopolistic firms choose prices (in this case banks choose deposit and loan interest rates). Therefore, it could be useful to make use of the Bertrand model to understand banking behaviour.

The Bertrand model predicts that, even in duopoly, the price would fall to the competitive level. In this model the only equilibrium would be at price equal to marginal costs, where no firm has an incentive either to lower or to raise prices, but where no profits are made. If we consider that an oligopoly model could not generate the same outcome as perfect competition, we can change some of the Bertrand model assumptions to make the model more realistic. The main assumptions of the Bertrand model are:

1. the firms produce identical products.
2. each firm has a constant marginal cost and no fixed costs.
3. costs are the same in each firm.
4. there are no capacity constraints.

With regard to the banking sector, some of these assumptions must be changed. For example, we can consider that banks produce heterogeneous products. In contrast to the homogeneous industry situation, more than one price logically may exist in the market at any time. We shall follow the oligopoly model developed by Cubbin (1983: 155–63). Price is the most common decision variable in a heterogeneous product industry. In the banking industry, banks can be considered as multiproduct firms (they offer assets with different characteristics with regard to risk, maturity or liquidity) so this approximation is especially appropriate. Another peculiarity of the banking sector as a multiproduct industry is the differences in location. People prefer to work with the nearest branch because to travel to another banking office is costly. Customers prefer to operate with their local banks (or the nearest branch), even if they obtain lower deposit interest rates, because to travel further to other bank is expensive, especially in terms of time. Furthermore, sometimes people can obtain advantages from working with their local branch or bank because personal knowledge can facilitate the obtaining of a loan. We cannot say, therefore, that banking services are perfect substitutes for each other. Finally, there is not consensus about the existence of scale economies (and, therefore, about the importance of fixed costs in the banking industry).

When we consider an oligopoly model without collusion, the solution (and the interest rates that banks fix) could be anywhere between the monopolistic and the competitive price. The result will depend on the conjectures of the bank about the reaction of its rivals.

III. Conclusions

To analyse the effects of regulation on banking behaviour, the first aspect it is necessary to consider is what is the objective function of a bank. In the case of commercial banks, we can assume that banks maximise banking profits. The case of universal banks is more complex. Mixed banks not only participate in the intermediation process but they invest in other activities such as industrial equities. Then, the main question is whether the objective function of universal banks is to maximise banking profits or to maximise the profits of the conglomerate (the bank and its affiliated firms). If there is interdependence between the bank and its participating firms, the maximisation of the conglomerate profits will be different from the maximisation of individual profits. The main reason for this is the existence of 'conflicts of interest' between the bank and the firms of the group.

A model where banks choose the rate of interest on deposits and loans has been provided. Within this model two possibilities were considered. First, a situation where there is no government intervention was examined. The first step looked at an extremely simple model where the volume of loans the bank lends is equal to the volume of deposits it takes. In this case, the main determinant of banking profits are the elasticities of the supply of deposits and the demand for loans which determines the spread between the monopolistic loan and deposit interest rates. Later, a more complex model was analysed where the volume of loans the bank makes is only a percentage of the total volume of deposits it takes. In the short term, when the volume of loans the bank lends is only a percentage of the total volume of deposits it takes, there is a lower level of profits than in the case where $L_i = D_i$. Banks sacrifice profits to achieve higher stability.

Second, the effects of regulation on profit-maximising behaviour were examined. Some considerations about the effect of reserve requirements and other regulatory measures which affect the proportion of deposits a bank can lend were included. When the authorities fix a binding deposit interest rate above the monopolistic interest rate, the volume of deposits and loans increases and the spread between the loan and deposit interest rate decreases. When the authorities introduce restrictions on the remunerations banks pay on deposits (and they fix a binding deposit interest rate below the monopolistic interest rate), these financial institutions respond to these constraints by engaging in non-price competition. The most important form of non-rate competition is to increase branches, but there are other alternative mechanisms for competing, for example, free services, raffle tickets, guaranteed credit lines, and so on. They were defined as 'implicit interest rates'. When the equilibrium deposit interest rate (or the market interest rate) is above the regulatory controlled limit (a binding deposit interest rate or a ceiling on the deposit interest rate) the only variables at a bank's discretion are the 'implicit interest rate', the number of branches and advertising costs. If these measures are effective, the demand for banking services will increase and banks will compensate for the initial loss in profits resulting from regulation. When the authorities introduce other complementary regulatory measures, such as branching restrictions, they restrict the possibility of banks evading interest rate constraints (at least, outside of the black market).

Usually banks do not lend the total volume of deposits they take to avoid liquidity problems. After the Great Depression, in many countries regulators introduced measures to guarantee the stability of the banking system such as reserve requirements, or other compulsory coefficients. The main effect of introducing a compulsory coefficient is an increase in the volume of deposits and a decrease in the volume of loans in comparison with a situation without compulsory coefficient. As a consequence of that, profits may fall with respect to an unregulated banking system.

If the authorities combine compulsory coefficients with a binding deposit interest rate below the monopolistic deposit interest rate, the volume of deposits and loans decreases. With a binding deposit interest rate above the monopolistic rate and a compulsory reserve requirement, the volume of deposits and loans may increase. The final effect on profits will depend on the elasticities of the supply of deposits and the demand for loans and the possibility of banks evading these interest rate restrictions. Banks can respond to deposit interest rate controls by paying implicit remuneration, increasing the number of branches or by advertising. If these mechanisms are effective, banks increase the volume of deposits and loans. However, as indicated above, if the authorities introduced other complementary regulations such as branching restrictions, they are limiting the capacity of banks to evade interest rate controls.

With regard to loan interest rate controls, the most usual case is when the authorities introduce a binding loan interest rate or a maximum loan interest rate. The main objective of these interest rate controls is to avoid banks charging a monopolistic interest rate. In a very simple model without compulsory coefficients, when the authorities fix a binding loan interest rate below the monopolistic interest rate, there is an increase in the volume of deposits and loans with respect to the volume of deposits and loans in a monopolistic market without public intervention. In a more complex model where the authorities combine a binding loan interest rate with a compulsory coefficient which restricts the percentage of deposits the bank can lend, it is possible that banks increase the volume of deposits and loans with respect to a situation with only a compulsory coefficient.

The authorities can affect banking behaviour not only through interest rate controls or compulsory coefficients but by other legal requirements such as a public bond coefficient, that is to say, a proportion of government bonds banks are obliged to hold. The main objective of the authorities is to obtain public finance and, especially, cheap banking finance. The major effect of a public bond coefficient would be to raise the loan interest rate and reduce the volume of deposits and loans. If the authorities combine this public bond coefficient with a binding loan interest rate, the negative effect on banking profits is clear.

The main effect of dividend controls is an increase in marginal costs. Since dividends cannot be paid out, they will be spent in advertising, more branches and so on. Some of this expenditure will provide a remuneration to depositors – and implicit remuneration too – and others will not.

The effects of regulation on universal banks are especially significant. Interest rate controls will change banking portfolio behaviour and reorient banking activity towards real investments. The existence of compulsory coefficients could have an influence on the supply of loans to the public and non-participating firms when the main interdependence between the firm and its affiliated firms is the guarantee of obtaining a loan.

With these results, there are many questions which require an empirical analysis because of their relevance for the Spanish economy between 1940 and 1975. First, do savers respond equally to an increase in implicit remuneration (in terms of increasing deposit demand) as to an increase in the deposit interest rate? Are savers less or more sensitive to a proportionate increase in the implicit interest rate as to an increase in the explicit interest rate? Burkett (1986: 88) considers that savers may respond by being less sensitive to increased implicit interest because 'payment of interest in non-monetary forms may cause saver's welfare to decrease, due to transaction costs involved in converting implicit interest into generalised purchasing power.' However, if banks respond to deposit rate ceilings by expanding the number of branches, these ceilings can be an effective tool for stimulating savings, especially in rural areas and then, the final effect on the volume of savings is not determined. Second, how does the substitution of non-price for price competition in the market for savings affect the evolution of profitability? If the cost of producing implicit interest rates is higher than the cost of explicit interest, and savers are less sensitive to an increase in implicit interest rates – in terms of increasing deposits, the final effect of this transition from explicit to implicit interest could be particularly costly for banks.[8] The idea is that if regulation forces banks to substitute implicit interest for monetary interest payments, may this regulation increase the cost of saving mobilisation? If these possible negative effects are compensated by an increase in saving banks thanks to the expansion of branch offices, this branching expansion could be an effective mechanism for promoting savings mobilisation and the final effect on profitability could be positive (Burkett 1986: 89).

Notes

1 To simplify, this model considers that the bank produces one output: loans. Hefferman (1996: 129) argued that deposits, in addition to loans, must be treated as bank products, because deposits provide customers with a liquidity and saving service. Berger and Humphrey (1992) also consider deposits as an output of the banking industry.

2 We consider only time and saving deposits. The incentives to maintain non-interest bearing deposits or current account deposits are different (to maintain liquid assets against future transaction requirements, for example). The analysis does not change if alternatively we consider the current account deposits separately, with zero interest rate. The main effect of considering current account deposits on the profit function are: a) that the volume of loans (*Li*) depends on the total volume of deposits the bank takes: $L_i = a_i.(D_i + D_{ci})$ where D_i are time and savings deposits and D_{ci} current account deposits, and b) that the non-financial cost depends on the total volume of deposits and loans: $C(D_i, D_{ci}, L_i)$.

3 According to Carnevali (1993: 2), banks with a more decentralised structure (in terms of organisation and existence of autonomous peripherical centres) and provincial banks, restrict credit to smaller customers to a lesser extent than other more centralised banks. The main reason for this behaviour is that provincial and decentralised banks have a better local knowledge than centralised banks. Local decision centres have less cost to obtain information than centralised banks because there is a closer bank-customer relationship.

4 According to Baltensperger (1980) model, we can consider a most general profit equation which includes capital and reserves:

$$\pi_i = (r_r.R_i + rl.L_i + ro.O_i) - rd.D_i - \rho K - C(D_i, L_i, O_i) \qquad (5.6)$$

where R_i are reserves, r_r is the rate of return on reserves, K is capital, and ρ is the cost of equity. For simplification, I will consider the first model.

5 A most realistic assumption is to assume that banks will maximise the rate of profitability ('profits/capital + reserves'). As indicated above, in this model I have not considered capital and reserves, however in my empirical estimates (Chapter 6) I will assume that Spanish banks maximised the rate of profitability (defined as 'profits/ (capital + reserves)'.

6 As Cable (1985: 122) indicates, usually mixed banks deny intervention in their affiliated firms, and probably this is true in relation to the day-to-day matters. However, as this author indicates 'it would be naive to assume that the representation of banks, with substantial reserve powers over both shareholders' voting rights and the supply of external finance, does not indirectly influence management's design and execution of policy.'

7 We can consider the simplest situation with only a bank and a participating firm:

$$\max\,[(\pi_b\,(X_1)) + (\pi_{fl}\,(X_2))] = \max\,(\pi_{cong})$$

where X_1 are the determinants of the bank profits π_b and X_2 are the determinants of the firm profits π_{fl}, and π_{cong} are the profits of the conglomerate (bank + firm). If $X1$ and $X2$ are independent:

$$\max\,(\pi_{cong}) = \max\,(\pi_b) + \max\,(\pi_{fl})$$
$$\partial\pi_{cong}/\partial X_1 = \pi_b'$$
$$\partial\pi_{cong}/\partial X_2 = \pi_{fl}'$$

However, if there is a relationship between X_1 and X_2 (for example, the loan interest rate is a determinant of bank profits, but it also affects firm profits $X_2 = f(X_1)$):

$$\max\,(\pi_{cong}) \neq \max\,(\pi_b) + \max\,(\pi_{fl})$$
$$\partial\pi_{cong}/\partial X_1 = (\partial\pi_b/\partial X_1) + (\partial\pi_{fl}/\partial X_1).$$

8 If implicit interest was less costly to produce than explicit interest, presumably banks would have paid interest in an implicit form even in a situation without deposit interest controls (Burkett 1986: 84).

I. Interest rate controls and Spanish banking behaviour

After the Spanish Civil War, all interest rates on deposits and credits were subject to specific controls set by the authorities. As indicated before, the government fixed a binding maximum rate of interest on deposits and a minimum on the rate of interest on loans. Additionally, the authorities introduced other complementary credit controls and they fixed some 'preferential' interest rates to finance some 'priority' sectors. These interest controls – a minimum loan interest rate – can be viewed as a way of compensating banks for their 'cheap' financing of priority sectors, although in most cases banks invested in these preferential sectors.

To understand the effects of these interest controls on the Spanish banking sector, it is necessary to examine: a) the market structure (a competitive or a monopolistic market), b) the way the authorities introduced these interest controls and c) the relationship between the regulated and the equilibrium rate of interest.

Market structure and interest rate controls

There are two indicators that show that the Spanish banking system during the Franco period did not perform as a competitive market: 1) the existence of barriers to entry, and 2) there were several agreements among private banks – at least until 1952 – to limit competition. In the following pages, the characteristics of these agreements will be explained.

Hence, the Spanish banking sector was not a competitive sector and we must analyse the effects of interest controls on an oligopolistic or monopolistic banking structure. To estimate the effects of interest controls we must know whether the interest rates banks paid for deposits and charged for loans were above or below the equilibrium interest rate. This task is all the more difficult because there is no information about the equilibrium interest rates during this period.

The SBC (1952, 1 December, Circular 431) reported the existence of several agreements among private banks to fix interest rates.[1] The government approved these agreements and it established an organisation to control their implementation.[2] Although the SBC reported the infringement of these agreements in some cases (1949, 10 December, Circular 199), it can be assumed that from 1939 to 1952 – the last year of evidence of these pacts – banks had a binding deposit interest rate on deposits which was fixed by these credit institutions. Banks that did not collaborate in these agreements were discriminated against compared with those banks that signed the agreement. For example, banks which did not sign the *Ordenación Reguladora de Condiciones Mínimas* did not benefit from the banking conditions fixed by and for the members of the cartel (SBC 1953, 29 January, Circular 446).

According to Tortella and García[3] (1999) the *Banco Central* was against the payment of 'extra-rates'. The *Banco Hispanoamericano*'s behaviour was very different. This bank broke the *Ordenación Reguladora de Condiciones Mínimas* agreement in 1949, and the amounts it paid as 'extra-rates' from 1949 to 1953 were high. From 10 March 1960 to the beginning of the 1970s there is no information about the remuneration the *Banco Hispanoamericano* paid on deposits. In the 1970s the *Banco Hispanoamericano* gave information about the payment of *intereses diferenciales* or *intereses elevados*.

As explained in Chapter 4, the official 'excuse' for supporting these private agreements was that low deposit interest rates would encourage low loan interest rates (Paris Eguilaz 1947: 196–7). However, this argument is clearly false, as there is no causal effect between low deposit rates and low loan rates.[4] Another alternative effect could have been to allow banks to exploit depositors to obtain monopolistic profits. The government looked for the collaboration of banks in the financing of the industrialisation programme of the regime and with this regulation the authorities allowed banks to exploit depositors as compensation for financing Francoís industrialisation programme.

To analyse the effectiveness of interest controls in Spain from 1940 to 1975 the 'total financial costs/deposits' ratio was estimated (see Figure 6.1) as an indicator of the actual costs of deposits for the five largest Spanish banks. The general structure of the profit and loss accounts of these five banks in this period is:[5]

1. Total revenues from all banking activities (loans, bonds, industrial investments and so on).
2. Financial costs: includes deposit costs, commissions, brokerages and some local taxes (a very small proportion of total taxes).
3. Gross profits: Total revenues – Financial costs.
4. General costs: includes operating and other costs.
5. Net profit: Gross profit – General costs.

Taking into account the general structure of the profit and loss accounts, the main problem in obtaining an estimate of the 'financial costs/deposits' ratio is that the Annual Banking Reports do not differentiate between interest payments and other costs such as commissions and brokerages. As the Annual Reports indicate, it is assumed that the major part of the item 'financial cost' is deposit costs.

Considering the composition of deposits in the Spanish banking system, I have estimated the 'maximum' deposit costs under the assumption that banks

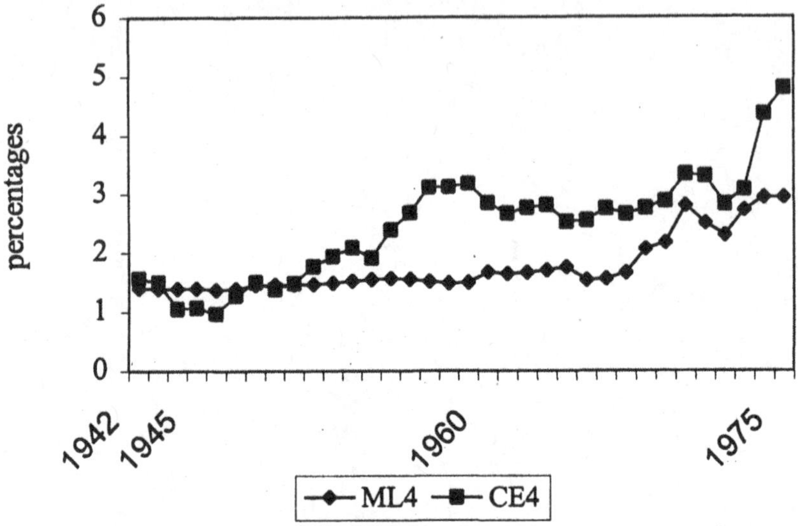

Figure 6.2 The financial cost/deposits ratio of the Big Four banks

Sources: Banking Annual Reports, *Banco Bilbao*, *Banco Central*, *Banco Español de Crédito*, *Banco Hispanoamericano*, *Banco Vizcaya*, several years.

The estimate shows that the effects of regulation were not exactly the same over the whole period (1939–1975). From 1940 to 1950 regulation was more restrictive (not in terms of legal coefficients but in terms of restriction of entry, branching expansion and mergers) and banks made some cartel agreements to fix banking conditions (SBC 1952, Circular 431). In this period the legal ceiling on the deposit rate was above the ratio 'financial costs/deposits' and regulation was not avoiding monopolistic behaviour. From 1950 the results are different. As Figure 6.1 indicates, the ratio 'financial costs/deposits' was above the legal maximum deposit interest rate. There are two possible explanations of this banking behaviour from the beginning of the 1950s: first that the deposit interest rate ceiling was below the monopolistic interest rate and banks adopted a collusive agreement to fix the deposit rate above the legal maximum or second that banks tried to compete. In both cases, banks increased deposit remunerations by paying 'extra-rates' or by engaging in non-price competition (they substituted explicit interest payments for implicit interest remunerations).

The last year I have found empirical evidence of the existence of a cartel agreement to fix the deposit interest rate below the maximum legal deposit interest rate is 30 June 1952. However, the ratio 'financial costs/deposits' was under the legal maximum from 1950. Then, empirical evidence shows that from 1950 banks broke cartel agreements (or they adopted a new cartel agreement to fix a deposit rate above the legal maximum) and they increased their financial costs through the payment of commissions and other instruments to take more deposits. The Report of the Overseas and Foreign Office of 1954 written by Macgilliaray (Bank of England Archives, 1954, OV61/5, 21 May: 11) about banking in Spain indicates:

> Although in theory there is a gentleman's agreement between the banks over commercial interest rates, little heed is paid to it and there is all-out competition. The Bank of London and South America which appears to stand alone in adhering to this Agreement has lost a considerable amount of custom by continuing to pay only the agreed 1/2 per cent on deposits – a rate exceeded by all the other banks.

In the report of 14 April 1962 (OV61/7: 8), there is a similar comment: 'Moreover since the unrealistically low rate of 1/2 per cent has been fixed for sight deposits and because of the absence of any really deterrent sanctions against breakers of the agreement, it is more than likely that banks will relapse into their old ways.'

Despite this empirical evidence, the SBC never accepted the existence of 'extra-rates' and it considered that this was not a general practice in the Spanish banking system (*Circulares del Consejo Superior Bancario*, several years).

Did economic conditions, and not only regulation, influence banking behaviour? It is possible that the difficult situation of the Spanish economy in the post-war years did not allow banks to pay higher deposit interest rates. The rates of profitability of the main banks in the post-war years were low and the investment opportunities too. It was in the 1950s, when the economic conditions improved, that banks increased deposit remunerations. But, in both cases banking behaviour was influenced by regulation: in the 1940s allowing banks to exploit depositors and in the 1950s and 1960s forcing banks to work in the black market and to make use of non-price instruments to compete.

Unfortunately, we cannot obtain the ratio 'revenues from loans/total loans' because the Annual Reports of the Big Five banks do not differentiate between revenues from loans and from other alternative banking activities such as bonds or industrial investments. The *Banco Español de Crédito* differentiated between a) revenues from loans, commissions and other sources and b) revenues from the selling of equities and bonds. This information indicates that the ratio 'total revenues (from loans, commissions and other sources)/total volume of loans' was around 14 per cent in the 1940s and it increased to 30 per cent in 1967. Data information from the *Banco Español de Crédito* indicates that there is not a significant difference between the ratio 'total revenues/loans' and 'revenues from loans, commissions and other sources/loans' (see Figure 6.3). However, we

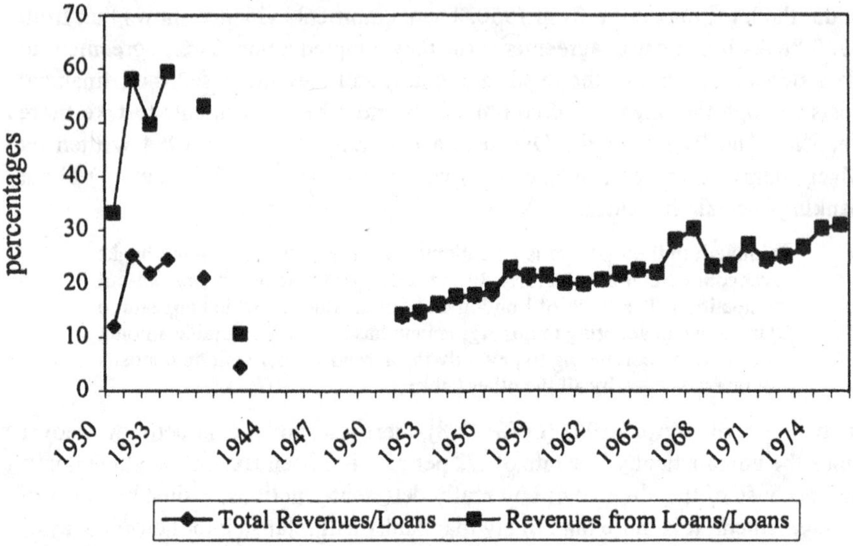

Figure 6.3 The total revenues/loans ratio and revenues from loans/loans ratio (*Banco Español de Crédito*)

Sources: Annual Reports, *Banco Español de Crédito*, several years.

cannot compare this ratio with the legal rate of interest on loans because profits from other alternative banking investments (public bonds, etc.) are also included in this ratio.

There is a possible relationship between interest controls – and other regulatory measures – and the 'mixed' character of Spanish banks. There are two main possible effects of interest rate controls on banking behaviour. First, when the authorities fix the rate of return on loans, banks try to maximise profits by investing in other alternative assets such as industrial investments. Second, when the government introduces 'preferential' interest rates, banks reorganise their investments to take advantage of these regulations. However, as seen in Chapter 2, the effect of regulations on the asset diversification of Spanish banks is not so clear as has generally been assumed. There is a general agreement about the 'mixed' character of the Spanish banking sector but Spanish banks' holdings of industrial securities represented only a small percentage of total assets (Martín Aceña and Pons 1994: 135). As Table 2.18 indicates, the percentage of industrial securities to the total assets decreased in this period, and the evolution is the same when we analyse the ratio 'industrial securities/total credits'. However, there was an extensive representation of banks on the supervisory boards of Spanish companies as a result of both their own shareholdings and the proxy votes they exercised on behalf of other shareholders who had deposited their shares with the banks for safekeeping (Muñoz 1969: 275–9). That is why it is necessary to take into account the links between banks and industrial firms through other different mechanisms than the industrial security portfolio.

Loan interest rate behaviour is related to the objective function of a mixed bank. Chapter 5 showed that mixed banks might have had two alternative objective functions. First, we can consider that the main objective of a bank is to maximise banking profits. Second, we can assume that the main objective of universal banks is to maximise the conglomerate profits. The links between banks and industrial firms can be a double-edged sword. As Edward and Fisher (1994: 125) indicate, supervisory board representation may disable a bank to monitor management closely or influence decision-making within the company. Banks can make use of their 'power' to exploit their participating firms charging higher rates of interest on loans to their own firms. However, representation on a company's supervisory board may increase the information available to a bank which is relevant for its lending decision. In this case mixed banks might be better positioned than other banks to know the 'quality' of a loan demanded by their affiliated firms. As a consequence of superior information or only because banks have an incentive to favour their participating firms, these firms will achieve advantageous lower loan interest rates or a higher volume of loans.

What is the possible influence of lending behaviour on banking profitability? If the bank makes use of its 'power' to exploit its participating firms, it may achieve super-normal profits. Alternatively, if the bank treats its subordinate firms favourably, lower profits for the mixed bank could be the result. However, universal banks may obtain super-normal profits without charging a higher loan interest rate to their participating firms because they are better informed about their affiliated firms, thus facing less risk when providing loans at the same (or even lower) rate as other banks. It is not easy, therefore, to obtain a general conclusion about the effects of loan interest controls on banking profitability.

In spite of these problems, an obvious feature to investigate is whether Spanish mixed banks were able to charge higher interest rates on loans to their participating firms, as Arruñada (1991: 24) affirms, or alternatively, whether they favoured their affiliated firms with cheaper financing or easy access to loans, as Poveda indicates (1981: 61). The main problem in obtaining information about Spanish banking lending behaviour is that data on interest rates charged on specific loans to individual firms is not available, so it is necessary to resort to indirect estimates.

Two different groups of firms were selected. The first was a group of firms with a very important banking participation. The second group was firms without a significant participation of banks. After selecting the firms, their financial costs were calculated. There are two main problems with this estimate. First, that some firms do not differentiate between financial costs and other operating costs. In these cases, we cannot obtain the financial cost paid by these firms. Second, even if we obtain the financial costs paid by different firms, and there are important differences among firms, the main problem is knowing whether these differences were the result of a policy of credit discrimination or were the result of different levels of risk. My estimates do not allow me to reach a conclusion about this problem, especially because I have not found a correlation between banking participation and higher or lower financial costs.

II. The main determinants of Spanish banking profitability and the influence of regulation

A simple and useful assumption is that the main objective of a bank is to maximise profitability, although as explained above, in the case of mixed banks this assumption is not realistic. Spanish banks obtained profits through three different activities: financial intermediating activity, investment in the industrial sector and the issue of new shares. Although this section primarily concentrates on the effects of regulation on profits derived from financial intermediating, reference will also be made to the other two questions.

Profitability and concentration

The relationship between concentration and profitability has a very important ambiguity. We can distinguish two different hypotheses. The traditional axiom of the 'structure-conduct-performance' paradigm is that high concentration lowers the cost of collusion, and collusion allows firms to obtain higher profits. The second hypothesis considers that some firms can earn more profits because of superior efficiency. When firms have superior efficiency, they obtain a high market share and, as a consequence, the market is more concentrated. If there are scale economies, when a firm increases in size it reduces costs and increases profits.

Thus, the relationship between the number of firms and the level of concentration depends on the cost structure of the industry. A small number of firms could be an indicator of the lack of competition because fewer firms lowers the cost of collusion. However, if we consider the possibility of scale economies in the banking industry, a high number of firms could be the result of the lack of competition in this sector. For example, if the increase in concentration of the Spanish banking system from 1942 to 1950 was the consequence of an attempt by banks to approximate the optimal size, the main question is how a significant number of small firms without the optimal size managed to remain in the banking industry.

Although there is an important body of literature which argues that there is a relationship between deregulation and an increase in competition,[6] in recent years the abolition of regulatory measures would seem to reflect the trend towards greater concentration to obtain standards of international competition. Hence, the interpretation of variations in concentration and the causal effect of regulation in this decrease in concentration are very ambiguous.

To sum up, in the analysis of the banking industry we cannot focus our attention exclusively on concentration. As explained before, larger firms in a concentrated system could be more profitable not because of collusion but because of efficiency.

Smirlock (1985: 69–83) proposed a methodology to test these two hypotheses (the 'structure-conduct-performance' and the 'efficiency' hypothesis), the estimation of a cross-sectional profit function. He estimated the following equation:

$$k = a + bMS + cCR + dMS.CR + fZ + u \qquad (6.1)$$

where k is the rate of profitability, MS the market share of the firm, CR is a measure of market concentration, Z is a vector of additional variables which affect banking profitability and u the error term. $MS.CR$ is an interaction term defined as MS multiplied by CR. He considers that, if $b > 0$ and $c = 0$, firms with a high market share are more efficient than their rivals and earn more profits because of efficiency. If $b = 0$ and $c > 0$, market share does not affect firm earnings and then higher profitability is the reflection of monopoly rents. Thus, $b > 0$, and $c = 0$ supports the efficient structure hypothesis, whereas $b = 0$ and $c > 0$ supports the collusion or traditional hypothesis. There are other possible combinations of b and c but in these cases, the interpretation of results is very ambiguous. When b and c are greater than zero, Smirlock defines an indirect test to interpret the results: he made use of the interaction variable. If high concentration is associated with collusion, then a positive coefficient on $MS.CR$ should be observed. If d is negative, then we can accept the efficiency hypothesis. In any case, this test must not be considered as unambiguous evidence in favour of one or another hypothesis.

This test, however, has serious problems. Shepard (1985), Berger (1995), or Maudos (1996) questioned the use of market share as a proxy for efficiency. The main reason for this criticism is that market share may capture the effect of other variables rather than efficiency. Berger (1995), for example, implemented a test that distinguished more clearly between these two hypotheses. He includes other variables as indicators of efficiency based on the estimation of the cost function. Unfortunately, in the Spanish case there is not enough information to estimate the cost function in this period (1942–1975).

To begin analysing the Spanish banking sector, a different methodology will be followed. One of the main purposes of this research is to examine the effects of the regulatory framework on banking behaviour and in this case on profitability. A comparison of cross-sectional relationships in a regulated and non-regulated regime could identify consequences of regulation on profitability. As homogeneous data are available only for the Big Five banks, a different methodology which incorporates cross-section and time series is proposed: the analysis of panel data. An equation to explain the evolution of profitability of the Big Five banks from 1920 to 1975 has been specified. The data were arranged in stacks, where π_i (profitability) is the pooled dependent variable, and all the equations have been estimated by ordinary least squares. A fixed effect model was used. This model assumes that differences across units (in this case banks) can be captured in differences in the constant term. Let π_i and X_i be the T observations for the *ith* bank and we may write:

$$\pi_i = 1.\alpha_i + \beta.X_i + \varepsilon_i \tag{6.2}$$

where π_i is the dependent variable, X_i is a vector of explanatory variables, ε_i is the associated vector of disturbances and each α_i is an unknown parameter to be estimated. We can rewrite this equation:

$$\pi = [d_1, d_2, \ldots, d_n X]\begin{pmatrix} \alpha \\ \beta \end{pmatrix} + \varepsilon \tag{6.2'}$$

where d_i is a dummy variable indicating the *ith* bank. Assembling all nT rows gives:

$$y = D.\alpha + \beta.X + \varepsilon \tag{6.3}$$

The data are composed of balance sheet information from 1920 to 1975 for the Big Five banks in Spain. To obtain the profit function the profit and loss accounts of the Big Five banks were reorganised because banks did not follow a homogeneous accounting criterion for classifying items. Because of the lack of information for the period 1936–1941, this regression was estimated without considering those years. Alternatively, an individual time-series equation for each bank was estimated, obtaining very similar results to those of the panel.

Spanish banking profitability

I define banking profitability as the ratio: 'profits/(reserves + paid up capital)'. Before examining the possible relationship between concentration and profitability, the evolution of banking profitability of the Big Five banks is described. After this, I analyse whether or not the changes in profitability coincided with changes in regulation – without considering causality. In examining this possible relationship between profitability and legislation I found it useful to include in my analysis the pre-war years.

There is no information about the average rate of profitability of the Spanish banking system during the Franco period. In some years the *Anuario Financiero y de Sociedades Anónimas* (an annual report where it is possible to find general information about the main national firms) gave these data for a sample of 75–85 per cent of the total banks in the Spanish banking system. For example, according to this information, in 1942 the average rate of profitability of a sample of 68 banks was 10.09 per cent. In 1952 this rate was 17.15 per cent. If we compare the average rate of profitability of the Big Five banks with the data from the *Anuario Financiero y de Sociedades Anónimas*, we do not obtain very important differences: it was 11.73 per cent in 1942 and 18.12 in 1952 (see Table 6.1). Then, at least in the 1940s and 1950s, the rate of profitability of the Big Five banks can be used as an indicator of the rate of profitability of the whole banking system (Martín Aceña and Pons 1995: 342–5). More recently, Tafunell (1997) estimated the average rate of profitability for different sectors of Spanish industry, including the banking sector, obtaining similar results.

In order to provide a broad picture of the evolution of profits and margins in Spanish banks, two complementary sources of data have been used: the data collected and compiled by the SBC (*Balances Consolidados de la Banca Privada*), and the Annual Reports of the main banks (*Banco Bilbao*, *Banco Central*, *Banco Hispanoamericano*, *Banco Español de Crédito* and *Banco Vizcaya*).

As explained above, Spanish banks did not have homogeneous accounts. For this reason, my initial work was to develop a general profit and loss account to obtain consistent profit figures. One of the main difficulties of the profit and loss accounts is that there was no convention about where to include depreciation costs. For this reason, the profit figures that banks show in their Annual Reports have different meanings.[7] For example, the *Banco Bilbao* does not offer any information about depreciation costs. We can only assume that these costs were included with the rest of the operating costs, but the Annual Reports of this

Table 6.1 Profitability of the Big Five banks and the average rate of profitability for a sample of banks, 1930–1952 (%)

	Profitability Spanish banking system		
	Number of banks	Average rate of Profitability	Profitability Big Five
1930	84	10.78	12.26
1931	82	7.17	9.05
1932	81	7.00	8.58
1933	80	7.04	7.94
1934	79	7.34	8.14
1935	77	8.11	8.79
1942	68	10.09	11.73
1943	67	11.28	11.86
1944	62	12.71	13.08
1945	108	13.40	14.11
1946	92	14.92	12.82
1947(1)	116	16.07	16.07
1948	130	17.40	17.96
1949	137	15.93	15.01
1950	135	16.51	16.15
1951	137	16.52	17.55
1952	138	17.16	18.12

Note: (1) = before 1947 these data include the *Banco de España, Banco de Crédito Industrial, Banco de Crédito Local* and *Banco Hipotecario*, all of them public banks. From this year on the sample includes only private banks.

Sources: *Anuario Financiero y de Sociedades Anónimas (Gardoqui)* and Annual Reports, Big Five banks, several years.

bank do not indicate anything at all. *Banco Vizcaya* and *Banco Español de Crédito* consider depreciation costs as a cost before obtaining profits. These banks give information about the volume of depreciation costs with the exception of the years 1973, 1974 and 1975 in the case of the *Banco Vizcaya* and 1967, 1968 and 1969 in the case of the *Banco Español de Crédito*. In these years the *Banco Vizcaya* and *Español* included depreciation costs with the rest of the operating costs. Finally, the *Banco Central* considers depreciation costs as a cost after obtaining profits. In order to make the figures homogeneous, in my estimate

significant decline in the ratio 'profits/(capital + reserves)' until 1934, especially in the *Banco Central*. From its foundation the *Banco Central* showed a clear preference to mix commercial banking with company promotion. In the 1920s and 1930s, the *Banco Central* experienced serious difficulties. There are two reasons which explain this circumstance. First, its mixed bank character. Although the depression of the 1930s was less serious in Spain than in other countries, it affected industrial and commercial sectors, and the stock yields and prices declined. So, the *Banco Central* – a mixed bank – suffered more than other banks from the evolution of the stock market. Second, there were some problems of mismanagement in this financial institution. These are the main reasons of the low rates of profitability in the pre-war years. It was in the mid-1940s when the situation of this bank changed completely (García and Tortella 1993: 10–22).

After the Civil War, and because of the negative effects of the war, the level of profitability of the Big Five banks was low, but it increased substantially in the 1940s and 1950s (see Figure 6.5). The *Banco Central* had a very slow recovery in the post-war years but after 1945 the ratio 'profits/(capital + reserves)' increased at a faster rate than for the other banks. The increase in profitability of the Big Five in the 1950s was high, but in 1958–1959 nominal profitability started to

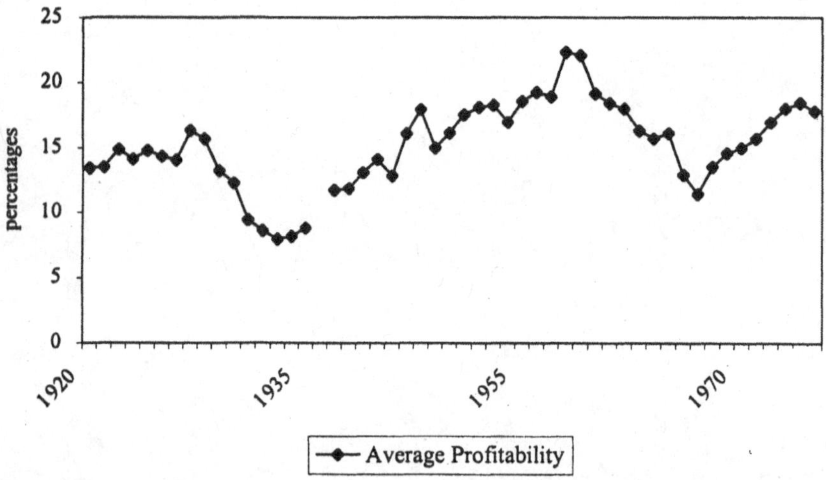

Figure 6.5 The average rate of profitability of the Big Five banks, 1920–1975

Sources: Banking Annual Reports and *Balances Consolidados de la banca privada* (SBC).

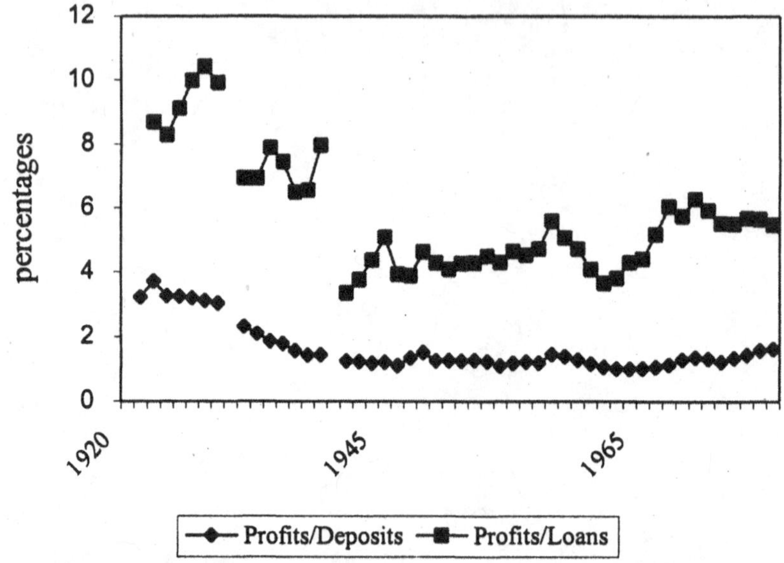

Figure 6.7 The profits/deposits and the profits/loans ratios of the Big Five banks

Sources: Banking Annual Reports and *Balances Consolidados de la banca privada* (SBC).

decreases again until 1954. From this year to 1958 there is a recovery of the 'profits/deposits' ratio. It decreases during the period 1958–64 but from 1964 the ratio has a growing trend. In spite of these small variations, the 'profits/deposits' ratio is quite stable: between 1–1.5 per cent during the entire period 1942–1975.

The 'profits/loans' ratio shows a significant breakdown after the Spanish Civil War: the ratio falls from 7.39 in 1935 to 3.3 in 1942. It has a positive trend from 1942 to 1958. From 1958 to 1962 the ratio decreases but from 1962 on the relationship between profits and loans increases again (see Figure 6.7).

In order to understand the evolution of profitability, we must examine the possible relationship between the evolution of this variable and changes in the regulatory framework. From 1920 to 1975 there were two important changes in financial legislation. The 1921 the BSL was to guide the Spanish banking system until 1946. From the end of the Civil War until 1962 banking activity in Spain was governed by a set of regulations adopted in the immediate post-war years and largely confirmed in 1946, as just indicated. The 1962 Banking Law introduced some changes to this legislation. Traditionally the economic literature has considered that thanks to regulation during the Franco regime banks achieved very high profitability rates (Muñoz: 379). In the following pages I will assess whether the changes in regulation in 1962 did in fact affect banking profitability.

As can be seen in Figure 6.5, after the Spanish Civil War profitability had a positive trend and the Big Five banks achieved higher rates than in the pre-war years. However, the decrease in profitability took place before the change in the Banking Law of 1962. If this decline in the ratio 'profits/(capital + reserves)' is an indicator of an increase in competition, there was no apparent relationship between this change in profitability and the 'relative' liberalisation of the regulatory framework. Moreover, from 1967 there was an important recovery of banking profitability. This result is similar when we consider the relationship between regulation and the 'profits/deposits' and 'profits/loans' ratios. The decrease in the 'profits/deposits' and 'profits/loans' ratios started in 1958 and, moreover, after the 1962 Banking Law there was an important recovery of these two ratios (from 1964 in the case of the 'profits/deposits' ratio and from 1962 in the case of the 'profits/loans' ratio).

Issues of capital

To analyse the influence of regulation on banking profitability we must consider not only the volume of profits derived from the profit and loss accounts but also other alternative ways of increasing their returns, especially investments in industrial sectors and profits derived from the issues of capital. From the beginning of the 1960s there were massive issues of capital. These issues of shares were linked to an extraordinary increase in the value of these shares in the stock market or *plusvalías*. In most cases, the cost of these issues for the shareholders was zero (Villar Arregui 1968: 6).

Lopez Muñoz[9] (1968: 49) analysed the effect of the issues of capital in the banking sector and the evolution of these shares in the stock market. They compared the value of 100,000 PTAs invested in 1960 in banking shares with the market value of these shares in 1967 and showed that the profits achieved by the shareholders where spectacular not only in nominal but also in real terms. For example, 100,000 PTAs invested in shares of the *Banco Español de Crédito* in 1960, with a cost of issue of 74,846 PTAs had a market share value of 980,967 PTAs in 1967. Then, with an investment of 174,846 PTAs investors obtained a profit of 806,121 PTAs (or 501,861 in PTAs of 1960). Results are very similar in the cases of the *Banco Central*, *Santander*, *Hispanoamericano* or *Popular* (Lopez Muñoz 1967: 17).

Muñoz (1968: 394) demonstrates that from 1950 to 1967 the total volume of dividends distributed by the *Banco Español de Crédito, Hispanoamericano* and *Central* was insignificant in relation to the increase in the stock market value. For example, from 1950 to 1967 the total volume of dividends distributed by these three banks were 612,816 PTAs and the capital gains achieved by the shareholders were 13,275,410 PTAs. To analyse in more detail the evolution of profits achieved by the big banks through this mechanism, the same criterion as Roldán, Muñoz and García Delgado has been followed. Table 6.2 shows the increase in the value of shares in the stock market[10] from 1940 to 1975 for these three banks.

Table 6.2 Capital gains achieved by the shareholders, 1940–1975 (millions PTAs)

	Español de Crédito	*Hispanoamericano*	*Central*
1940–1945	379.1	422.0	130.8
1945–1950	322.3	336.0	244.5
1950–1955	2,067.2	1,730.0	1,186.5
1955–1960	775.7	28.0	383.0
1960–1965	13,483.4	8,374.5	8,788.0
1965–1970	27,582.6	28,587.7	34,140.8
1970–1975	31,218.1	8,001.9	56,649.2

Sources: *Anuario de Cotizaciones Oficiales de la Bolsa de Madrid* and Annual Reports, *Banco Español de Crédito, Hispanoamericano* and *Central*.

The main conclusion reached is that from 1960 there was a spectacular increase in the value of banking shares in the stock market. From the end of the Civil War to 1960, the evolution of the shares of the main banks in the stock market was related to the distribution of dividends and the general evolution of the banking business. In the 1960s this trend changed. There existed a speculative phenomenon: the issues of capital coincided with the increase in the value of banking shares and the shareholders achieved quick profits. What were the main reasons for this change? (Muñoz 1969: 389–90.)

First, the Law of 31 December 1946, section VIII, established that when a limited company issued new shares or equivalent titles with preference rights of subscription, it required not only the payment of the shares but in addition the proportional part of the reserves corresponding to these shares. In 1958 the Decree Law of 24 October eliminated this requirement reducing the 'costs' of issuing new shares.

Second, the Tax Reform Law of 1964 considered the profits achieved through the issue of capital to be tax-free. Third, the Banking Law of 1962 linked the size of the portfolio of banks to their volume of capital plus reserves; then, those banks which tried to increase or maintain the size of their portfolio, had to increase the volume of their own assets. Fourth, mixed banks increased the value of their shares on the stock market as a consequence of their own shareholdings. As they owned a very important volume of their own shares, they intervened in the market to maintain the high price of their shares. Finally, part of the increase in the volume of capital in the banking sector was a consequence of the *Ley de Regularización de Balances* (Law 76/1961 and Decree 3836/1965 of 16 December). This law regularised the value of capital and reserves of banks to narrow the difference between the market value of banking 'capital + reserves' and the value registered in the balance accounts.

If we examine the relationship between the total profits (profits derived from financial intermediating activity and profits derived from the issues of capital and the evolution of banking shares on the stock market) and the changes in the regulatory framework we conclude that it is not possible to find a relationship between the evolution of total profits and the change in regulation. It was after the Banking Law of 1962 when the shareholders achieved higher profits. Although the profits derived from the financial intermediating activity decreased from 1959 to recover again in the late 1960s, capital gains rose spectacularly in the 1960s and the beginning of the 1970s. The relative liberalisation of the banking system did not impede the achievement of extraordinary profits for the shareholders.

The existence of 'super-normal' profits in the Spanish banking sector

Was the rate of profitability of the Big Five banks higher or lower than the average rate of profitability of the industrial sector? This is one way of deciding whether banks obtained supernormal profits or not. The main problem with this kind of comparison is that, as Martínez Méndez (1991: 137) indicates, differences in profitability could be a consequence of a different accounting criterion between financial and non-financial firms and a different effect of inflation on the evolution of profitability for financial and non-financial firms. These are the main difficulties of comparing the rates of profitability of two different sectors. For this reason, the results obtained from this exercise must be interpreted with caution.

Unfortunately, we do not have accurate information from the end of the Spanish Civil War to 1962. Guerrero (1988) obtained an indicator of the average rate of profitability of Spanish firms from 1952 to the mid-1970s.

However, the quality of this data is uncertain. First, Guerrero does not indicate the source of the information and second, he does not explain the way the indicator was estimated. Although we cannot accept this information as full proof in reaching a conclusion about the relationship between the rate of profitability of the Big Five banks and the rest of firms, Figure 6.8 shows Guerrero's results. The data does not indicate that banks obtained supernormal profits in this period. As indicated above, Tafunell (1997) also estimated the average rate of profitability for Spanish firms. This series was obtained from a sample of 372 firms. It is not an indicator of the profitability of Spanish industry but of big and medium-size firm profitability. It is this latter data that I have concentrated on.

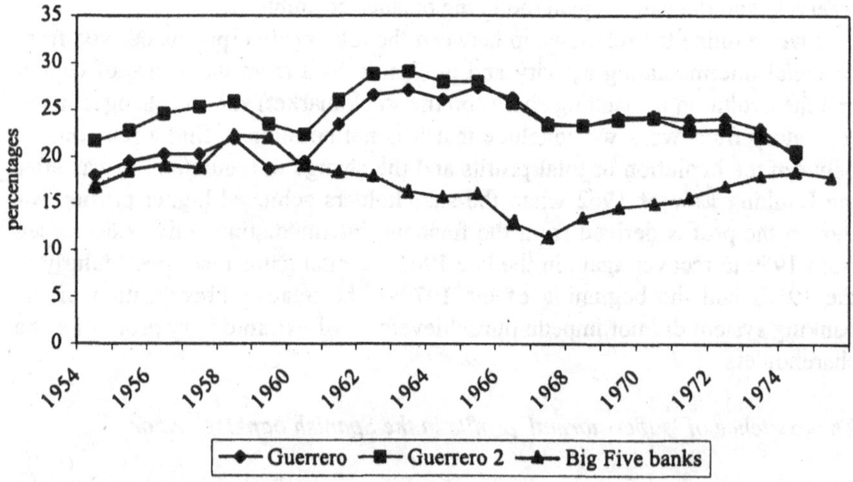

Figure 6.8 The profitability of banks and the rest of firms

Sources: Banking Annual Reports and Guerrero (1988).

Tafunell (1997) defines profitability as: '(profits + depreciation costs)/(paid up capital + reserves)'. This criterion has some problems however, as for some years there is no information about depreciation costs. Thus, the rate of profitability was re-estimated assuming that the percentage of depreciation costs in the years where there is no information (1967, 1968, 1969 for the *Banco Español de Crédito* and 1973, 1974 and 1975 for the *Banco Vizcaya*) was similar to that of the previous years. This is an *ad hoc* assumption, because in some cases the evolution of depreciation costs is very erratic. However, this variable was more

Table 6.3 The profitability of the Big Five banks and the profitability of big and medium size firms

	Big Five banks (a)	Big Five banks (b)	Total banking industry (c)	Industrial sector (d)
1920	13.43	14.58	14.60	16.20
1925	14.33	13.76	13.00	13.40
1930	12.26	12.90	12.80	13.60
1935	8.79	9.32	10.03	9.50
1942	11.73	12.19	10.70	13.10
1943	11.86	13.07	12.50	13.60
1944	13.08	14.42	13.90	14.40
1945	14.11	15.42	15.90	15.80
1946	12.82	13.87	16.00	15.00
1947	16.07	17.15	17.90	15.30
1948	17.96	19.09	17.60	14.70
1949	15.01	16.70	15.50	14.50
1950	16.15	17.33	16.00	15.50
1951	17.55	18.84	17.50	16.70
1952	18.12	19.63	17.90	15.90
1953	18.29	18.89	18.80	16.90
1954	16.96	18.55	18.40	16.90
1955	18.57	20.17	19.80	19.60
1956	19.26	29.70	21.40	18.60
1957	18.91	20.40	20.70	19.80
1958	22.37	23.74	21.90	20.20
1959	22.13	23.74	20.80	18.20
1960	19.17	20.95	20.30	18.70
1961	18.42	20.12	18.70	18.90
1962	18.01	19.57	18.90	17.60
1963	16.31	17.68	17.50	15.20
1964	15.71	16.96	16.20	14.50
1965	16.11	17.16	18.00	16.40
1966	12.93	14.03	15.20	15.40
1967	11.42	12.29	14.70	14.10
1968	13.54	14.56	16.70	15.10
1969	14.58	15.89	17.50	16.30
1970	14.98	16.53	17.70	16.40
1971	15.70	17.40	17.90	15.10
1972	16.95	18.72	20.10	16.10
1973	18.02	21.18	21.20	18.50
1974	18.45	20.06	22.00	15.00
1975	17.83	19.86	21.40	13.30

Notes: (a) Profitability of Big Five banks without depreciation costs.
(b) Profitability of Big Five banks with depreciation costs.
(c) Tafunell's estimates for the total banking industry.
(d) Tafunell's estimates for the industrial sector.

Sources: Tafunell (1996) and Annual Banking Reports and *Balances Consolidados de la Banca Privada* (SBC).

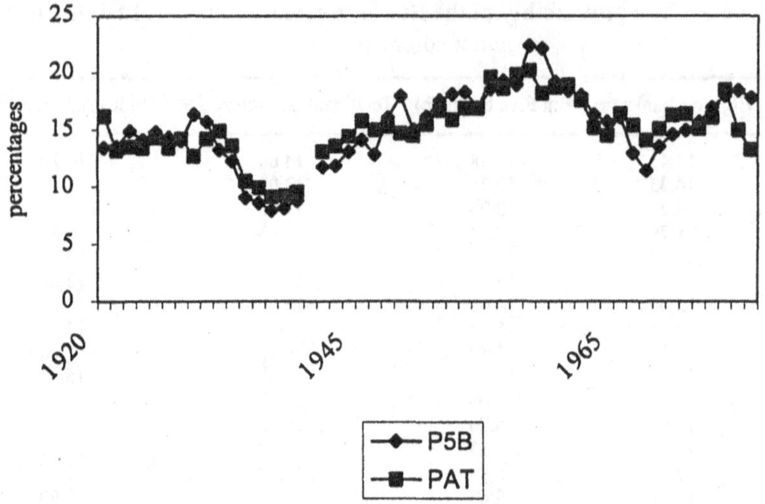

Figure 6.9 The profitability of the Big Five banks (P5B) and the rest of firms (PAT)

Sources: Banking Annual Reports and Tafunell (1999).

erratic in the 1940s and 1950s than in the 1960s and 1970s and for this reason such an assumption does not significantly alter my results.

Table 6.3 and Figure 6.9 suggest that, with the exception of the post-war years,[11] the average rate of profitability of the Big Five banks was higher than the average rate of profitability of Spanish firms. In the immediate post-war years (1942–1946) the recovery of banking profitability was slower than the recovery of profitability of the rest of firms. The situation changed in 1947. From this year to 1975 banking profitability was above the profitability of the big and medium-size firms. However, a conclusion cannot be reached about the relationship between these differences in profitability and the legal framework. After the Civil War the differences between the rates of profitability of the Big Five banks and the rest of firms increased. With the post-war regulatory framework, the Big Five banks achieved higher 'super-normal' profits than the rest of firms than in the pre-war period. However, if the process of liberalisation of the banking system which started in 1962 had a positive effect on the evolution of profitability, we must expect a decrease in the 'spread' between the banks' profit rate and the average rate of profitability of the rest of firms. My data indicates that although the rates of the big banks' profitability approached the rate of profitability of the rest of firms between 1965 and 1966, from this year the spread between these two profitability rates increased again. This information shows that the higher rates of growth of banking profits – in comparison with the rest of firms – occurred after the Banking Law Reform of 1962, especially from 1970 on.

Did Spanish banks manipulate their accounts to hide profits? There are four possible reasons for reporting lower profits. First, the existence of taxes on profits. Second, a 'moral' justification. There was a commonly held view about the monopolistic nature of the banking sector. Banks would try to hide 'super-normal' profits to project a better 'image'. Third, the existence of dividend controls. Fourth, to hide profits from the shareholders. In the Spanish case, we cannot accept the first reason because taxes were not very important. With respect to the remaining reasons, I have not found any empirical evidence to support them. Thus, it is possible that banks hid profits but there is no evidence that this was so. Muñoz (1969: 282–83) made reference to the existence of fraud in Spanish firms and the banking industry as, for example, *Diario Pueblo*, 9 December 1968, for the whole Spanish firms or the Report of the *Sección Social del Sindicato Provicial de Banca, Bolsa y Ahorro*, 23 November 1967 (*Cuadernos para el Dialogo, 1968, April VIII*: 55). However, we cannot affirm that fraud in banking was higher than in other sectors. This fact, therefore, did not alter inter-sector comparisons.

Other indicators of competition

Another variable that many researchers used as an indicator of the degree of competition is the 'spread' between the rate of return on loans and the cost of deposits – the difference between interests received and interest paid out by banks. One would expect that low competitive pressure would translate into high interest spreads. In this case, the hypothesis I aim to test is whether the changes in regulation affected interest margins between the banks' lending rate and the borrowing rate.

The profit and loss accounts of Spanish banks do not differentiate between revenues from loans and revenues from other alternative investments (public bonds, securities, etc) with the exception of the *Banco Español de Crédito*. With the information available from the Annual Reports of the Big Five we have obtained the following indicator:

(total revenues/total loans) – (total financial costs/total deposits)

This is not the spread between loan and deposit interest rates or the interest margin, but it can be seen, although not without reservation, as an indicator of the evolution of this variable.

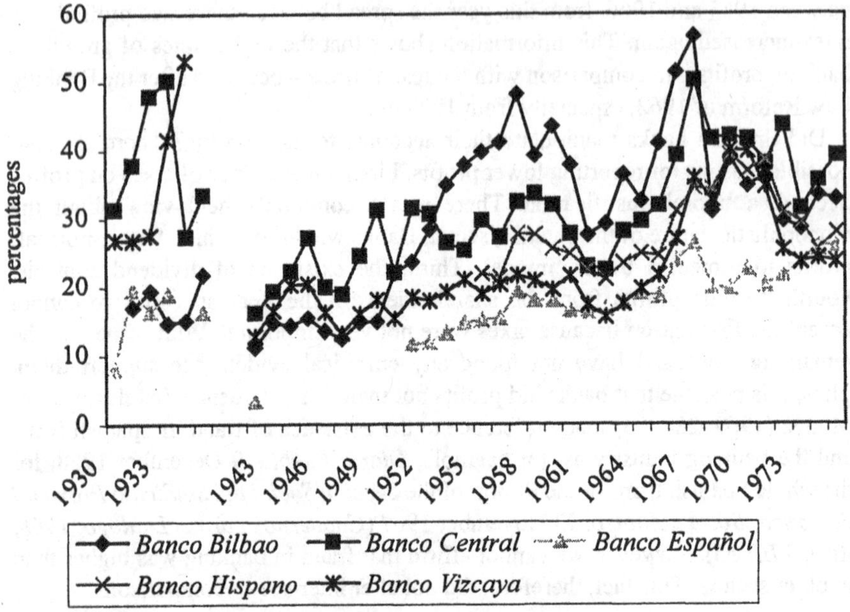

Figure 6.10 Interest margin of the Big Five banks

Sources: Banking Annual Reports, several years.

My results show that there was an increase in the 'spread' from 1942 (10.9 per cent) to 1957 (29.8 per cent), with substantial differences among banks (see Figure 6.10). After 1957 the interest margin declined until 1962. From 1962 to 1967 the spread increased spectacularly from 21.01 to 40.7. In 1967, however, the positive trend in the interest margin was interrupted and this variable decreased from 40.7 in 1967 to 27.2 in 1973.

In summary, according to this information we cannot accept that as a consequence of the regulatory change in 1962 the interest margin decreased. If we are to believe the interest margin as an indicator of competitiveness, competition did not increase after 1962. There are at least two interpretations of this fact. First, that the relative liberalisation of the legal framework which started in 1962 did not have a positive effect on efficiency, at least in the short term. Second, that the effects of the process of liberalisation of the Spanish banking system did not become apparent until after 1967.

Pérez and Quesada (1992: 139–42) hold an alternative definition of the interest margin, and they define this intermediation margin as 'revenues on loans –

cost of deposits)' and they present their results as a percentage of total assets. The ratio 'intermediation margin/total assets' had very high rates in the 1940s but later followed a downward trend until the mid-1960s. The *Banco Vizcaya, Central* and *Español de Crédito* had a similar trend. However, the trend changed and the ratio rose from 1964–1970 in the *Banco Vizcaya,* from 1965–1970 in the *Banco Español de Crédito* and from 1963–1967 in the *Banco Central.* The *Banco Bilbao* and *Hispano* had a different evolution. The *Banco Bilbao* had a positive trend from 1942 to 1957. After this year the trend was very similar to the *Banco Central* and *Vizcaya*: it decreased from this year until 1965. After this year the ratio 'intermediation margin/total assets' had many ups and downs. The *Banco Hispano* only offers information from 1955 and the ratio increased from 1955 to 1959, and it had a negative trend from this year until 1962. The ratio increased again from 1962 to 1970.

The general picture that emerges from the data is as follows. There was a change in the functioning of the Spanish banking system from the late 1950s. This change was reflected in an increase in financial costs, a decrease in concentration, a decrease in profitability and a reduction in the interest spread and the 'intermediation margin/total assets' ratio (with the exception of the *Banco Hispanoamericano*). There is no correlation between these changes and the legal framework, because this change took place before the *Ley de Bases* of 1962. Moreover, there was a recovery of the interest margin and the 'intermediation margin/total assets' ratio after 1962. It was in 1967 when the interest margin was once again reduced, although the average spread from 1967 to 1975 was higher than in the 1940s and 1950s. Something similar occurred with the ratio 'intermediation margin/total assets': all the banks under consideration had a positive trend in the 1960s and only in the 1970s it is possible to observe a change in this trend.

A general profit equation for the Spanish banking sector, 1940–1975

After obtaining a banking profitability series, the next step is to analyse the main determinants of this variable. As explained above, Smirlock (1985) proposed a cross-sectional profit function estimation to discriminate between the efficient hypothesis (the relationship between profitability and size) and the market power hypothesis (the relationship between concentration and profitability). The main problem of this simple regression is the omission of other relevant variables, for example, an indicator of the demand for banking services or an indicator of the management ability of assets and liabilities of banks. For this reason, this section presents a more general model including other variables which go toward explaining the evolution of profitability.

Chapter 5 developed a theoretical model regarding the profit maximisation behaviour of banks. When the authorities introduce deposit interest rate controls, the profit identity is defined as:

$$\pi_i = rl.L_i + r_o.O_i - rd.D_i - m.D_i - C(B_i) - C(A_i) - C(L_i, D_i) \tag{6.4}$$

where π_i are profits, $rl.L_i$ revenues from loans, $ro.O_i$ revenues from other alternative investments, $rd.D_i$ the interest cost of deposits, $m.D_i$ the non-interest costs of taking more deposits (free services, lottery, and so on) and what we called implicit remunerations, $C(B_i)$ the costs of increasing the number of branches, $C(A_i)$ the advertising costs and $C(L_i,D_i)$ the operating costs.

Although the elasticity of demand is an important factor in determining profitability, empirical work has left this variable out of the estimations. Following Waterson (1988: 191), the main reason is that 'estimates of elasticities of demand for industrial goods are difficult to obtain.' As we do not know what the value of the demand elasticity on deposits and loans was in each year of the period under analysis, I will introduce into the profitability function one of the main determinants of the deposits demand function: the per capita GDP. As the implicit interest rate is an unobservable variable too, some 'proxies' of this variable were included.

In the selection of the relevant variables I have followed the works of Fanjul and Maravall (1985) who analysed the main determinants of Spanish banking profitability in 1979, and Lloyds-Williams and Molyneaux (1994) who tested the structure-conduct-performance and the efficiency hypothesis for the Spanish banking industry from 1986 to 1988. Considering the lack of information about several variables and the characteristics of the period, I have estimated a profitability function (where profitability = profits/(capital + reserves)) for the Big Five banks including:

1. A concentration index (*CR*). To measure market concentration I have considered two possibilities:
   a) an absolute index of concentration, or the percentage of total volume of deposits of the Big Five banks, and
   b) the Herfindahl index, defined as $\sum s_i^2$, where s_i is the percentage of deposits in the hands of every firm in the banking sector. This index goes from unity in the monopoly case to zero in a market with many small firms.
2. The market share of this bank (*MS*) as an indicator of size, or the volume of deposits of the bank i with respect to the volume of deposits of the

Spanish banking system. The bank's market share of the firm is defined as $MS = D_i/D$.

3. Two indicators of the assets structure of the bank. The idea is to include some indicators of the management of assets and liabilities of each bank. These two indicators are:

   a) the relationship between loans and securities plus commercial bills as an indicator of asset composition (*Cred*).
   b) the percentage of public bonds bank holds with respect to the total assets of the bank (*fp*). The bank's portfolio of securities was composed of two items: government bonds and private bonds and shares, of which the former was considerably more important.

   A descriptive analysis of these two variables shows the following results. There is a possible negative relationship between the 'loans/(securities + commercial bills)' ratio and profitability. Those banks with higher proportions of 'public bonds/total assets', had lower rates of profitability.
4. The ratio short-term deposits total deposits as an indicator of the composition of liabilities (*Dc*). This variable was influenced by regulation. As I have just mentioned, regulation controlled the rate of interest on deposits and this affected the incentives to hold long-term deposits. The ratio did not fluctuate very much between 1942 and 1951. After this year the proportion of short-term deposits to the total volume of deposits had a downward trend.
5. The relationship between the total non-financial cost and the total own assets (G). When regulations restrict competition through price controls, banks make use of other alternative mechanisms to increase their market share. And this 'non-price' competition has a direct impact on financial (through commissions and other payments) and non-financial (more branches, gifts, and so on) remunerations. For this reason, the sign of the relationship between this variable and profitability can be ambiguous. *Ceteris paribus*, when cost increases profitability must decline. However, in the banking sector there are other possible explanations of this relationship (Martínez Méndez 1991). First, in many cases an increase in profitability has meant a necessary increase in costs, especially to finance banking expansion and to increase market share. Second, an increase in costs could have raised the volume of deposits taken by banks and then the final effect would have been a positive effect on profitability.

Some evidence of the evolution of banking costs is provided in Table 6.4.

The ratio 'operating costs/(capital + reserves)' grew from 1942 to the mid-1960s and declined from 1967 to 1970. The main reason for this

Table 6.4 The evolution of Spanish banking costs for the Big Five banks

	Operating costs/ (K + R) (percentages)	Operating costs/ Total assets (percentages)	Ratio profits/ Operating costs
1942	22.5	14.5	0.57
1945	23.6	14.6	0.73
1950	30.7	12.1	0.64
1955	35.5	12.4	0.63
1960	35.1	14.0	0.63
1965	36.8	13.6	0.39
1970	31.9	14.3	0.46
1975	38.5	15.4	0.46

Sources: Annual Banking Reports, Big Five banks.

result is the *Ley de Regularización de Balances* of 1967. This law regularised the value of the capital and reserves of banks to narrow the difference between the market value of banking (capital + reserves) and the value registered in the balance accounts. With the ratio of profits to operating costs, the index grew from 1942 to 1948 but it shows a smooth downward trend from 1948 to 1965. After this year the index is around (0.42–0.46).

Unfortunately it is not possible to estimate the bank cost function because for this period there is no information about some of its main determinants (for example, wages).[12] The analysis of the relationship between the cost 'per unit' (operating costs/own assets) and own assets (as a measure of size) for the Big Five banks (Figure 6.11) in 1946, 1952, 1962 and 1973 indicates that, with the exception of 1973, there was a positive relationship between size and costs 'per unit' (Martin Aceña and Pons 1995: 334–39). Thus, there is no evidence of increasing efficiency after the 1962 Banking Law.

6. The ratio between own assets and total assets (CG=RP/A). The sign of this relationship depends on the cost of own assets and the cost of external funds.

   The relationship between own assets and total assets has a downward trend from 1942 to 1957. From this year the index has many ups (1957–1960 and 1965–1967) and downs (1960–1965 and 1967–1975).

7. The per capita income (gGDPpc). Demand conditions in the market are measured by per capita NI. When the per capita NI increases there are

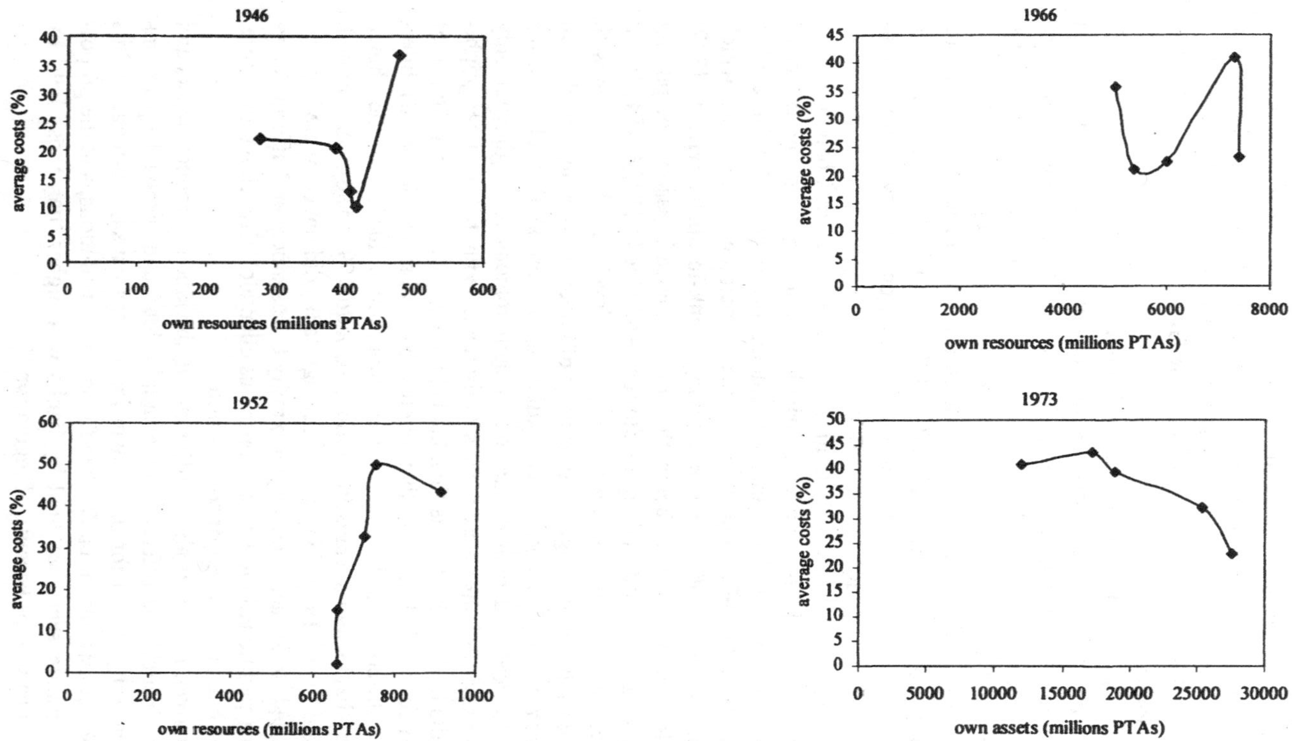

Figure 6.11 The relationship between size and cost of the Big Five banks

Sources: Annual Reports and *Balances Consolidados de la Banca Privada* (SBC).

more incentives to save than with low-income levels. Then, the sign of this relationship must be positive. I have made use of the per head GDP series instead of the per capita NI because this series has been revised recently (Prados 1995).[13] The rate of growth of the GDP may include the effect of the economic cycle.

I have also included the proportion of the GDP produced by the agricultural sector as an indicator of structural change (Ag). It is assumed that when a country is more developed the demand for banking services increases. Then, when the relative size of the agricultural sector decreases, the demand for banking services increases and banking profitability too.

8. With respect to the conjectural variations, it is very difficult to accept that they were constant over the period and that the Big Five banks had the same conjectural variations. Unfortunately, we do not have any information about the evolution of this variable.

9. Competition from savings institutions (Sav). As said in Chapter 2, it is extremely difficult to include a variable which 'captures' the effect of competition from savings banks on banking profitability. Recent studies indicate (Coello 1997) that there are many sociological variables which explain the choice of a bank or a savings bank in Spain. Wright (1977: 110), for example, spoke about the 'psychological' reasons for putting money in a non-profit making institution. And Coello (1997: 184) found that people with low incomes, with a low level of education or with unskilled jobs have a higher probability of choosing a savings bank than people with a higher level of education and a more skilled job. Savings banks concentrated their expansion in their regions of origin, not only because savings banks were more strictly regulated in terms of geographical limits to their operations than banks, but because of the importance of the non-economic links with their clients (cultural and sociological). Interest rate differentials did not have an important influence on the choice between banks and savings institutions (Coello 1997: 186). As Caminal, Gual and Vives (1990: 281) assert, savings banks did not compete in price. They tried 'to attract clients by proximity to customers and offering services to a traditionally less price-conscious clientele'. Branching, therefore, was the main instrument of competition.

Moreover, there was also a difference in the kind of products banks and savings institutions offered. For example, loan and discount operations were more important for banks than for savings banks. Mortgage credits were less important for banks than for savings institutions, and the proportion of public securities held by banks was higher than those held by savings institutions because of regulation.[14]

As an indicator of the competition from savings banks the ratio between the total volume of deposits in the hands of savings banks and the total volume of deposits in the hands of the banking sector was included. When savings institutions increase their market share (and so increasing the ratio (Sav)), the profitability of banks will decrease.

10. Dummy (t). This dummy variable reflects the change in regulation after the 1962 Banking Law.

The complete regression equation to be estimated is:

$$\begin{aligned}\text{Profitability} = {} & a_0 + a_1 MS + a_2 CR + a_3 CRMS + a_4 cred + a_5 fp + a_6 DC \\ & + a_7 G + a_8 CG + a_9 .L/D + a_{10} gGDPpc + a_{11} Ag + a_{12} Sav \\ & + Dummyt + dummies \end{aligned} \tag{6.5}$$

The regressions results are reported in Tables 6.5 and 6.6. As explained above, I estimated four regressions: (eq. 6.5.1) and (eq. 6.6.1) use an absolute index of concentration whereas regressions (eq. 6.5.2) and (eq. 6.6.2) use the Herfindahl index. As we can see, below the results of each regression there is an F-test. With this F-test we can see whether the dummy variables as a group are significant or not. Only in equation 6.6.2, are the dummy variables not significant at a level of 95 per cent, although they are on the limit of being acceptable.

With respect to the period 1920–1975, when we consider an absolute index of concentration (eq. 6.5.1), *MS* is significant and has the sign the theory predicts. This result is consistent with those obtained in other previous results (Maudos 1996). *CR* is not significant and it has the opposite sign of that hypothesised. When we consider the Herfindahl index as an indicator of the level of concentration of the banking industry, both variables *MS* and *H* are significant at a 95 per cent level (eq. 6.5.2). However, the sign of *H* is the opposite of the one the theory predicts (if we accept the collusion hypothesis). According to Smirlock's test, we cannot accept the collusion hypothesis.

The results of the regression for the period 1942–1975 are different. When we use an absolute index of concentration the variables *MS* and *CR* are significant at a 95 per cent level and both variables have the expected sign. According to Smirlock (1985), when *MS* and *CR* are significant, we can make use of the 'interaction' variable to interpret the result: if the interaction variable is positive, we accept the collusion hypothesis and if the interaction variable is negative, we accept the efficient hypothesis. In equation 6.6.1, the interaction variable *CRMS* has a negative sign. When we alternatively include the Herfindahl index *H*, neither the market share nor the concentration index are significant at a 95 per cent level.

In the light of the effect of per capita income on banking profitability, rather surprisingly, per capita gGDP does not affect banking profitability. The indicator of structural change *Ag* (the relative participation of the agricultural sector in the economy) is significant and with the sign the theory predicts in the regression for the period 1920–1945: when the participation of the agricultural sector in the economy is reduced, banking profitability increases.

The main result obtained is that the main variables which explain profitability are related more to the management by these five banks of their resources than to concentration. The ratio between non-financial costs and the own assets *G*, the composition of deposits *Dc*, and the percentage of 'loans/(securities + commercial bills)' 'Cred' were statistically significant.[15] The variable which represents savings banks competition *Sav* is also significant and with the expected sign. Finally, the dummy included to 'capture' the effect of the 1962 Banking Law is also significant.

As we can see, the relationship between profitability and the ratio 'non-financial cost/own resources' is positive. As explained before, when the authorities control the rate of interest, banks try to attract deposits by inducements in the addition to the payment of explicit deposit rates. The main problem is that this implicit rate of interest is non-observable, although we must expect that an increase in the implicit interest rate would be reflected in an increase in the non-financial costs of banks. In this case, my results show that profitability was linked to the ability of banks to produce 'implicit' remunerations.

The negative relationship between 'loans/(securities+commercial bills)' and profitability could be an indicator of the advantages of a more 'universal' or mixed banking orientation: those banks less 'commercially orientated' were more profitable.

The results for the regression for the period 1942–1975 are very similar. The variables which explain banking profitability are: the market share *MS*, the percentage of short-term deposits with respect to the total volume of deposits *Dc*, the relationship between non-financial cost and own assets *G*, the ratio *own assets/total assets CG*, the savings banks competition *Sav* and the *Dummyt*. With respect to the ratio *loans/(securities+commercial bills)* Cred, although it has the same sign as in the 1920–1975 estimate, in (eq. 6.6.1) it is not significant at a 95 per cent level. Only the absolute index of concentration *CR* is significant at a 95 per cent level.

In general, the main variables which explain banking profitability are related to the management that the Big Five banks made of their assets and liabilities. Those banks with a lower ratio of own assets/total assets, a lower percentage of short-term deposits with respect to total deposits, and a higher ratio *non-financial costs/own assets*, obtained a higher rate of profitability. The sign of the relationship between the percentage of short-term deposits and profitability is difficult to interpret. As these results indicate, lower financial costs have a positive effect on profitability, and short-term deposits are less costly to banks than long-term deposits. However, a greater percentage of short-term deposits increases banking instability and this fact can affect investment decisions. Throughout most of the period under study the cost of deposits (even long-term deposits) was relatively low, and so it is possible that the advantages of having more long-term deposits (in terms of stability) were greater than the costs (in terms of interest rates) of these deposits.

With respect to the ratio *own assets/total assets*, this ratio was affected directly and indirectly by regulation. For example, dividend controls encourage banks to accumulate more reserves. Alternatively these dividends which could not be paid out could be invested in higher costs or *G* (for example, if they were spent in branch proliferation). My econometric results show that in the estimated regressions for the period 1920–1975, *CG* is not significant. However, in the period 1942–1975, those banks with lower ratio *own assets/total assets* obtained higher rates of profitability. As regulation on dividends affects *G* and *CG*, it is not possible to affirm that the final effect of dividend controls on profitability was negative.

If, as showed above, market share has a positive effect on profitability, can these results be interpreted as support of the efficiency structure hypothesis? Is market share a proxy for efficiency? As Berger (1995) pointed out, market share cannot be interpreted as a proxy for efficiency. But in the same line, concentration is not a good indicator of collusion. The main conclusion reached is that it is necessary to look at other variables different to concentration and market share to come to any clear conclusion about the level of competition of the Spanish banking sector in this period.

The influence of the character of 'mixed' banks on banking profitability

My research does not allow me to reach a conclusion about the existence of different interest rates for participating and non-participating firms. Table 6.5 indicates that for the period 1920–1975 those banks with a lower *loans/(securities + commercial bills)* ratio obtained higher rates of profitability. However, this variable is not significant at a 95 per cent level in the period 1942–1975. For this reason, other 'qualitative' information has been analysed regarding the relationship between banks and their subsidiary firms and the existence of credit discrimination.

With respect to banking representation on firm supervisory boards and its lending practices, Villalonga (President of the *Banco Central* from 1943 to relationship between the percentage of short-term deposits and profitability [illegible]. As these results indicate, lower financial costs are positively [illegible] profitability, and [illegible] short-term deposits [illegible]. [illegible] that long-term deposits [illegible]. However, a greater percentage of short-term deposits [illegible] and has [illegible] effect [illegible]. Throughout [illegible] of the period [illegible] deposits [illegible] [illegible]

With respect to the [illegible] was affected [illegible] dividend [illegible] dividends which could not [illegible] if they were [illegible] in the period [illegible]. However, in the period 1962–[illegible] obtained higher rates of profitability [illegible]. It is [illegible] that the [illegible] of dividend policy on profitability was negative.

[illegible] above [illegible] efficiency [illegible] [illegible] Spanish banking sector [illegible].

The influence of the size variable on the ratios of banking profitability

[illegible] allow us to [illegible] conclusion about the existence of [illegible] the period 1962–1975 [illegible] higher rates of profitability. However, [illegible] is not significant [illegible] in the period 1962–1975. For this reason, [illegible] has been analysed [illegible] between banks [illegible] concentration.

With respect to banking [illegible] supervisory boards [illegible]

Table 6.6 Regression of the profitability function, 1942–1975

Dependent Variable PROF – Estimation by Least Squares
Panel(50) of Undated Data From 1//01 To 5//50
Usable Observations: 170 Degrees of Freedom: 153
Total Observations: 250 Skipped/Missing: 80
Centred R≤: 0.61999 Mean of Dependent Variable: 16.3548
Std Error of Dependent Variable: 3.28573 Standard Error of Estimate: 2.128739
Sum of Squared Residuals: 693.3416 Regression F(14,121): 15.6014

	Eq (6.6.1)			Eq (6.6.2)	
	Coeff	T-Stat		Coeff	T-Stat
1.Constant	18.9283	1.3544	1.Constant	51.2163	7.1742
2.MS	2.0481	2.1894	2.MS	0.0971	0.9104
3.CR	0.3716	2.1864	3.H	–0.6486	–1.2789
4.CRMS	–0.0292	–2.0979			
5.CG	–0.5144	–3.8651	4.CG	–0.5120	–2.1043
6.Dc	–0.1853	–3.8651	5.Dc	–0.1613	–3.2910
7.Cred	–0.0496	–1.6826	6.Cred	–0.0845	–3.0178
8.G	0.11577	3.7121	7.G	0.0938	3.1445
9.Fp	–0.0848	–1.3321	8.Fp	–0.1018	–1.6000
10.Caj	–0.1762	–2.0311	9.Caj	–0.2385	–2.7781
11.gGDPpc	–0.1009	–1.6804	10.gGDPpc	–0.0766	1.2835
12.Ag	–0.1596	–1.6921	11.Ag	–0.0998	–1.0051
13.Dummyt	–4.3071	–4.7268	12.Dummyt	–5.0001	–5.3343
14.DUM1	1.2432	1.1646	13.DUM1	–0.1093	–0.1142
15.DUM2	1.3086	1.3924	14.DUM2	0.5792	0.6705
16.DUM3	0.0600	0.0790	15.DUM3	0.7619	1.0395
17.DUM4	3.1107	2.3747	16.DUM4	1.5578	1.5041

F-Test: significance of the dummy variables
F(4,157) = 3.01846 with Significance Level 0.01968
F(4,158) = 2.40472 with Significance Level 0.051927.

With the information of the *Central de Información de Riesgos* (Centre for Informational Risks), Rubio, Barbé, Taules and Aranguren (1972) analysed the existence of credit discrimination in the Spanish banking sector from 1968 to 1970. The hypothesis they tested was whether in crisis periods banks supplied more loans to large firms rather than to small ones. If we consider that banks had a higher participation in big firms, the analysis of the volume of credit supplied to small and large firms could be an indicator of the existence of credit discrimination in favour of the 'subordinate' firms. Their evidence allowed them to accept this hypothesis. However, small firms are in most cases more risky than big firms and, then, to reduce the volume of credits supplied to small firms in periods of crisis, may be the result of the profit maximising behaviour of banks and not the result of credit discrimination in favour of participating firms.

De Miguel and Linz (1963) interviewed many firms to establish the attitude of entrepreneurs towards banks. The interviews were conducted with 466 firms classified into small firms (firms between 50–99 workers) and big firms (more than 99 workers), in 13 provinces (Madrid, Barcelona, Vizcaya, Guipuzcoa, Sevilla, Asturias, Valencia, Alicante, Zaragoza, Cadiz, Cordoba, Coruña and Pontevedra). The main conclusions they obtained were:

1. Big firms were more satisfied with the services supplied by the banking sector than small firms.
2. There is no evidence that small firms preferred small banks.
3. Large firms had a higher dependency with respect to credit than small firms. In the sample, 18 per cent of the small firms had links with a bank and 52 per cent of large firms had links with a bank. In general, firms with banking participation (in terms of capital participation or common members on the board of directors) had a higher volume of credit than non-participating firms.
4. The characteristics of the entrepreneurs (age, education, province, etc.) were very significant in understanding their lending behaviour. For example, young managers had a higher recourse of external finance than old managers. There are also significant differences among regions. Catalan entrepreneurs demanded less credit than in the North of Spain or Madrid (especially in the case of big firms).

All this information, therefore, shows that participating firms had higher volumes of credit than non-participating firms. This effect could be the result of credit discrimination or the result of lesser risk. There is no information with respect to the cost of credit. To know what the main lending practices were it would be necessary to have information about the operations; in this sense, only confidential bank records could offer empirical evidence about the role of Spanish banks in the industrial finance of small business. Only with this information would it be possible to reach a conclusion about the convenience (or not) of considering Spanish banks as profit-maximising firms.

Table 6.7 Coefficients of variations, Big Five banks

A. The coefficient of variation of the *profits/(capital + reserves)* ratio, Big Five banks

	Bilbao	Central	Español	Hispano	Vizcaya	Average
1942–52	0.1672	0.2898	0.2389	0.1483	0.1638	0.1638
1953–62	0.0666	0.1407	0.1154	0.1468	0.0687	0.0687
1962–75	0.23	0.1688	0.1927	0.2825	0.2825	0.1802

B. The coefficient of variation of the *profits/deposits* ratio, Big Five banks

	Bilbao	Central	Español	Hispano	Vizcaya	Average
1942–52	0.2619	0.2426	0.2295	0.1273	0.0894	0.7996
1953–62	0.1168	0.1709	0.1185	0.1634	0.0095	0.0982
1962–75	0.1303	0.0513	0.2777	0.1543	0.1206	0.1663

C. The coefficient of variation of profits, Big Five banks

	Bilbao	Central	Español	Hispano	Vizcaya	Average
1942–52	0.512	0.8345	0.5672	0.4132	0.4893	0.5447
1953–62	0.4	0.3169	0.3838	0.4358	0.3593	0.378
1962–75	0.7828	0.9043	0.8305	0.6538	0.7087	0.7736

D. The coefficient of variation of deposits, Big Five banks

	Bilbao	Central	Español	Hispano	Vizcaya	Average
1942–52	0.4869	0.7323	0.4963	0.4515	0.5112	0.4622
1953–62	0.4727	0.4148	0.384	0.3742	0.4198	0.4023
1962–75	0.6923	0.7025	0.581	0.5491	0.617	0.6225

Sources: Annual Reports Big Five banks and *Balances Consolidados de la Banca Privada* (SBC).

Table 6.8 The coefficient of variation of profits, deposits and loans in real terms (average Big Five banks)

	Profits	Deposits	Loans
1942–52	0.1588	0.125137	0.507176
1953–62	0.2185	0.23194	0.445854
1963–75	0.5435	0.404979	0.751609

Sources: Annual Reports Big Five banks, *Balances Consolidados de la Banca Privada* (SBC) and for prices, De Ojeda Eiseley (1988).

III. Banking regulation and risk

Until now I have assumed that financial regulation could reinforce monopoly power and this would have an impact on profitability. Another possibility is that banks with monopoly power do not achieve higher benefits but that they may be more secure. As Heggestad (1977: 1209) indicates, 'part of the potential profits inherent in monopoly power are being taken in the form of reduced risk.' In this section I have estimated a measure of risk for different periods characterised by significantly different regulatory environments to analyse the possible changes in this variable.

I have estimated the coefficient of variation of two indicators of profitability: *profits/(capital + reserves)*, and *profits/deposits* for the Big Five banks. I have divided the sample 1942–1975 into three sub-samples: 1942–1952, where a higher level of risk and instability is assumed because of the consequences of the Civil War; 1953–1962, a period where – thanks to protective regulation – banks had a very stable framework; and finally, 1963–1975, a period with a priory higher instability as a consequence of the regulatory change that occurred in 1962 with the *Ley de Bases*.

Table 6.7 shows significant stability from 1942–1962 (especially in the period 1953–1962) and an increase in risk in the last period, 1963–1975, with the exception of the *Banco Central* (with a lower coefficient of variation of the ratio *profits/deposits* in the period 1963–1975).

If we take into account prices, results are very similar. The evolution of profits, deposits and loans in real terms shows that the most 'risky' period was 1962–1970. These results demonstrate that the change in regulation after the 1962 Banking Law was an important determinant in the stability of real bank profits, deposits and loans (see Table 6.8).

IV. Conclusion

In this chapter the effect of regulation on banking behaviour was estimated. In particular I concentrated on:

a) the effects of interest controls on bank strategies,
b) the relationship between the regulatory framework, concentration and profitability,
c) the main determinants of the Spanish banking profitability and
d) the relationship between regulation and risk.

As explained in Chapter 5, when banks cannot compete in price for customer deposits, they have an incentive to engage in various forms of non-price competition. The first question asked, therefore, is whether it is possible to obtain an indicator of these various forms of competition.

In considering the effect of interest controls on the behaviour of the Big Five Spanish banks, the major implication of this study is that bank strategy to compete for customer deposits changed during this period. Private banks signed several agreements to fix interest rates: they fixed the rate of interest on deposits below the legal maximum and the loan interest rate under the legal minimum. The government supported these private agreements. But the main question is: was banking behaviour conditioned by these cartel agreements? As we do not have information about the loan side of the market, I have concentrated on deposits.

When we compare the ratio *financial cost of deposits/total deposits* with the legal maximum interest rate on deposits the results are clear. In the 1940s interest controls did not prevent collusion and banks paid a deposit interest rate lower than the legal ceiling. In the 1950s banking behaviour was different. Although I have found empirical evidence of the existence of cartel agreements to fix banking conditions until 1952, from 1950 financial costs were under the legal maximum deposit interest rate. The main explanation for this fact is that banks developed strategies to take more deposits through 'extra-rates' or implicit interest remuneration. There are two possibilities. First, that the legal maximum deposit interest rate was below the monopolistic deposit interest rate, and banks adopted an agreement to pay 'extra-rates' or other implicit remuneration. Second, that banks competed to take deposits. The difference between the financial cost of deposits and the legal ceiling was very important from 1957 to 1968. Both the Reports from the Bank of England Archives about the evolution of the Spanish banking system and the Tortella and García (1999) work suggest that banks broke interest rate agreements and paid 'extra-rates'.

To sum up, in the 1940s interest rate regulation allowed banks to use monopoly power to exploit depositors. However, from 1950, in spite of cartel agreements, banks paid remunerations on deposits higher than the regulated deposit interest rate. This empirical evolution of financial costs shows how the regulatory measures affect the strategy variables banks choose to maximise profits. When the authorities regulate prices they introduce other mechanisms – that we have defined as 'implicit interest rates' – or pay 'extra-rates' in order to take more deposits.

Then, evidence shows that there was a change in banking performance from the beginning of the 1950s and the question is whether this change was the result of an increase in competition or not. Various indicators of competition have been used. First of all, we looked at the degree of concentration. In general, one would expect collusion to be easier among a small number of larger banks than in a more atomistic industry. In terms of deposits, concentration increased from the end of the Civil War to the 1950s. From 1950 (when we made use of the Herfindhal index) or from 1959 (when we made use of an absolute index of concentration) the positive trend in the level of concentration of the Spanish banking system was interrupted. This fact has been used as an indicator of an increase in competition in the Spanish banking system in this period. However, concentration is not a good indicator of competition, especially as it does not reflect the cost structure of firms. For this reason I have used other alternative indicators of the degree of competition.

The second variable considered is profitability. One would expect that low competitive pressure would translate into high profits. Figure 6.5 presents the rate of profitability of the Big Five banks. In the post-war years, the rate of profitability was low. However, it increased substantially in the 1940s and 1950s. This positive trend changed in 1958. The decrease in profitability was interrupted in 1968, although banks obtained lower levels of profitability than in the 1950s. The main result obtained is that the decrease in profitability took place before the *Ley de Bases* of 1962. The evolution of profitability does not show an apparent relationship between this variable and the changes in the regulatory framework.

When we compare the rate of profitability of the Big Five banks with the average rate of profitability of Spanish firms results are difficult to interpret. With respect to the spread between the profitability of the Big Five banks and an estimation of the rate of profitability of Spanish firms, I have not obtained a relationship between the evolution of this 'spread' and the changes in the financial regulation. In fact, the 'spread' between bank profitability rates and the average rate of profitability of the rest of firms increased from 1966, especially from 1970. If we take into account that from the end of the 1950s Spain experienced a general process of liberalisation of the Spanish economy, this fact may reflect a slower process of liberalisation in banking than in the rest of the sectors. It may also reflect the problems of comparing different indicators of profitability.

If we look at the intermediation margins (with all the imperfections and problems that my indicator has), my estimates show that there was an important increase in the spread from 1942 to 1957. In this year the trend changed and the interest margin declined until 1962. The spread rose from 1962 to decrease again in 1967. From 1967 this variable increased again. Then, we cannot affirm that the interest margin decreased as a consequence of the process of liberalisation which started with the Banking Law of 1962. We obtain similar results when we consider the profits derived from the issues of capital and the evolution of the stock market or *plusvalías*. In this case, the higher profits were obtained in the post-1962 period. In the 1940s and 1950s, banks aimed to increase their profitability rates and achieved moderately increased profits through the new issues of capital. Although we can consider that in this period private banks consolidated their monopolistic power thanks to the existence of barriers to entry, there were some regulatory measures which constrained the banking performance such as the restrictions in the distribution of profits, in branch expansion, and so on. In the 1960s, theoretically there started a period of relative liberalisation of the banking sector in some areas. Branching restrictions were removed and entry was in theory less restricted. The removal of some restrictions and the maintainance of some privileges in certain areas (especially, the existence of barriers to entry to foreign banks, or the new regulatory changes which favoured the issues of capital) allowed Spanish banks not only not to decrease substantially their rates of profitability but also to obtain important profits through the issues of capital and the control of the stock market.

On the whole, the following picture emerges: the evolution of concentration, financial cost, profitability and the intermediation margin of the Big Five banks indicate that there was a change in the performance of the Spanish banking system from 1950 in comparison with the 1940s. We cannot identify this change with an increase in competition because there were many regulatory constraints that avoided competition. Despite this, the estimate of the ratio *financial costs/deposits*, the Tortella and García Ruiz research and the Reports from the Bank of England Archives indicate that the largest banks adopted different strategies in their interest rate policies. However, the increase in the interest spread, the average rate of profitability of the Big Five banks and the *plusvalias* from the late 1960s do not allow us to draw any conclusions about the links between the change in the regulatory framework associated with the *Ley de Bases* of 1962 and the degree of competition of the Spanish banking system.

An econometric analysis has been carried out to determine the main determinants of the profitability of the Big Five banks from 1920 to 1975. Empirical results do not provide clear evidence either about the efficiency hypothesis or the market power hypotheses.

An important result is the link found between profitability and those variables related to bank management of their resources: the ratio *non-financial costs/own resources*, the ratio *own resources/total assets*, the percentage of short-term deposits to the total volume of deposits and the ratio *loans/(securities + commercial bills)*. Profitability falls with the ratio of short-term deposits to total deposits. Banks heavily committed to short-term deposits earn considerably lower returns. Furthermore, those banks with a lower percentage of loans securities and commercial bills obtain higher rates of profitability. The ratio *non-financial cost/own resources*, shows a positive relationship between this variable and profitability. There are two interpretations of this fact. First, because regulation forced banks to limit explicit pricing of payments in an attempt to retain their deposit base, banks competed through various forms of implicit interest payments. This non-price competition took the form of free financial services and additional branches to provide customers with closer geographic services. As banking is traditionally a labour-intensive industry, the main result of this policy was an important increase in the operating cost. According to our estimates, the influence of this increase in operating costs on profitability was positive. Second, we can change the direction of the causality and consider that the availability to banks of increasing implicit remunerations – especially, through branches – was linked to the profitability of banks. Only banks with very high levels of profitability were allowed to increase the number of branches and the remuneration to take more deposits.

The evolution of banking costs does not indicate the existence of scale economies. Banks of a greater size had higher ratios of cost to own assets. The situation changed at the beginning of the 1970s when banks of a greater size had a lower ratio *cost/own assets*.

The main conclusion reached is that concentration and market share do not offer much information about the level of competition of the banking sector in this period.

Finally, I have analysed the influence of regulation on risk. The main result obtained is that the regulatory framework reduced the instability of the Spanish banking system in nominal terms. In real terms the result obtained is the same: the highest coefficient of variation in the evolution of profits, deposits and loans in real terms was in the period 1962–1975.

Notes

1 The SBC called these agreements *Ordenación Reguladora de Condiciones Mínimas*. The first reference regarding these 'formal' agreements is found in 1949 in *España Económica y Financiera* (Tortella and García Ruiz 1993: 153), although it is impossible to know if there were previous agreements.
2 The government established the '*Junta de Vigilancia*' and the '*Junta Superior*' to control these agreements.
3 I would like to thank Gabriel Tortella and Jose Luis García Ruiz for showing me the main results of their unpublished work.
4 We can assume that when loan rates are high, banks have a higher incentive to pay higher interest rates on deposits. However, in a monopolistic market, banks can maintain low deposit interest rates and high loan interest rates to obtain monopolistic profits.
5 There were some important differences among the way these banks presented their financial statements, but I have re-estimated the amount of gross and net profits to make them homogeneous. I will explain this in more detail in the following section.
6 See, for example, the arguments of Fanjul and Maravall (1985), about the increase in competition in the late 1950s and 1960s as a consequence of a reduction in administrative controls in the Spanish financial system.
7 This is a very important limitation because banks can make use of these depreciation costs to 'manipulate' their volume of profits.
8 Real profitability is defined as: $\pi_r(t)/K_r(t) = ((1+r_n)/(1+p) - 1)$.
There is a relationship between the total volume of capital K and the yield on this capital r_n. We know that:

$$K(t+1) = (1 + r_n).K(t) \quad (1)$$

if we consider the influence of prices p:

$$p(t+1).K(t+1) = (1 + r_n).K(t).p(t) \quad (2)$$

then, in real terms K_r we have

$$K_r(t+1) = (1 + r_n).(p(t)/p(t+1)).K_r(t) \text{ or } K_r(t+1) = [(1 + r_n)/(1 + \dot{p})].K_r(t) \quad (3)$$

where $\dot{p}$ is the rate of inflation.

$$\text{If } K(t+1) = (1 + r_n).K(t) = K(t) + (\pi t) \quad (4)$$

where π are profits. Then,

$$K_r(t+1) = K_r(t) + [(1 + r_n)/(1 + \dot{p})) - 1].K_r(t) \quad (5)$$

where $[(1 + r_n)/(1 + \dot{p}) - 1]$ are profits in real terms $\pi_r(t)$

$$K_r(t+1) = K_r(t) + \pi r(t)$$

If we divide this expression by K_t:

$$K(t+1)/K_r(t) = 1 + (\pi_r(t)/K_r(t))$$

and reorganising and considering equation (5), we obtain:

$$\pi_r(t)/K_r(t) = ((1 + r_n)/(1 + \dot{p}) - 1).$$

9 Lopez Muñoz was the pseudonym that Santiago Roldán, Juan Muñoz, Arturo Cabello and Jose Luis García Delgado used to publish some articles in different newspapers and journals about the situation of the Spanish economy in the 1960s. Most of these articles were summarised in Lopez Muñoz (1967) and Lopez Muñoz (1968).

10 *Plusvalía* = [value of capital in the stock market in (t) – value of capital in the stock market in (t–n)] – [capital in (t) – capital in (t–n)] where the value of capital in the stock market = the number of shares × the nominal value of the share × the stock market index.

11 The average rate of profitability of the Big Five banks was influenced by the bad results of the Banco Central until 1945.

12 The Annual Reports indicate that wages were around 85–90 per cent of the 'operating cost'. However, I do not have information about the number of employees in the banking sector. For this reason I cannot estimate the average wage paid by banks.

13 Prados (1995: 4–11) explains the main shortcomings of a set of national accounts for Spain: the CEN, Alcaide, Schwartz, Naredo and Carreras estimates.

14 Ross Hombravella (1967: 138–9) compares the investment structure of Spanish savings institutions in a sample of 15 countries. His results show that the percentage of public securities was higher in Spain than in the rest of the countries considered. The main reason for this is that Spanish savings banks were legally required to invest a minimum of 60 per cent of their deposits in public securities.

15 I have obtained very similar results when I have estimated an individual profitability equation for each of the Big Five banks. The estimated profitability function for the period 1920–1975 shows that only in two cases the index of concentration (*CR*) is significant. The effect of market share is very ambiguous. This variable is significant at the 1 per cent level in three cases but only in the *Banco Central* is the effect of market share on profitability positive. Then, we cannot accept the efficient structure. The main variables which explain profitability are: a) the ratio *non-financial costs/own assets* (*G*). This variable was significant for four banks, b) the ratio *own resources/total assets* (*CG*). This was significant for two banks and c) the percentage of short-term deposits (*Dc*). This variable was significant for two banks also.

CHAPTER SEVEN

Conclusions

The literature on regulation suggests two alternative reasons for the Spanish banking legislation in the period 1940–1975. The first suggests that regulation offsets market failures. The second, that regulation is a means of using state power to further an industry's own interests. Conventional wisdom emphasises the importance of the links between banks and government, which are seen as evidence of the capture of the Franco government by the banking sector. The Franco government has been seen as a passive actor that regulated in response to pressures from society, especially industrial and banking pressures (Braña, Buesa and Molero 1984 or Lukauskas 1992). Although this view is widespread, it ignores the fact that the regime itself had a programme of industrialisation and it needed the collaboration of the banking sector to achieve its goals. As explained in Chapter 4, the interest of the banking sector in minimising risk and maximising profits and the objective of accelerated industrialisation of the Franco government, both had a strong influence on Spanish financial legislation under the Franco regime. Nevertheless, this latter intention of the Franco government to use financial regulation as an instrument to develop its economic programme was the most prominent.

The Franco government did not 'officially' justify interventionism in the banking sector. However, if we take into consideration the works of some authors closely linked to the Franco government such as Paris Eguilaz, who was the Chairman of the National Economic Council, or Sáez de Ibarra, who was the Deputy-Governor of the Bank of Spain and Vice-president of the SBC and who, according to the Bank of Spain Directors' Minutes had a very important role in the design of the 1946 BSL, we can consider that the main 'declared' reasons for regulating the banking sector were:

a) as a necessity for the reconstruction of the banking sector after the Civil War,
b) as a means of avoiding monopolistic behaviour, and
c) for allocative purposes.

The Franco authorities established two sorts of measures for stability. The first was designed to curb the 'excessive' expansion of the banking system and the second was connected with monetary policy. The former group included different measures such as prohibitions on the constitution of new banks and restrictions in the opening of branches. After the Civil War there were relatively few failures or bankruptcies. There are two main reasons for this absence of failures: banks in difficulties merged with bigger banks; the Bank of Spain always helped banks with financial problems. But the cost of this stability was high. First, in terms of efficiency. From the end of the Civil War to the late 1950s there was a significant number of mergers and the level of concentration increased substantially. However, there was an important number of small banks. These banks played a very small role in the banking system and they were not forced to increase their efficiency or to compete. In general, there was little growth in the average size of banks, and from the end of the Spanish Civil War to the 1980s there were no mergers among the 'core' banks. Although the low level of economic development and the weakness of the industrial sector (the demand side of the market) are other explanatory factors of the Spanish financial structure, it remains true that the lack of competition was the main determinant of the survival of most of the very small banks.

The existence of barriers to entry not only affected the banking structure's size but its diversification too, as shown in Chapter 2. Financial regulation limited the development of other alternative financial institutions such as savings institutions, insurance companies and other financial markets such as the bond or equity markets. The main effect of the small diversification of the Spanish banking system is clear. Banks maintained their dominant position in the financial market not only because regulation encouraged savers to keep their savings in the form of deposits but because they were the main suppliers of loans.

The second effect of this relative stability was an increase in moral hazard. A large number of risky and illegal banking practises were accumulated in these years because banks knew that the Bank of Spain would intervene if they were in difficulties. The international crisis and the increase in competition – as a consequence of the process of liberalisation and deregulation of the Spanish financial system – increased risk levels in the late 1970s. Moreover, banks oriented towards corporate investment were hardly hit by the stock market recession. These factors and the unprofessional banking practices mentioned above explain the Spanish financial crisis which started in 1978. In this year there were 110 banks in Spain and as a consequence of the crisis 51 were involved in solvency crises to a greater or lesser degree.

The objective of stability can be interpreted not only in terms of the number of failures or bankruptcies but in terms of monetary stability too. The second group of measures linked to the objective of stability tried to achieve monetary stability. At the end of the Civil War the Franco authorities adopted some measures to control inflation such as the *Ley de Desbloqueo* or the issue of

Treasury bonds to use up monetary funds. They also established some credit controls. The Minister Decree Law of 1942 prohibited banks and bankers from granting new credits secured on mortgages without authorisation from the General Directorate for Banking and the Stock Market. It also prohibited the granting of credits in the form of overdrafts on current accounts for a period exceeding 15 days. Empirical evidence shows, however, that the authorities sacrificed the goal of controlling inflation to promote industrialisation. But this fact is no different from the situation in other European countries where the inflationary movement was similar to that in Spain. In this period the influence of post-war policies and Keynesianism downgraded monetary policy to a macroeconomic instrument. However, in Spain the massive use of inflationary methods of public financing and the passive monetary policy indicate that the Franco authorities were less sensitive to the risks of inflation than other European governments. Minimum monetary control became possible at the end of the 1950s, but even so we cannot say that monetary policy was at all active. Monetary measures in the 1960s were unsophisticated, with quantitative limits on the amount of credit advanced by banks. This rudimentary instrument was not very effective and inflation rose considerably from the mid-1960s.

Therefore, we cannot accept that the main objective of the banking regulation during the Franco regime was to assure the stability of the banking system. If this were the main objective of the Franco regime, they would have considered other measures typical for prudential regulation such as deposit insurance, or legal requirements. These measures would have allowed stability in both senses, in terms of bankruptcies and in providing instruments to control monetary policy. Moreover, they would have avoided the high costs of the measures they established (such as inefficiency and moral hazard behaviour).

The second justification for Spanish banking regulation was the interest in avoiding monopolistic behaviour. However, the way the interest rate restrictions were employed does not allow this claim to be accepted. The authorities fixed a 'ceiling' on the rate of interest on deposit and a 'floor' on the rate of interest on loans. Only a binding interest rate or a minimum for deposits and a maximum for loans would have prevented monopolistic behaviour.

The SBC (Circular 431, 1952) reported several agreements among private banks to fix the deposit rate below the legal maximum and the loan interest rate above the legal minimum. The government approved these agreements and it established an organisation to control their implementation. Therefore (and also considering the evolution of the ratio financial cost/deposits in this period), we can say that from the end of the Civil War to the early 1950s banks operated with a binding rate of interest on deposits and loans, these interest rates being fixed by the banking industry.

As of 1952, there is no evidence of these kinds of agreements. The increase in financial and operating costs could indicate that banks paid 'extra-rates' or developed strategies to compete for deposits by substituting implicit interest payments for explicit interest remunerations. Banks attracted deposits by inducements in addition to the payment of explicit interest rates. They provided commissions and free services and opened more branches, and the result of this was an increase in the financial and non-financial costs of providing deposits.

The official purpose of avoiding monopolistic banking behaviour was not a real intention. The differences between the Bill of the 1946 BSL (where the government fixed a binding interest rate on deposits and loans) and the final version of the law reflect the pressures of private banks.

Finally, the Franco government used financial regulation as an instrument to accelerate industrialisation. As explained in Chapter 2, the authorities believed that the market allocation of resources was sub-optimal and they introduced compensating mechanisms. Many authors (Muñoz 1969 or Tamames 1965) consider that this intervention resulted from pressures brought to bear on politicians and government officials by organised interest groups. However, as shown in Chapter 4, state intervention in the banking sector was motivated by the political ideology of the Regime. The collaboration of the banking system was essential for the Franco regime and the government tried to involve the banking sector in its development programme. Under these circumstances the close links which existed between banks and firms gave financial institutions a powerful position in the economy.

The main elements of the Regime's ideology were reflected in the Law of Protection and Development of National Industry of 1939, the Law of Regulation and Defence of National Industry of 1939 and the establishment of the INI, a state holding company. Most of these initial investments and economic incentives were meant for public industries (electricity, mining, chemical fertilisers, or shipbuilding). Other traditional industrial sectors, which constituted important lobbies before the Civil War (Fraile 1991: 112–15), were not the main beneficiaries of Franco's economic policy. In the 1960s, however, the authorities decided to reduce their support for the public sector and to increase incentives for the private sector. It may have been in this period that the interests of the elite sector had a stronger influence over government actions.

Although the only objective of some regulations was to protect the interest of traditional lobbies, it is clear that government intervention also had a strong ideological motivation. That is why we can find several measures which in fact did not benefit the banking system. Some examples of these are the branch expansion restrictions, the limits on dividends and the monopolistic position of some public banks such as the *Banco Exterior de España* in foreign trade (this bank was specifically authorised to affect all banking operations in Spain connected with the interchange of goods, services and capital between Spain and foreign countries). The serious criticisms of the SBC and the *Banco de Vizcaya* (Bank of Spain Archives, *Informe sobre el Proyecto de Ley de Ordenación Bancaria de 1946*, unclassified) about the *Proyecto de Ley de Ordenación Bancaria de 1946* (Bill of the 1946 BSL) and the non-acceptance of some of the main proposed amendments by the Franco government is yet another example of this lack of coincidence between banking and government interests. Finally, the 'fight' between the INI and the *Banco Urquijo* for the opening of the first automobile firm in Spain also tends to corroborate this argument.

My research, then, demonstrates that government and banking interests did not always coincide. On the one hand, there was the interest of the Franco government in involving the banking sector in their strategy of development. Banks and saving institutions were used as instruments of industrialisation and they were also used to obtain cheap financing. On the other hand, there was the banking interest in maximising profits and minimising risk. The Franco government offered some advantages to the banking sector to obtain their collaboration and banks tried to take advantage of this situation by investing in preferential sectors. The final financial regulatory framework was the result of both pressures.

The 1962 Banking Law and the subsequent reforms were a result of the political and economic changes which took place in this period. In the 1950s political and economic problems forced Franco to initiate a very cautious liberalisation process. International pressures greatly influenced these changes, too (Pérez 1997: 96–97). The OEEC and the FMI recommended that the Franco government reform the financial regulatory framework. The 1960s were a period of financial liberalisation in many European countries and these international agencies (OEEC, FMI) considered financial liberalisation as a pre-condition for Spanish modernisation. In spite of this, this financial reform showed serious contradictions as a consequence of ideological constraints. On the one hand, in the 1960s the government reinforced intervention for allocation purposes. There was an attempt to increase the importance of public credit and the government strengthened the mechanism to finance national interest industries. So, the changes of financial regulation in the 1960s, in spite of international and internal pressures, do not suggest that liberalisation was in practice very influential. On the other hand, the links between the government and the banking sector became stronger in this period, as Table 4.3 indicates. The weakness of the regime forced them to look for 'allies'. It was only in the mid-1970s, in the transition from a dictatorship to a democracy, that the liberalisation of the Spanish financial system took place.

It is not possible to separate the 1962 Banking Law from the rest of the political and economic changes that took place in Spain in the late 1950s. These transformations had several origins. First, there were the limitations of autarky. As explained in Chapter 1, economic and political problems forced the Franco regime to introduce many reforms. There was substantial social instability during the 1960s, with an increase in the number of strikes and student protests, and the Franco authorities deemed that strong economic growth was the best means of ensuring the stability of the regime. The authorities, supported by the Bank of Spain and the Minister of Finance (the 'technocrats') but with the opposition of the Ministers of Industry and Agriculture, believed that the main instrument to promote economic growth was liberalisation. And this liberalisation process also affected the banking sector. Second, it is necessary to take into account international pressures. The reports from the different international institutions that Spain joined in the late 1950s (OEEC, IMF) were severely critical of the Spanish financial structure and they recommended a reform of the regulatory framework (*Informe del Comité Económico sobre la ejecución del Programa de Estabilización*, Report D-1191 Bank of Spain, 1960, section 8). Finally, we must not forget that the 1960s were a period of financial liberalisation in other European countries. In fact, most of these reforms were a clear copy of the French laws and regulatory institutions (Anderson 1970: 164–67). In this period very similar forms of financial regulation were also adopted in countries with very different political regimes from the Spanish one such as those of Norway and Sweden as well as that of France.

After analysing the reasons behind the regulation of the Spanish banking system during the Franco regime, the main consequences of this regulatory framework on banking behaviour, and especially on profitability, have been studied. As explained in Chapter 3, after the Spanish Civil War the authorities introduced a very restrictive regulatory framework. Maximum and minimum interest rates were fixed, and the government extended its control over other aspects of banking activity such as lending. Entry was restricted and mergers and branching expansion were under strict governmental controls. Financial regulation was reinforced by a private cartel agreement which determined price conditions in the first part of the period.

Spanish banks were mixed or universal banks. This characteristic is very relevant in order to study the effects of regulation on banking behaviour. The main objective of financial conglomerates must be to maximise profits. The main problem is to know whether banks and participating firms will maximise profits individually or, alternatively, whether the financial group will maximise the global profitability. As the banking output (in particular, loans) is an input for the affiliated firms, there is an interdependence between banking and participating-firm profits. If banks decide to make use of their 'power' to 'exploit' their firms, they will charge higher loan interest rates to participating than to non-participating firms. Alternatively, banks may favour their affiliated firms by offering lower loan interest rates. So, loan interest rate behaviour and credit discrimination are essential elements in the study of the objective function of Spanish banks and the repercussions of the character of mixed banks on profitability. There is no clear evidence about the existence of credit discrimination, at least in terms of lower interest rates for participating firms. A correlation between banking participation and higher or lower loan interest rates has not been found. Other qualitative information about the relationship between banks and their subordinate firms and the existence of credit discrimination indicates that participating firms had a higher volume of credit than non-participating firms. However, this higher volume of credit could be the result of credit discrimination or the result of a lower risk factor. Without more information it is impossible to come to any clear conclusion about the existence of credit discrimination.

Therefore, the conclusions reached in this research do not allow me to be certain about the convenience of maintaining the assumption of profit-maximising behaviour for the Big Five Spanish banks. Comín and Martín Aceña (1996: 26) consider that one of the main objectives of Spanish banks in their strategy of industrial investment was to look for 'clients'. Banking participating firms are 'captive clients'. If we accept this argument, profit-maximising behaviour seems quite a reasonable assumption. However, there are important differences among banks. Only if the private archives of the main banks are opened, will information about banking operations decisions and the possible existence of credit discrimination be available. The present research maintains the banking profitability-maximising assumption, although the influence of industrial participation on banking profitability has also been examined. Furthermore, it must be taken into account that Spanish banks not only obtained profits from intermediating activities, but also from other mechanisms such as profits derived from the issues of shares. This was an important source of profits for Spanish banks from the mid-1960s.

When the authorities regulate the banking system and restrict profit-maximising behaviour, banks respond to these constraints by engaging in various forms of non-price competition and by modifying their strategy of assets and liabilities diversification. So the main objective of Chapter 6 was to analyse the effects of interest rate controls and other regulatory measures on banking strategies and profitability.

With interest rate controls, as shown in Chapter 5, if regulation was binding, banks would have responded to this constraint by substituting implicit interest payments (branches, commissions and so on) for explicit remunerations (deposit interest rates). However, the final effect of regulation depended on the market structure and the opportunities for banks to evade controls and pay 'extra-rates' or implicit interest remunerations. If the implicit interest rate had equalled the explicit interest rate paid before regulation, the effects of removing constraints – in terms of volume of deposits – would have been more shadow than substance. However, this situation seems unlikely.

To assess the effectiveness of interest controls in Spain from 1940 to 1975 the ratio 'total financial costs/deposits' has been estimated as an indicator of the actual costs of deposits for the four and five larger Spanish banks. This indicator has also been compared with the maximum deposit costs – the maximum cost banks incurred if they paid the legal ceiling.

My estimates suggest that the effects of regulation were not the same throughout the period (1939–1975). Results show that from 1942 to 1950 the remuneration that banks paid to depositors was below (or equal to) the legal deposit rate. In the 1940s and mid-1950s regulation was more restrictive (not in terms of legal ratios but in terms of restriction of entry, branching expansion and mergers) but it allowed cartel agreements to fix banking conditions. From 1950 the results are again different. After that year the ratio 'financial costs/deposits' was above the legal maximum deposit interest rate, and it increased substantially from the mid-1950s.

There are two possible explanations for this financial cost increase. Either banks adopted a new cartel agreement to pay interest rates above the legal ceiling or 'extra-rates', or, there was an increase in competition because of the difficulties in maintaining a cartel agreement and banks made use of 'extra-rates' or implicit remuneration (free commissions, and so on) to take more deposits. From 1952 there is no evidence of the existence of formal agreements and as explained above, the general impression is that in this period the pact was not effective.

From 1967 the authorities changed the ceiling more frequently. In 1969 they liberalised some interest rates. If the modification of ceilings had reduced the spread between the regulated and the monopolistic – or the equilibrium – interest rate, the main effect of regulation would have been to reduce implicit interest payments; that is to say, banks would have substituted explicit interest rates for implicit interest remunerations. If changes in the legal ceilings were a result of changes in the equilibrium interest rates – and, therefore, did not modify the relationship between the equilibrium and the regulated interest rate – they would not have decreased implicit remunerations. My estimates show that from 1968/69 the spread between the legal ceiling and the deposit remuneration (the ratio 'financial costs/deposits') decreased.

Empirical evidence, then, shows that banks tried to avoid regulation and they 'competed' through 'extra-rates' and other mechanisms rather than price. The are two main questions which remain to be answered. First, what was the level of competition through these instruments (more branches, free services, lottery and raffle tickets, and so on)? Second, what was the effect of these competitive banking strategies on profitability?

With respect to the level of competition, the 'structure-conduct-performance' predicts that one of the main indicators of the competition of an industry is the degree of concentration. However, concentration could also be an indicator of the existence of scale economies in the banking industry. So, I have made use of other alternative indicators of the degree of competition such as profitability or the 'intermediation' margins.

Concentration in Spanish banking was high, especially until the mid-1950s but not very different from that of other European countries. The percentage of deposits in the hands of the larger banks was lower than in the UK, similar to France and higher than in Italy. The main difference between Spain and other European countries was the lack of diversification of the financial system.

The decline of Spanish banking concentration started in the 1950s. This change occurred before the regulatory switch. So to understand the evolution of concentration we must take into account other aspects in addition to that of regulation. The decrease in concentration from the 1950s without a significant change in the number of banks could indicate an increase in competition when these financial institutions tried to expand towards the optimal size.

The main variable I used to measure the effects of competition has been the evolution of profitability or 'profits/(paid up capital+reserves)'. The idea is that when the level of competition of an industry is low, this translates into high profits. After the Civil War, banking profitability reached nominal rates of 14 per cent – similar to those obtained in the 1920s. Nominal banking profitability reached a maximum in 1958/59. From this year profitability declined to rates around 14 per cent. The fall in profitability started before the change in the regulatory framework (*Ley de Bases* of 1962) and there was an important recovery of this variable from 1967. The 'profits/deposits' and 'profits/loans' ratios show a similar evolution. The two ratios decreased from 1958, before the regulatory change. The ratio 'profits/deposits' increased again from 1965 and the recovery of the ratio 'profits/loans' took place in 1963.

Although the rates of profitability increased in the 1940s and 1950s, empirical evidence about the existence of supernormal profits in the banking industry has not been found. The rate of profitability of the banking industry was higher than the rate of profitability of the medium and large-sized non-financial firms, but the gap was quite small. Furthermore, the main result obtained when we try to link the evolution of profitability with the changes in regulation is that the major differences between the banking sector and the rest of firms increased from the mid-1960s in favour of the banking sector.

In my panel estimates of the profitability function for the Big Five Spanish banks I have not found evidence of a relationship between profitability and concentration or profitability and size. In the period 1920–1975, when we consider an absolute index of concentration, this variable is not significant and it has the opposite sign of that hypothesised, but the market share is significant and has the sign the theory predicts. When we consider the Herfindahl index as an indicator of the level of concentration of the banking industry, both variables (market share and concentration) are significant at a 95 per cent level, but again the sign of concentration is the opposite of the one the theory predicts if we accept the collusion hypothesis. Therefore, according to Smirlock's test, we cannot accept the collusion hypothesis.

For the period 1942–1975 I have obtained very different results. In this period, when we use an absolute index of concentration the variables market share and concentration are significant at a 95 per cent level and both variables have the expected sign. According to Smirlock (1985), when *MS* and *CR* are significant, we can make use of the 'interaction' variable to interpret the result: if the interaction variable is positive, we accept the collusion hypothesis and if the interaction variable is negative, we accept the efficient hypothesis. In our estimates, the interaction variable *CRMS* has a negative sign. When we alternatively include the Herfindahl index *H*, neither the market share nor the concentration index are significant at a 95 per cent level. We have not obtained, therefore, very conclusive results about the significance of concentration and market share.

My empirical estimates show that the variables which explain profitability are more related to a bank's management of its resources than to its size or concentration. Regulation could guarantee banks a minimum level of profitability, although the differences in profitability among the Big Five banks were a consequence of the policy of asset and liability diversification of each bank. The ratio between non-financial costs and own assets, the percentage of loans with respect to securities and commercial bills and the compositions of deposits are the main variables which explain the evolution of banking profitability from 1920 to 1975. Those banks with a higher percentage of long-term deposits earn higher returns. With regard to asset diversification, banks with a less commercially orientated activity, that is to say, with a lower percentage of loans with respect to securities and commercial bills, obtained higher rates of profitability. These results may explain the universal banking character of the Spanish banks. I have also found a positive relationship between the ratio 'non-financial costs/

own resources' and the evolution of profitability. When the authorities controlled interest rates, banks made use of other alternative mechanisms to compete, such as free financial services or the increase in the number of branches to provide customers with advantages in terms of closer geographic services. These non-price forms of competition increased the non-financial costs of the banking sector but they had a positive effect on profitability. In fact we can change the direction of the causality and say that only banks which had the opportunity to increase their non-interest rate remunerations, especially in the form of new branches, obtained increases in profitability. The variable which represents savings banks competition is also significant and with the expected sign. Finally, the dummy I have included to 'capture' the effect of the 1962 Banking Law is also significant.

Following my estimates, regulation had ambiguous effects on profitability. I cannot affirm that the strength of regulation in terms of barriers to entry and other regulatory constraints only had positive effects on profitability. In fact, profitability was more related with managerial variables than with indicators of the size or the power market. This result could be the consequence of the inadequacy of using concentration as an indicator of market power. Regulation may have guaranteed banks a minimum rate of profitability but the differences in profitability among banks depended on management.

It is important to mention the implications of these results in terms of the influence of regulation. As I indicated before, there is no clear relationship between changes in profitability and changes in regulation. In fact the changes in profitability anticipated the changes in regulation. However, there are three variables which affected banking profitability and were strictly regulated by the Spanish government. First, the number of branches. As explained before, the Spanish banking regulation tended to favour the concentration of branches in the hands of the larger banks. Therefore, national banks had an advantage in terms of regulation to expand the number of branches and this fact had a positive effect on the rate of profitability obtained by these banks. Second, the Franco regime tried to involve banks in their programme of industrialisation through the establishment of preferential interest rates to national interest industries and compulsory coefficients to finance these sectors. This fact explains the negative relationship between the ratio 'loans/(securities+commercial bills)' and profitability and explains the banks' strategy of increasing their participation in the industrial sector and their character of mixed banks. Finally, my estimates show that saving competition had a negative effect on banking profitability. From the end of the Civil War to the mid-1970s regulation discriminated against savings banks in favour of banks. In this sense, the Spanish regulatory framework favoured banking profitability.

I have made use of other indicators of the level of competition such as the 'intermediation' margin or the change in the evolution of costs. According to the former indicator we cannot accept that the change in the regulatory framework in 1962, which apparently increased the level of competition in the banking industry by reducing branching restriction and removing barriers to entry, had any effect on the interest margin. One would expect that an increase in competition would translate into a lower spread between interest received and interest paid out by banks, but this interest margin increased from 1962 to 1967 for all the banks under consideration. This fact indicates that financial liberalisation did not have a real effect on banking competition until the late 1970s.

The evidence of the ratio 'operating cost/own assets' refutes the existence of scale economies. Larger banks had a higher ratio 'operating cost/own assets' in 1946, 1952 and 1962. Only in 1973 have I found a negative relationship between size and the evolution of costs.

The second hypothesis I have tested is whether financial regulation reinforced monopoly power by reducing risk. Banks can make use of their power not to obtain higher profits but to work in a more secure environment. I calculated the coefficient of variation of the profitability of the Big Five banks in three periods, the post-war years 1942–1951 (a period with higher instability as a consequence of the aftermath of the Civil War), an intermediate period 1952–1961 (the period when banks consolidated their monopolistic power), and finally the years 1962–1970 (a period of higher instability as a consequence of the change in regulation which started with the *Ley de Bases* of 1962).

My estimates show that banking profitability was more stable from 1952–1961. The period with lower stability (in nominal and real terms) was 1962–1970. Empirical results, then, provide evidence to support the position that the most regulated period (1940–1962) was more secure, at least in terms of profitability variations.

To summarise, the evolution of profitability, interest margins and operating costs indicate that the *Ley de Bases* of 1962 did not have a significant effect on banking efficiency. The Spanish authorities missed an opportunity to liberalise the Spanish banking sector with the consequent positive effect on competition.

Sources and Bibliography

Sources

Anuario financiero y de S.A. Gardoquí.
Anuario Estadístico de España. Instituto Nacional de Estadística (INE).
Annuario Statístico Italiano.
Bank of England Archives. OV61 (SPAIN).
Bank of Spain Archives
Reports about the demand for branches 1945–1955.
Directors' Minutes Bank of Spain 1940–1955 (Actas del Banco de España, Secretaría).
Report about the 1946 Banking Supervision Law. Supreme Banking Council. Unclassified.
Report about the 1946 Banking Supervision Law. Banco de Vizcaya. Unclassified.
Banco de España
(1972): *Propuesta de Memoria del Banco de España al Ministerio de Hacienda sobre el limite de la circulación fiduciaria*. Informe D-3850.
(1961): *Informe Memorandum sobre el sistema bancario y sus problemas*. Informe D-20748.
(1960): *Informe de la misión de la OECE que vino a España en Diciembre de 1959 para estudiar el Programa de Estabilización*. Informe D-1191.
(1960): *Informe del Comité director del acuerdo monetario europeo sobre la ejecución del programa de estabilización*. Informe D-1191.
(1960): *Informe del Comité de la OCDE sobre la ejecución del programa de estabilización del gobierno español*. Informe D-1191.
(1945–1956): *Informes varios sobre España y extranjero*. Informe D-6462.
(1941): *Informe sobre el Balance de Diciembre de 1941 y Régimen de Desbloqueos*. Informe D-6824.
(1938): *Estudio sobre la restauración de la comunidad dineraria española*. Informe D-6402/03.
(1933–45): *Informe sobre la situación económica, la reconstrucción y el crédito*. Informe D-6421.
Boletín Estadístico del Banco de España. Banco de España.
Boletín de Cotizaciones de la Bolsa de Madrid. Bolsa de Madrid.
Comisaria del Plan de Desarrollo Económico y Social (1965): *Summary of the*

Spanish Economic and Social Development Plan, 1964–1967. Presidencia del Gobierno, Oficina de Relaciones Públicas, Madrid.

(1965): *Development Plan and Incentives in Industrial Centers*. Presidencia del Gobierno, Oficina de Relaciones Públicas, Madrid.

(1967): *The Spanish Development Plan Summarized, 1964–1967*, Presidencia del Gobierno, Oficina de Relaciones Públicas, Madrid.

Consejo Superior Bancario. *Anuario Estadistico de la Banca privada.*

Consejo Superior Bancario. *Balances Consolidados de la Banca Privada.*

Consejo Superior Bancario. *Recopilación de Circulares.*

The International Bank for Reconstruction and Development (1963): *The Economic Development of Spain*, Report of a Mission Organized by the International Bank for Reconstruction at the Request of the Government of Spain. Baltimore. The Johns Hopkins Press.

The Handbook of Statistic Federal Republic of Germany.

Memorias del Banco de Bilbao.

Memorias de Banco Central.

Memorias del Banco Hispano Americano.

Memorias del Banco Urquijo.

Memorias Banco de Vizcaya.

Memorias del Crédito Oficial.

Overseas Economic Surveys for Spain. London. Her Majesty's Stationery Office.

Public Record Office, Western Department, WS 1103/2, no. 82, 1101/22/50, 15 March: *The economic situation of Spain*.

Bibliography

Alhadeff, D.A. (1968): *Competition and Controls in Banking, a Study of the Regulation of Bank Competition in Italy, France and England*. Los Angeles. University of California Press.

Almenar, S. (1999): 'The development of economic studies and research in Spain (1939–1995): an overview', in Coats, A. W. (ed.): *The Development of Economics in Western Europe since 1945*. London. Routledge, pp. 191–226.

Altunbas, Y. and Molyneaux, P. (1993): 'Scale and scope economies in European banking'. University College of North Wales, Bangor, School of Accounting, Banking, and Economics, and Institute of European Finance, Research Paper, no. 93/11.

Alvarez LLano, R. (1984): *Evolución de la estructura económica regional de España en la historia: Una aproximación*. s.n.

the Italian Banking System: An International Comparison. Rome. Banca Nationale del Lavoro.

Beaulac, W.L. (1986): *Franco. Silent Ally in World War Two*. Southern Illinois University Press.

Berger, A.N. and Humphrey, D.B. (1992): 'Measurement and efficiency issues in commercial banking', in Griliche, Z., ed.: *Output Measurement in the Service Sectors*. Chicago. NBER. University of Chicago Press, pp. 245–79.

Binder, J.J. and Brown, D.F. (1991): 'Bank rates of return and entry restrictions, 1864–1914'. *The Journal of Economic History*, vol. 51, no. 1, March, pp. 47–66.

Biscani (1979): 'La estrutura finanziaria. Aspetti quantitativi du longo periodo', in Vicarelli, F.: *Capitale industrial e capital finanziario. Il caso Italiano*. Bologne. Il Mulino, pp. 93–134.

Braña, J., Buesa, M. and Molero, J. (1984): *El Estado y el cambio tecnológico en la industrialización tardía*. Madrid. F.C.E.

Bruni (1991, 2nd edn): 'Banking and financial reregulation: the Italian case', in Dermine, J., ed.: *European Banking in the 1990s*. Oxford. Blackwell, pp. 241–67.

Burkett, P. (1986): 'Interest rate restrictions and deposit opportunities for small savers in developing countries: an analytical view'. *Journal of Development Studies*, vol. 23, pp. 77–92.

Cable, J.R. (1985): 'The bank-industry relationship in West Germany: performance and policy aspects', in Schwalbach, J., ed.: *Industry Structure and Performace*. Berlin. Edition Sigma, pp. 17–140.

Cairncross, A. (1992): *The British Economy since 1945*. Oxford. Blackwell.

Caminal, R., Gual, J. and Vives, X. (1990): 'Competition in Spanish banking', in Dermine, J., ed.: *European Banking in the 1990s*. Oxford. Blackwell, pp. 261–321.

Canals, J. (1996): *Bancos Universales y diversificacion empresarial*. Madrid Alianza Ed.

Capie, F. and Collins, M. (1992): *Have the Banks failed British Industry?* Institute of Economic Affairs. Hobart Papers.

Capie, F. and Webber, A. (1985): *A Monetary History of the United Kingdom, 1870–1981*. London. George Allen & Unwin.

Carande, R. (1941): 'Bases de una política económica de reconstrucción'. *Revista de Estudios Políticos*, no. 1, pp. 43–81.

Carbó, S. (1994): *Institutional, Structural and Supervisory Developments in Spanish Banking*. Institute of European Finance. University College of North Wales, Working Paper no. 18.

Carnevali, F. (1993): *Finance in the Regions: The Case of Britain after 1945*. Colloquium of the European Association for Banking History. Zurich, 27/28 May. Unpublished.

Carr, R. (1970): *España 1808–1975*. Barcelona. Ed. Ariel.

Carreras, A. comp. (1989): *Estadísticas históricas de España, siglos XlX y XX*. Madrid. Fundación Banco Exterior.

Carreras, A. (1992): 'La producción industrial en el muy largo plazo: una comparación entre España e Italia de 1861 a 1980', in Prados de la Escosura, L. and Zamagni, V., eds: *El desarrollo económico en la Europa del Sur: España e Italia en perspectiva histórica*. Madrid. Alianza Universidad, pp. 173–210.

(1989): 'Depresión económica y cambio estructural durante el decenio bélico (1936–1945)', in Delgado, J.L., ed.: *El primer franquismo, España durante la II Guerra Mundial*. Madrid. Siglo XXl, pp. 127–57.

(1984): 'La producción industrial española, 1842–1981: construcción de un índice anual'. *Revista de Historia Económica*, II, no. 1, pp. 127–57.

Catalán, J. (1992): 'Reconstrucción, política económica y desarrollo industrial: tres economías del sur de Europa, 1944–1953', in Prados de la Escosura, L. and Vera Zamagni, V., eds: *El desarrollo económico en la Europa del Sur: España e Italia en perspectiva histórica*. Madrid. Alianza Universidad, pp. 359–95.

Cerani, L. (1962): 'Italy: the commercial banks and financial institutions', in Sayers, R.S.: *Banking in Western Europe*. Oxford. Oxford Clarendon Press, pp. 124–54.

Cesarini, F., Grillo, M., Marti, M. and Onedo, M., eds: *Banca e mercato: Riflessioni su evoluzione e pospettive dell'industria bancaria in Italia*. Bologne. Il Mulino.

Clayton, G. (1962): 'Spain', in Sayers R.S.: *Banking in Western Europe*. Oxford. Oxford. Clarendon Press, pp. 347–82.

Clode, S. (1986): *The Mix of Price and Non-price Competition for Retail Transaction Balances*. Institute of Finance. Bangor. University College of North Wales, 86/6.

Coello, J. (1997): 'Determinantes del comportamiento de los españoles en la elección de entidad financiera'. *Moneda y Crédito*, 0(205), pp. 165–92.

Collins, M. (1991): *Banks and Industrial Finance in Britain, 1800–1939*. Studies in Economic and Social History. London. Macmillan.

(1990): *Money and banking in the UK: A History*. London. Routledge.

Comín, F. and Martín Aceña, P. (1996): *Los rasgos históricos de las empresas en España: un panorama*. Fundación Empresa pública, Documento de trabajo 9605.

(1991): *INI. Cincuenta años de industrialización en España*. Madrid. Espasa Calpe.

Committee to Review the Functioning of Financial Institutions (1980). Report. London. Her Majesty's Stationery Office.

Confederación Española de Cajas de Ahorro (1986): 'La red de oficinas de cajas de ahorro en España (1950–1985). *Temas económicos*, no. 39. August.

Courakis, A.S. (1984): 'Constraints on bank choices and financial repression in less developed countries'. *Oxford Bulletin of Economics and Statistics*, 46(4), November, pp. 341–70.

Cowling, K. and Waterson, M. (1976): 'Price cost and market structure'. *Económica*, 43(171), August, pp. 267–74.

Cuadrado Roura, J.R. (1977): 'Financiación privilegiada al sector privado y desequilibrios regionales'. *Información Comercial Española*, no. 526–27, p. 120.

Cubbin, J. (1983): 'Apparent collusion and conjectural variations in differential oligopoly'. *International Journal of Industrial Organization*, no.1, pp. 155–63.

Cuervo-Arango, C. (1990): 'La relación Banca-Industria: perspectiva desde España'. *Rev. Economista*, no. 41, pp. 82–84.

(1988): 'La competitividad del sistema bancario español: perspectivas futuras'. *Hacienda Pública Española*, no. 10, pp. 134–46.

Cuervo, A. (1988): 'Banca e industrialización en el período 1960–88', in *Banca e industrialización: presente, pasado y futuro*. Madrid. Ed. Banco Español de Crédito, pp. 73–90.

De Boissieu, Ch. (1990): 'The French banking sector in the light of European financial legislation', in Dermine J, ed.: *European Banking in the 1990s*. Oxford. Blackwell, pp. 193–236.

De la Sierra, F. (1953): *La concentración económica de las industrias básicas españolas*. Madrid. Instituto de Estudios Políticos.

De Miguel, A. and Linz, J.J. (1963): 'Los empresarios españoles y la banca'. *Moneda y Crédito*, no. 84, March, pp. 3–112.

De Ojeda Eiseley, A. (1988): 'Indices de precios en España en el período 1913–1987'. *Serie de estudios de Historia Económica del Banco de España*, no. 17.

Di Battista, M.L. and and Grillo, M. (1988): 'La concorrenza nell'industria bancaria italiana', in Cesarini, F., Grillo, M. and Onedo, M., eds: *Banca e mercato: riflessioni su evoluzione e prospettive dell'industria bancaria in Italia*. Bologne. Il Mulino.

Diez Nicolás, J. (1985): 'La mortalidad en la guerra civil española', *Boletín de la Asociación de Demografía Histórica*, no. 3, pp. 41–55.

Donges, J.B. (1976): *La industrialización en España, políticas, logros perspectivas*. Barcelona. Oikos-Tau.

Dowd, K. (1992): *The Experience of Free Banking*, London and New York. Routledge.

Downs, A. (1957): *An Economic Theory of Democracy*. New York. Harper and Row.

The Economist (1962), 12 May.

Edwards, J. and Fischer, K. (1994): *Banks, Finance and Investment in Germany*. Cambridge. Cambridge University Press.

Ercolani, P. (1978): 'Documentazione Statistica di Base', in Fuá, G., ed.: *Lo svilupo economico in Italia*. Milan. Franco Angeli, pp. 388–472.

Estapé, F. (1966): 'Política industrial', in *España ante la integración económica europea*. Barcelona. Ed. Ariel.

Fanjul, E. (1981): '1951–1957. El despegue de la industrialización en España', in *Lecturas de Economía Española e Internacional. 50 Aniversario del Cuerpo de Técnicos Comerciales del Estado*. Madrid. Ministerio de Economía y Comercio.

Fanjul, O. and Maravall, F. (1985): *La eficiencia del sistema financiero español*. Madrid. Alianza.

Fanjul Martín, E., Fernández Navarrete, D. and Rodríguez Prada, G. (1987): 'La política monetaria española (1940–1978)', *Monografías del Instituto de Estudios Fiscales*, no. 7.

Farré-Escofet, E. (1980): 'Inflación y bloqueo de la inversión (1939–1953). *Banca Catalana*, no. 57, pp. 1–21.

Fernández, V. (1975): 'La deuda pública', in *Datos básicos para la Historia financiera de España*. Madrid. IEF.

Fontana, J. and Nadal, J. (1980): *España*, in Cipolla, C.M.: *Historia Económica de Europa*, vol. 6. Barcelona. Ariel, pp. 95–163.

Fornies, J.F. (1991): 'Interpretación básica de la historia de las cajas de ahorro españolas'. *Papeles de Economía Española*, no. 46, pp. 39–51.

Fraile, P. (1991): *Industrialización y grupos de presión. La economía de la protección en España, 1900–1950*. Madrid. Alianza.

Fua, G. (1981): *Lo sviluppo economico in Italia: storia dell' economia italiana negli ultimo cento anni*. Milano. Ed. Franco Angeli.

Fuentes Quintana, E. (1986): 'La economía española desde el Plan de Estabilización de 1959: el papel del sector exterior', in Martínez Vara, T., ed.: *Mercado y desarrollo económico de la España Contemporánea*. Santander. Junta del Puerto de Santander, pp. 131–57.

Gamir, L. (1975): *Política Económica de España. Madrid*. Ed. Guadiana.

García Delgado, J.L. (1987): 'La industrialización y el desarrollo económico de España durante el franquismo', in Nadal, J., Carreras, A. et al., eds: *La economía española en el siglo XX. Una perspectiva histórica*. Barcelona. Ed. Ariel, pp. 164–89.

García Delgado, J.L. and Segura, J. (1977): *Reformismo y crisis económica*. Madrid. Ed. Saltés.

García Ruiz, J.L. and Tortella, G. (1999): *Una Historia de los Banco Central e Hispanoamericano, 1900–2000: Un siglo de gran banca en España*. Unpublished work (with internal and external sources).

(1994): *Divergent, parallel and convergent Trajectories: the history of the Hispanoamericano and the Banco Central, 1901–1965*. Colloquium of the European Association for Banking History. Zurich.

(1993): *Una Historia de los bancos Central e Hispanoamericano (1901–1991). Noventa años de gran banca en España*. Unpublished work (with external sources).

Gibson, N.J. (1967): *Financial Intermediaries and Monetary Policy: The Instruments of Economics Affairs*. London.

Glasner, D. (1989): *Free Banking and Monetary Reform*. Cambridge. Cambridge University Press.

Goldsmith, R. (1975): 'The Quantitative International Comparison of Financial Structure and Development'. *Journal of Economic History*, 35(1), March, pp. 216–37.

(1969): *Financial structure and Development*. New Haven. Yale University Press.

González, M.J. (1979): *La economía política del franquismo (1940–70)*. Madrid. Ed. Tecnos. Madrid.

González Temprano, A., Sánchez Robayna, D. and Torres Villanueva, E. (1981): *La banca y el estado en la España contemporánea (1939–1979)*. Madrid. Ed. El Espejo.

Goodhart, C.A.E. (1989): *Money, Information and Uncertanty*. London. Macmillan.

Gowland, D. (1990): *The Regulation of Financial Markets in the 1990s*. Worcester. Edward Elgar.

Guerrero D. (1988): *Acumulación de capital, distribución de la renta y crisis de rentabilidad en España (1954–1987)*. Unpublished Thesis. Madrid.

Hall, S.G., Henry, S.G.B. and Wilcox, J.B. (1989): *The Long-run Determination of the UK Monetary Aggregate*. Bank of England Discussion Papers, no. 41, August.

The Handbook of Statistic Federal Republic of Germany (1961).

Harrison, J. (1993): *The Spanish Economy. From the Civil War to the European Community*. London. Macmillan.

(1985): *The Spanish Economy in the Twentieth Century*. London and Sydney. Hoom & Helm.

Heffernan, S. (1996): *Modern Banking in Theory and Practice*. Chichester. John Wiley and Sons.

Heggestad, A.A. (1977): 'Market structure, risk and profitability in commercial banking'. *The Journal of Finance*, vol. XXXll, no. 4. September, pp. 1207–16.

Humphrey, D. (1992): 'Flow versus stock indicators of bank output: effects on productivity and scale economy measurement'. *Journal of Financial Services Research*, 6(2), pp. 55–135.

Italian International Bank (1987): *An Introduction to the Published Accounts of Italian Banks*. Italian International Bank.

Kroszner, R.S. and Strahan, P.E. (1999): 'Bankers on boards: monitoring, conflicts of interest, and lender liability'. NBER. Working Paper 7319. August.

Krouse, C.G. (1990): *Theory of Industrial Economics*. Oxford. Blackwell.

Krummel, H.J. (1980): 'German universal banking scrutinized'. *Journal of Banking and Finance*, vol. 4, pp. 33–55.

Lacomba, J.A. and Ruiz, G. (1990): *Una Historia del Banco Hipotecario de España (1872–1986)*. Madrid. Alianza Editorial.

Larraz, J. (1940): 'Resumen provisional sobre la evolución de la Hacienda desde el 18 de julio de 1936 hasta el presente'. *Boletín Oficial del Estado*, 4 August.

Laurence, P.H. (1950): *The Economic Situation in Spain. Comments on the enclosed Memorandum by Mr Pelham, Commercial Counseller which analyses the Present Economic Situation*. Public Record Office, Western Department, WS 1103/2, no. 82, 1101/22/50, 15 March.

Lawrence, C. (1989): 'Banking costs, generalized functional forms and estimations of economies of scale and scope'. *Journal of Money, Credit and Banking*, 21(3), pp. 368–79.

Levine (1997): 'Financial development and economic growth: views and agenda'. *Journal of Economic Literature*, vol. XXXV. June, pp. 688–726.

Lieberman, S. (1982): *The Contemporary Spanish Economy: A Historical Perspective*. London. George Allen & Unwin.

Liesner, T. (1985): *One Hundred Years of Economic Statistics: USA, Australia, Canada, France, Germany, Italy, Japan, Sweden*. London. Economist.

Lopez Muñoz, A. (1968): 'Análisis de la banca privada española'. *Cuadernos para el diálogo*. April, pp. 3–49.

(1967): *Crecimiento y crisis del capitalismo en España*. Madrid. Edicusa.

López Roa, A. (1981): *Sistema financiero español*. Alicante. Nueva Generación de Editores.

Lopez Yepes, J. (1973): *Historia Urgente de Cajas de Ahorro y Montes de Piedad en España*. Madrid. Confederación Española de Cajs de Ahorro.

Lukauskas (1992): *The Political Economy of Financial Deregulation: The Case of Spain*. A dissertation in International Relations. University of Pensylvania.

Lluch, C. (1974): *La industria española del futuro*. Madrid. Ed. Guadiana.

Mankiw, N.G. and Whinston, M.D. (1986): 'Free entry and social inefficiency'. *RAND Journal of Economics*, vol. 17, pp. 48–58.

Martín Aceña, P. (1991): *Los problemas monetarios al término de la guerra civil*. Instituto Universitario Ortega y Gasset. Papeles de Trabajo, Historia Contemporánea. Febrero.

(1989): *Economic Growth and Financial Development in Spain, 1900–1930*. Unpublished paper.

(1988): *Una estimación de los principales agregados monetarios en España: 1940–1962*. Servicio de Estudios Banco de España. Documento de trabajo, no. 8807.

Martin Aceña, P. (1985): 'Desarrollo y modernización del sistema financiero español', in Sánchez-Albornoz, N.: *La modernización económica de España 1830–1930*. Madrid. Alianza Editorial.

(1984): *La política monetaria en España 1919–1935*. Ministerio de Economía y Hacienda. Madrid. I.E.F.

Martín Aceña, P. and Pons, M.A. (1995): *Estructura y rentabilidad de las empresas financieras en España, 1874–1975*. Fundación Empresa Pública. Documento de trabajo 9501. Madrid.

(1994): 'Spanish Banking after the Civil War, 1940–1962'. *Financial History Review*, no. 1, pp. 121–38.

Martínez Cortiña, R. (1971): *Crédito y banca en España: análisis y estructura*. Madrid. Ed. Moneda y Crédito.

Martínez Méndez, P. (1991): *Los beneficios de la banca privada, 1970–1989*. Madrid. Banco de España.

Martínez Serrano, J.A. and others (1982): *Economía española 1960–1980. Crecimiento y cambio estructural*. Madrid. Ed. Blume.

Mathieson, D.J. (1983): 'Estimating models of financial behaviour during periods of extensive structural reform: the experience of Chile'. *IMF Staff Papers*, vol. 30, pp. 350–93.

(1982): 'Inflation, interest rates, and the balance of payments during a financial reform: the case of Argentina'. *World Development*, vol. 10, no. 9, pp. 813–27.

Melitz, J. and Pardue, M. (1973): 'The demand and supply of commercial bank loans'. *Journal of Money, Credit and Banking*. vol. V, no. 2, May, pp. 669–92.

Mckinnon, R.I. (1981): 'Financial repression and the liberalization problem within less developed countries', in Grassman, S. and Landberg, E., eds: *The World Economic Order. Past and Prospects*. Hong Kong. Macmillan Press.

(1976): *Money and Finance in Economic Growth and Development. Essays in Honor of Edward. S. Shaw*. New York. Marcel Decker. Inc.

Ministerio de Hacienda (1961): *Informe del Banco de España, Consejo Superior de Camaras de Comercio, Industria y Navegación, Consejo Superior bancario, Organización Sindical, Instituto de Estudios Políticos, CECA y Consejo de Economía Nacional, sobre el Memorandum del Ministerio de Hacienda sobre el sistema bancario y crediticio*. Madrid. Ministerio de Hacienda.

Mitchell, B.R. (1988): *British Historical Statistics*. Cambridge. Cambridge University Press.

Moltó, L., Uriel, E. and Cucarella, V. (1995): *Contabilidad Nacional de España. Series 1954–1993*. IVIE. Valencia.

Morella, E. (1992): 'El producto industrial de posguerra: una revisión (Indices sectoriales, 1940–1958)'. *Revista de Historia Económica*, no. 1, pp. 125–43.

Moreno, A. (1954): 'The Spanish capital market', in the seventh International Banking Summer School: *The Post-war Functioning of Banking Returns to Normal?* Madrid. Consejo Superior Bancario, pp. 213–29.

Muñoz, J. (1978): 'La expansión bancaria entre 1916 y 1926: La formación de una banca nacional'. *Cuadernos de Información Comercial Española*.

(1969): *El poder de la banca en España*. Ed. Zero. Madrid.

Muñoz, J., Roldan, S. and García Delgado, J.L. (1973): *La formación de la sociedad capitalista en España, 1914–1920*. Madrid. CECA.

Muns, J. (1986): *Historia de la relaciones entre España y el FMI, 1958–1982*. Madrid. Alianza.

Nadal, J. and Sudriá, C. (1983): *Historia de la Caja de Pensiones*. Barcelona. Ed. 62.

Nevin, E. and Davis, E.W. (1970): *The London Clearing Banks*. London. Elek Books.

Olariaga, L. (1951): 'La liquidabilidad de los bancos de depósitos españoles'. *Moneda y Crédito*, no. 38, pp.12–67.

Opie, R.G. (1962): 'Western Germany', in Sayers, R.S., ed.: *Banking in Western Europe*. Oxford. Oxford Clarendon Press, pp. 53–123.

Overseas Economic Surveys for Spain. London. Her Majesty's Stationery Office. Several years.

Paris Eguilaz, H. (1947): 'El problema de la reforma bancaria en España'. *Anales de Economía*, no. 26, pp. 161–232.

(1945): 'Sobre algunos problemas de la Ley de Desbloqueos'. *Moneda y Crédito*, no. 14, p. 31.

Pelham, M. (1950): *Analysis of Spanish economic situation*. Public Record Office. Western Department, WS 1103/2, no. 82, 1101/22/50, 15 March.

Peltzman, S. (1976): 'Toward a more general theory of regulation'. *Journal of Law and Economics*, no. 19, pp. 211–40.

(1970): 'Capital Investment in Commercial Banking and its Relationships to portfolio regulation'. *Journal of Political Economy*. January, pp. 1–26.

Perez, S. (1997): *Banking on privilege: the politics of Spanish financial reform*. Ithaca and London. Cornell University Press.

Perez de Armiñan, G. (1980): *Legislación bancaria española*. Madrid. Banco de España.

Pérez, F. and Quesada, J. (1992): 'La eficiencia del sistema bancario español en la perspectiva europea'. *Moneda y Crédito*, no. 195, pp. 137–84.

Plaza Prieto, J. (1971): *El ahorro y la formación de capital en España (1939–1968)*. Madrid. CECA.

Poveda, R. (1981): 'Funcionamiento del mercado financiero español'. *Papeles de Economía*, no. 9, pp. 42–67.

Prados Arrate, J. (1958): *El sistema bancario español*. Madrid. Ed. Aguilar.

Prados de la Escosura, L. (1995): *Spain's Gross Domestic Product, 1850–1993: Quantitative Conjectures*. Working Paper 95–05. Universidad Carlos III de Madrid.

Prados de la Escosura and Zamagni, V., eds (1992b): *El desarrollo económico en la Europa del Sur: España e Italia en perspectiva histórica*. Madrid Alianza Universidad.

Pueyo, J. (1998) 'La concentración económica de la banca privada en España en el s.XX'. Revised version of the paper presented to the third session of the VI Congreso de Historia Económica de Gerona, 15–17 September 1997.

Rafart Febrer, J. (1959): 'El ahorro en España'. *Cuadernos de Información Económica y sociológica*, no. 7.

Repullo (1990): 'Comment to the Caminal, Gual and Vives paper', in Dermine, J., ed. (1990): *European Banking in the 1990s*. Oxford. Blackwell, pp. 322–24.

Revell, J. (1987): *Comparative concentration of banks*. Institute of European Finance. Research Papers in Banking and Finance RP 87/13. Bangor. University College of North Wales.

(1985): *Mergers and the role of large banks*. Institute of European Finance. Research Monographs in Banking and Finance, no. 2.

Ridruejo, E. (1954a): 'El sistema bancario español'. *Moneda y Crédito*, no. 51. English version in (1954b): 'The Spanish banking system', in the seventh

International Banking Summer School: *The Post-war Functioning of Banking Returns to Normal?*. Madrid. Consejo Superior Bancario, pp. 141–203.

Rodriguez (1977): *El problema regional en España*. s.n.

Rodriguez, J.M. (1989): 'The crisis in Spanish private banks: an empirical analysis'. *Rivista Internazionale di Scienze Economiche e Commerciali*, vol. 36, no. 10–11, pp. 1033–55.

Roldán, S., García Delgado, J.L. and Muñoz, J. (1973): *La formación de la sociedad capitalista en España*. Madrid. CECA.

Rojo, L.A. (1963): 'La política monetaria', in Fuentes Quintana, E., ed.: *El desarrollo económico de España*. Madrid. Revista de Occidente.

Ros Hombravella, J. (1967): *Las Cajas Generales de Ahorro en la economía española*. Madrid. CECA.

Rubio, M., Barbé, L., Taules, M. and Aranguren, J. (1972): *Discriminación y crédito bancario*. Banco de España.

Sáez de Ibarra, L. (1956): *'La regulación de la banca en España'*. Madrid. Consejo Superior Bancario. Madrid.

(1954a): 'La regulación de la banca en España'. *Moneda y Crédito*. no. 51.

(1954b): 'Regulations of Spanish banking', in the seventh International Banking Summer School: *The Post-war Functioning of Banking Return to Normal?*. Madrid. Consejo Superior Bancario, pp. 89–140.

Sánchez Pedreño, A.J. (1961): 'Tres casos de banca comparada'. *Revista de banca y Seguros*. II trimestre, pp. 3–21.

Sandberg, L.G. (1978): 'Banking and economic growth in Sweden before World War I'. *Journal of Economic History*, 38(3), September, pp. 650–80.

San Román, E. (1995): *El nacimiento de la SEAT*. Documento de Trabajo de la Madrid. Fundación Empresa Pública.

Sardá, J. (1968a): *Le financement du development industrial. Paris*. O.C.D.E.

(1968b): *El Banco de España, 1930–1962. Una Historia Económica*. Madrid. Banco de España.

(1967): *The Financing of Industrial Development. Paris*. O.C.D.E.

Saunders, A. and Walter, I. (1994): *Universal Banking in the United States*. New York and Oxford. Oxford University Press.

Sebastián, A. and Suarez, J.L. (1992): *Análisis de la rentabilidad histórica de la inversión en acciones, deuda pública y renta fija privada en el mercado de capitales español*. Madrid. Ed. Bolsa de Madrid.

Schwartz, P. (1977): *El Producto Nacional de España en el siglo XX*. Madrid. IEF.

Shaw, E.S. (1973): *Financial Deepening in Economic Development*. Oxford and London. Oxford University Press.

Sheppard, D.K. (1971): *The Growth and Role of the UK Financial Institutions, 1880–1962*. London. Methuen.

Sklivas, S.D. (1987): 'The strategic choice of manegerial incentives'. *RAND Journal of Economics*. vol. 18, no. 3, pp. 452–58.

Smirlock, M. (1985): 'Evidence and (non)relationship between concentration and profability on banking'. *Journal of Money, Credit and Banking*, 17(1), February, pp. 69–83.

Spellman, L.J. (1980): 'Deposit ceiling and the efficiency of financial intermediation'. *The Journal of Finance*, vol. 35, no. 1, March, pp. 129–36.

Startz, R. (1979): 'Implicit interest on demand deposits'. *Journal of Monetary Economics*, 5(4), October, pp. 515–34.

Steinherr, A. (1996): 'Performance of universal banks: historical review and appraisal', in Saunders, A. and Walter, I., eds: *Universal Banking: Financial System Design Reconsidered*. Chicago, London and Singapore. Irwin, pp. 2–30.

Stigler, G.J. (1971): 'The economic theory of regulation'. *Bell Journal of Economics*, no. 2, pp. 3–21.

(1964): 'A theory of oligopoly'. *Journal of Political Economy*, no. 72, February, pp. 255–65.

Stigler, G.J. and Friedland, C. (1962): 'What can regulations regulate? The case of electricity'. *Journal of Law and Economics*, no. 5(1), October.

Stiglitz, J.E. and Weiss, A. (1981): 'Credit rationing in markets with imperfect information'. *American Economic Review*, 71(3), pp. 393–410.

Superior Banking Council. *Circulares*, 1942–1975.

Tafunell, X. (1998): 'Los beneficios empresariales en España 1880–1981'. *Revista de Historia Económica*, no. 3, pp. 707–47.

(1997): *Los beneficios empresariales en España*. II Encuentro de Historia Económica. UIMP Valencia. Unpublished paper.

Tamames, R. (1970, 1976): *Estructura económica de España*. Madrid. Ed Guadiana.

(1966): *La lucha contra los monopolios*. Madrid. Tecnos.

Tena, A. (1992): 'Protección y productividad en España e Italia, 1890–1960', in Prados de la Escosura, L. and Zamagni, V., eds: *El desarrollo económico en la Europa del Sur: España e Italia en perspectiva histórica*. Madrid. Alianza Universidad, pp. 321–58.

Titos Martinez, M. (1991): 'La respuesta histórica de las Cajas de Ahorro a las demandas de la sociedad española'. *Papeles de Economía*, no. 46, pp. 12–38.

Velarde, J. (1988): 'Banca e industrialización: la etapa autarquica (1939–59)', in *Banca e Industria en España: presente, pasado y futuro*. Madrid. Ed. Banco Español de Crédito.

(1962): 'Algunos problemas de la estructura y desarrollo de la economía española'. *Revista de Economía Política*. January–April, pp. 1–20.
Villalonga, I. (1962): 'La banca española en lo que va de siglo'. *Arbor*, no. 189–190.
Villar Arregui, M. (1968): 'Un proyecto de Ley. Reflexiones sobre las incompatibilidades de los banqueros y otros temas olvidados o relegados que despiertan'. *Diario Ya* , 10 July, p. 6.
Viñas, A. et al. (1979): *Política exterior the España, 1931–1975*. Madrid. Banco Exterior de España.
Viñas, A. (1982): *Guerra, dinero, ayuda fascista y autarquía en la España de Franco*. Barcelona. Ed. Crítica.
(1976): *El oro español en la guerra civil*. Madrid. I.E.F.
Vives, X. (1988): 'Concentración bancaria y competitividad'. *Papeles de Economía Española*, no. 41, pp. 62–76.
Viver Pi-Sunyer, C. (1978): *El personal político de Franco (1936–1945). Contribución empírica a una teoría del régimen franquista*. Barcelona. Ed. Vicens-Vives.
Waterson, M. (1990, 9th edn): *Economic Theory of the Industry*. Cambridge. Cambridge University Press.
(1988): *Regulation of the Firm and Natural Monopoly*. Oxford. Blackwell.
White, L.H. (1984): *Free Banking in Britain. Theory, Experience and Debate, 1800–1845*. Cambridge. Cambridge University Press.
Wright, A. (1977): *The Spanish Economy, 1959–1976*. London. Macmillan.

Index

Page references in italics indicate that the reference is within a figure or table.